Sociology of the E

Also by Adrian Favell
PHILOSOPHIES OF INTEGRATION
EUROSTARS AND EUROCITIES

Also by Virginia Guiraudon
IMMIGRATION POLITICS IN EUROPE: The Politics of Control

Sociology of the European Union

Edited by

Adrian Favell
*Professor of European and International Studies,
Aarhus University, Denmark*

and

Virginie Guiraudon
*Research Professor at the National Centre for
Scientific Research (CNRS), University of Lille, France*

palgrave
macmillan

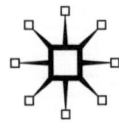

Selection and editorial matter © Adrian Favell and Virginie Guiraudon 2011

Introduction and chapters (in order) © Adrian Favell and Virginie Guiraudon; Juan Díez Medrano; Adrian Favell and Ettore Recchi; Alberta Andreotti and Patrick Le Galès; Neil Fligstein; Virginie Guiraudon; Niilo Kauppi; Frédéric Mérand; Hans-Jörg Trenz 2011
Postscript © George Ross 2011

All rights reserved. No reproduction, copy or transmission of this publication may be made without written permission.

No portion of this publication may be reproduced, copied or transmitted save with written permission or in accordance with the provisions of the Copyright, Designs and Patents Act 1988, or under the terms of any licence permitting limited copying issued by the Copyright Licensing Agency, Saffron House, 6–10 Kirby Street, London EC1N 8TS.

Any person who does any unauthorized act in relation to this publication may be liable to criminal prosecution and civil claims for damages.

The authors have asserted their rights to be identified as the authors of this work in accordance with the Copyright, Designs and Patents Act 1988.

First published 2011 by
PALGRAVE MACMILLAN

Palgrave Macmillan in the UK is an imprint of Macmillan Publishers Limited, registered in England, company number 785998, of Houndmills, Basingstoke, Hampshire RG21 6XS.

Palgrave Macmillan in the US is a division of St Martin's Press LLC, 175 Fifth Avenue, New York, NY 10010.

Palgrave Macmillan is the global academic imprint of the above companies and has companies and representatives throughout the world.

Palgrave® and Macmillan® are registered trademarks in the United States, the United Kingdom, Europe and other countries

ISBN 978–0–230–20711–0 hardback
ISBN 978–0–230–20712–7 paperback

This book is printed on paper suitable for recycling and made from fully managed and sustained forest sources. Logging, pulping and manufacturing processes are expected to conform to the environmental regulations of the country of origin.

A catalogue record for this book is available from the British Library.

A catalog record for this book is available from the Library of Congress.

10 9 8 7 6 5 4 3 2 1
20 19 18 17 16 15 14 13 12 11

Printed in China

Contents

Analytical Contents	vii
List of Figures and Tables	x
Notes on the Contributors	xi
Acknowledgements	xiii
1 Sociology of the European Union: An Introduction *Adrian Favell and Virginie Guiraudon*	1

PART I: SOCIAL FOUNDATIONS — 25

2 Social Class and Identity *Juan Díez Medrano*	28
3 Social Mobility and Spatial Mobility *Adrian Favell and Ettore Recchi*	50
4 Elites, Middle Classes and Cities *Alberta Andreotti and Patrick Le Galès*	76
5 Markets and Firms *Neil Fligstein*	100

PART II: POLITICS AND POLICIES — 125

6 Mobilization, Social Movements and the Media *Virginie Guiraudon*	128
7 EU Politics *Niilo Kauppi*	150
8 EU Policies *Frédéric Mérand*	172

9	**Social Theory and European Integration** *Hans-Jörg Trenz*	193
	Postscript *George Ross*	215
	Bibliography	225
	Index	257

Analytical Contents

1	**Sociology of the European Union: An Introduction**	**1**
	Adrian Favell and Virginie Guiraudon	
	Sociological approaches in EU studies from neo-functionalism to social constructivism	4
	Comparative sociologies of Europe	11
	The political sociology of EU politics	18
	How to do a sociology of the European Union	23
	PART I: SOCIAL FOUNDATIONS	**25**
2	**Social Class and Identity**	**28**
	Juan Díez Medrano	
	Social groups and classes in the sociology of Europe	29
	Class, social structure and Europeanization	30
	Europeanization or European social classes?	32
	Identity	35
	Social ties	37
	Mobilization	40
	Why is there no European society (yet)?	42
	Social transactions	42
	Socialization	43
	Security	45
	The enduring salience of the national	46
	Conclusion: the prospect for European classes	48
3	**Social Mobility and Spatial Mobility**	**50**
	Adrian Favell and Ettore Recchi	
	Social and spatial mobility in Europe	52
	Mobility and immobility in Western societies	52
	Analyzing social mobility data	54
	The problem of methodological nationalism	57
	Hypotheses about social and spatial mobility in Europe	60
	Operationalization 1: a quantitative approach	61
	Operationalization 2: a qualitative approach	65
	Conclusion: a European field of mobility	73

4 Elites, Middle Classes and Cities — 76
Alberta Andreotti and Patrick Le Galès

Social theory, nation building and globalization — 78
Between rootedness in urban life and international mobility: the dynamics of middle-class formation — 82
Operationalization: a comparison of upper-middle classes in European cities — 86
   Social categories and selection of interviewees — 86
   Selection of cities and local contexts — 88
   Construction of questionnaire — 89
Mobile but rooted: the upper-middle classes as part of a virtual global society — 92
   Transnational networks — 93
   Geographical mobility — 94
   Practices — 96
   Feeling of belonging to Europe — 97
Conclusion — 98

5 Markets and Firms — 100
Neil Fligstein

Economic sociology and the study of integrated market economies — 102
Globalization or Europeanization? — 107
A case study: the telecommunications industry — 113
Costs and benefits of Europeanization — 120
Conclusion: economic sociology and EU studies — 123

PART II: POLITICS AND POLICIES — 125

6 Mobilization, Social Movements and the Media — 128
Virginie Guiraudon

European mobilizations: symptom or cause of European integration? — 132
From theory to research design: studying EU-related contention — 135
A mixed method approach to studying mobilization: the politics of immigration, race and gender in comparative perspective — 139
   Operationalization 1: a quantitative analysis of claims-making — 139
   Operationalization 2: a qualitative study of EU immigration and race politics — 142
   Operationalization 3: bringing in gender politics as a comparative control case — 145
Conclusion — 147

7 EU Politics — 150
Niilo Kauppi

Fields and power — 151
Roles and resources — 154

Contents   ix

    Advantages of the sociological approach   157
    The Strasbourg school   160
    Social practices in the European Parliament   163
    Conclusion   169

8 **EU Policies**   172
  Frédéric Mérand

    Political science approaches to EU policies   173
    EU policy-making: a sociological approach   177
        Social fields   177
        Social representations   179
        Bricolage as practice   182
    The case of European defence policy   185
        Going beyond common sense   186
        Constructing the research object   187
        Taking practices seriously   188
        Keeping a critical perspective   191
    Conclusion   191

9 **Social Theory and European Integration**   193
  Hans-Jörg Trenz

    Weberian approaches in the study of the European Union   194
    Durkheimian approaches in the study of the European Union   195
    Contemporary social theory and European integration   200
        Integration as macro-structural transformation   202
        Integration as micro-structural transformation   206
        Integration as meso-structural transformation   208
    Conclusion   212

**Postscript: Arriving Late at the EU Studies Ball – Dilemmas,
Prospects and Strategies for a Sociology of the European Union**   215
George Ross

List of Figures and Tables

Figures

2.1	Dimensions of European social groups	35
4.1	Urban options for European elites and middle classes	84
7.1	Political space as field	153
8.1	A typology of EU policies	174
8.2	The European Security and Defence Policy	185

Tables

2.1	Trends in relative identification (1992–2004)	36
3.1	Intergenerational social mobility in the five largest countries of EU15	55
3.2	Proportion of foreign-born residents in EU member states, end of 2006	59
3.3	Class position of EU stayers and movers by country of residence and nationality	63
3.4	Patterns of intragenerational class mobility of EU movers	64
4.1	Number and percentage of legislators and managers plus professionals in Europe, 2002	87
5.1	Regional structure of world merchandise trade in exports, 1993 and 2005	107
5.2	Percentage of total manufacturing trade of selected EU countries with others in the European Union	108
5.3	Merchandise trade exports for Eastern Europe (without Russia), 1994–2003	110
5.4	Comparison of the world's largest multinationals, 1987 and 1997	112
5.5	Privatization of European telecommunications companies	118
5.6	Shareholdings of main European telecommunications companies, circa 2003	119
7.1	European Parliament, national and international experience of MEPs, 1979–1994	167

Notes on the Contributors

Alberta Andreotti is permanent research fellow in Sociology at the University of Milan-Bicocca, Italy.

Juan Díez Medrano is Professor at the IBEI (Institut Barcelona d'Estudis Internacionals) and Catedrático Rafael del Pino at the Universidad Carlos III de Madrid.

Adrian Favell is Professor of European and International Studies at Aarhus University, Denmark.

Neil Fligstein is the Class of 1939 Chancellor's Professor in the Department of Sociology at the University of California, Berkeley, USA.

Virginie Guiraudon is Research Professor at the French National Centre for Scientific Research (CNRS) posted at the Ceraps (Lille Centre for Politics), Lille, France.

Niilo Kauppi is Research Professor at the French National Centre for Scientific Research (CNRS) posted at the GSPE-PRISME (European Political Sociology Group), Strasbourg, France.

Patrick Le Galès is Research Professor at the French National Centre for Scientific Research (CNRS) posted at the CEE (Centre for European Studies), Sciences Po, Paris, France.

Frédéric Mérand is Associate Professor in the Department of Political Science at the University of Montreal, Canada.

Ettore Recchi is Professor of Political Sociology at the University of Chieti-Pescara, Italy.

George Ross is *ad personam* Chair Jean Monnet at the University of Montreal, Canada, and Morris Hillquit Professor of Labor and Social Thought, Emeritus, Brandeis University, USA.

Hans-Jörg Trenz is Research Professor at ARENA, the Centre for European Studies at the University of Oslo, Norway.

Acknowledgements

This book is a story of intellectual companionship. It represents both a network of colleagues, and a group of friends whose vision of what sociology can do for the study of the European Union is unusually complementary. For once, it is a textbook that benefits from the fact that it is a collection of different voices. It has been a long story, and it could not have been completed without the enduring resilience of an old alliance between the editors. Between the moment when a few of us first discussed the ideas behind this book and today when we can write these acknowledgements, most of the authors changed jobs, moved to different cities, countries or continents, had babies and life changes, not to mention publishing other books along the way. Bringing it all together has been an honour and a labour of love.

We organized our first panel back in 2005 at the European Union Studies Association (EUSA) in Austin, Texas. Our first official book meeting took place in Montreal at the invitation of Frédéric Mérand in April 2006, where our group decided about the structure and content of the book. Our collective commitment reflected the excitement of finding others with a similar diagnosis of EU studies and the sheer joy of working with people whose work had in some way inspired one another. The framing agenda behind the book was then presented at various venues, notably EUSA, UACES, ECPR, and in seminars at Sciences Po, the London School of Economics and Political Science, the University of Edinburgh and the University of Copenhagen. We received constructive comments and challenging questions from a number of discussants at these events, including Alberta Sbragia, Renaud Dehousse, Sophie Duchesne, Craig Parsons, Damian Chalmers, Andy Smith, Morten Rasmussen, Caitriona Carter and Simon Hix. We also gratefully acknowledge the constant support of George Ross for the project.

Now came the hard part: making sure that the book would meet our own original high expectations and making time in between other projects. We thank our editors at Palgrave Macmillan for their constant support and practical wisdom. One of the reasons why we kept working on the book project was the enthusiasm of younger colleagues, such as Rebecca Adler-Nissen or Virginie Ingelgom, writing their PhD dissertations at the time, who wanted to see the book out there because they felt that a sociology of the EU was missing from the bookshelves when they had started their project. We hope that they were right in pushing us and that other young scholars will seize upon our agenda.

It is usual to express gratitude to one's partners in the acknowledgements. We know that they are happy that we are done. We even got to celebrate together in a Paris bistro. Our loving thanks to Stine, whom we hope will like and assign the book, and to Arnaud for his unfailing support. Not to mention our three cats, perfect pets for writing projects.

Aarhus   ADRIAN FAVELL
Paris   VIRGINIE GUIRAUDON

The authors and publishers wish to thank the following publishers, organizations and authors for granting permission to reproduce copyright material: the Office for National Statistics, for Table 3.2, originally from *ONS: Labour Force Survey: Employment Status by Occupation and Sex, April–June 2006* (Office for National Statistics, 2006) reproduced under Crown Copyright; the World Trade Organization for Table 5.1, originally from *World Trade Organization Annual Report 1996*, and the *World Trade Organization Annual Report 2006*, and Table 5.3, originally from www.wto.org; OECD Publishing, for Table 5.2, originally from *OECD Economic Outlook*, Volume 1998, Issue 2, p. 154, www.oecd.org/oecdEconomicOutlook (OECD, 1998); and McGraw-Hill, for Tables 5.5 and 5.6, originally from *Standard Corporation Descriptions* (New York: Standard & Poor's, 1999), reprinted with permission of Standard & Poor's Financial Services LLC, a wholly owned subsidiary of the McGraw-Hill Companies. All rights reserved.

CHAPTER 1

Sociology of the European Union: An Introduction[1]

Adrian Favell and Virginie Guiraudon

> **Key concepts:** Europeanization, operationalization, functionalism, neo-functionalism, transactionalism, socialization, meta-theory, ontology, epistemology, social constructivism, identity, institutionalism, globalization, nation building, social theory, comparative sociology, political sociology, socio-history
>
> **Key references:** Deutsch, Haas, Parsons, Barry, Katzenstein, Hall and Taylor, Fligstein, Crouch, Milward, Kaelble, Esping-Andersen, Bourdieu

After many years in the wilderness, sociology is finally being called for by mainstream studies of the European Union (EU) seeking new inspiration. Sociologists on the whole have been curiously absent from EU studies. Not that they don't study Europe. They have 'Europeanized' their projects and objects of study along with all the other disciplines chasing after European research funding; they have their own European networks, associations and journals; sociology additions to courses on the EU are popping up everywhere. Yet over the

---

[1] In what follows, we would like to acknowledge our contributors' many thoughts on this subject during the development of this project. Their earlier formulations on the question of 'What is a sociology of the European Union?', which were included in some cases in their original drafts, are reflected throughout the volume's introduction. We would especially like to thank Patrick Le Galès for his draft notes towards the historiography of comparative sociologies of Europe reflected in the third section of the introduction.

years sociologists have participated little in the characteristic approaches and debates of mainstream EU studies which focus on the production and implementation of policies and laws coming out of the European institutions. Nor have they been much heard in the now broad range of work considering 'Europeanization', seen as the way in which political and legal institutions at the national level have been transformed by processes of European integration. This is despite the notion that such Europeanization ought to be taking EU studies down and out into studying the full effects of the EU across and within European societies, an issue with obvious sociological implications.

However, recently things have changed. Sociology in EU studies is now on everyone's lips. In the last few years, the adjective 'sociological' has been used in all kinds of international relations (IR) and comparative politics studies as a synonym for anti-rationalist, institutionalist, ideas-driven or cultural approaches in political science. Critical theorists and others that use contemporary social theory extensively in their work, meanwhile, have also come to discuss Europe and the EU. Viewed more broadly, there are longer standing, if somewhat marginal, currents in EU studies involving anthropologists and historians which share many of the same questions that a sociology of the EU might pose. Sociology clearly means many things to many people: it is an impossible discipline to define exhaustively. Our goal in this volume is more specific. In relation to these various currents, we seek to take a distinct line on what the *empirical* sociology of the EU is and might be: that is, make explicit what questions, research design and methodologies such an approach might involve, and show how it can make a distinctive contribution to the mainstream of EU studies.

As a rule of thumb, the sociologists collected in this book are unified by three things. First, there is an enduring interest in the influence of the sociological classics – in this volume you will find references to Weber, Durkheim and Marx, as well as Goffman, Gellner and Goldthorpe. Second, there is an insistence on the importance of studying the specifically social dimension of the European Union, whether it is the possible social foundations of the political and legal construction, the social characteristics of political actors or policy networks, or the consequences for society of European integration. Third, there is a belief in research that combines the virtues of qualitative ethnographic research and quantitative demographic work. One of the key goals of the collection here is to show how relevant sociological questions about the European Union can be specified and hence operationalized as data-driven empirical projects.

An empirical sociology of the European Union thus will not only offer an alternative approach to answering the usual questions about familiar EU political actors, policies and institutions. Rather, it also poses different questions about the causes, consequences and scope of the European Union, proposing to answer them via the introduction of quantitative and qualitative methodologies not yet used in EU studies. One consequence is that the turn to sociology reopens the bigger questions about the 'Europeanization' of European societies – in terms, say, of the emergence of European class structures, mobility patterns, or transnational networks – that are usually defined by scholars in EU studies in terms of a narrower focus on institutional change, policy implementation and compliance at national levels. Sociology in EU studies, in short, would change the *object* of study, as well as offering a different understanding of Europeanization.

In this introduction and those which preface each half of the book, we explain these choices, via an interpretation of the existing literature in EU studies and the sociology of Europe.

First, we trace the rise, fall and return of 'sociological' concerns in mainstream EU studies: from neo-functionalism through new institutionalism to social constructivism. The presence of sociological approaches among political scientists offers opportunities for a new sociology of the European Union, yet certain limitations and errors in understanding what sociology might bring to EU studies first need diagnosing.

In the following section, after briefly reviewing how the European Union has appeared as a theme in contemporary social theorists such as Jürgen Habermas and Ulrich Beck, we move on to what will be much less familiar terrain in EU studies: the contributions of the comparative sociology of Europe since the 1980s – involving figures such as Hartmut Kaelble, Henri Mendras, Colin Crouch, Göran Therborn and Gøsta Esping-Andersen. The comparative sociology of Europe debates how European societies might converge on a distinctively European economic or social model, but they are not *yet* necessarily the same thing as a sociology of the European Union. This would go further by taking the notion of sociological Europeanization seriously, and focusing on the social, economic, cultural and political practices that underpin or are induced by the making of the EU.

A similar basic introduction is then offered to a neglected, distinctive school of political sociology that has emerged among EU studies specialists who work with a framework that uses the work of Pierre Bourdieu and his notions of 'field', 'capital' and 'habitus'. This leads to a rather different interpretation of EU politics and policy than that found in the mainstream, one which locates the determination of familiar European institutions, laws and policies studied by political scientists elsewhere – in the social positions and trajectories of actors and their symbolic conflicts about meaning, legitimacy and social power. It is a quite fresh empirical approach to the political sociology of the EU that is reflected in second half of this volume.

Following the contours of the two latter sections in the introduction, the volume is split into two distinct halves: the first, 'Social Foundations', presents a variety of studies that offer empirical studies of the social structures and social change associated with European Union, and the second, 'Politics and Policies', applies sociological approaches to classical areas of EU political action and policy-making. In the short introductions that preface each half, we thus guide readers briefly through the chapters that follow as a 'how to do' the sociology of the European Union. This is both a question of how to re-think the EU as an object of study – in terms of recognisable sociological questions that take up the concepts and themes of classic and contemporary sociologists – and, even more importantly, of how to turn these questions into fully operationalized research projects with practical, data-driven methodologies. Taking a range of topics – from the impact of European Union on class formation or mobility to the sociological underpinnings of EU policy-making and parliamentary politics – we show what a sociology of European can and should be doing (see also Favell and Guiraudon 2009).

Sociological approaches in EU studies from neo-functionalism to social constructivism

Although nominal sociologists have not been much present in EU studies over the past decades, sociology and distinctly sociological forms of reasoning were highly present in the original work of the field's forefathers in the 1950s. No survey of the canon of EU integration theory, for example, would omit the names of Karl Deutsch or Ernst Haas. These famous names at the origins of the research field both proposed visions of the European Union that were grounded in clearly sociological-style arguments (see also Rosamond 2000: 171–5).

The first oft-mentioned name of the period, Karl Deutsch, was a sociologically minded IR scholar with an abiding concern for rational, economic regional integration as the master process uniting nations in ever more international structures (1957). It was a view embedded in the archetypal modernist developmental perspective that dominated progressive social science in its heyday in the 1950s and 60s: a classic kind of functionalist theory, predicting that the form of future political structures would evolve from a growing functional need in the world for such forms. Through the influence of sociologist Talcott Parsons (1951) – the most famous figure associated with the functionalist paradigm – sociology and sociological theory was pervasive in the dominant 'systems-based' logic of much political science of that time. For functionalists, the modernization of society would lead to ever more abstract legal–rational forms that would gradually supersede the antiquated ethnic or cultural preoccupations of nations.

The emergent European Community, for some, seemed one more form of this developmental process. Deutsch's transactionalist theory thus posited macro-regional integration as a larger-scale version of the dynamics that had built nation-states in an earlier era. He set out to empirically investigate the degree to which regional integration projects were beginning to display these forms in the more integrated post-war world. In these terms, it was possible to consider measuring the everyday cross-border interactions of European elites, policy actors and (potentially) everyday citizens, as an indicator of cross-border integration – a process that might one day form a European society as the sum of all the European transactions, and which would be a parallel process to the historical dynamic that formed societies on a national scale.

The dynamic of micro-level socialization leading to macro-level integration was developed further in the other major sociological-style thinker on European integration of that period, Ernst Haas. His massively influential early study of the forerunner to the European Community, the European Coal and Steel Union (1958), emphasized how international institutions might socialize bureaucrats and policy actors such that they engage in building cooperation and policy instruments across an ever-expanding range of policy areas beyond the nation-state. 'Neo-functionalism', as it has come to be known by generations of EU studies students, thus offered a broad macro-theory of how European regional integration proceeds through a cumulative dynamic. Through a functional mechanism called 'spillover', supranational integration in one policy area creates incentives for integration in others, and in the process national policy actors come to identify with the European level and hence 'supranational' forms of governance as a more effective way of regulating matters that would normally be left to national law or politics. Once again, the theoretical paradigm that lay behind the basic explanatory logic at work in this model was a Parsonsian-style modernist functionalism.

The influence of these classic readings remains high today, especially in institutionalist, multilevel governance, and social constructivist accounts of European integration. In particular, the notion of 'socialization' has been used by a new generation of scholars interested in studying the internal dynamics of European institutions through the way these institutions may or may not Europeanize these actors. A number of scholars have revisited Haas's ideas to see whether EU institutions become laboratories of social engineering, in which actors are internationalized and therefore promote further internationalization in their own self-image (Hooghe 2001, 2005; Checkel 2005; Börzel 2006). The opening of the black box of socialization, and hence the return to the more sociological questions of the 1950s and 60s, associated with Haas and the Parsonian style of political science dominant in that era, inevitably challenges narrower rational choice models of political action. Deutsch's main influence, meanwhile, was through scholars who have continued to pursue large-scale studies on regional integration, even as the topic has waxed and waned in popularity. He has enjoyed a substantial comeback in the work of political economists re-introducing the big regional integration questions (Mattli 1999; Warleigh 2004; Katzenstein 2005; Bartolini 2005), economic geographers pointing to the dynamics of trade, mobility and welfare as core (Rodríguez-Pose 2002), and, most spectacularly, in the fully worked out Deutschian development of a sociology of the European Union by Neil Fligstein (2008 and Chapter 5 in this volume). In this, and in the accompanying work here of Díez Medrano, Favell and Recchi, and Andreotti and Le Galès, there is a clear positing of Deutschian-like assumptions about the micro-level roots of macro-level integration, that each is answering in clear empirical terms. While empirically the evidence for Deutsch's hypotheses was generally sceptical and remains so – as it was indeed for tests of Haas's theory – the theories of integration of Haas and Deutsch established clear sociological hypotheses about the underlying drivers of an ever closer Union.

However, despite the underlying influence, sociological reasoning about the EU has not always been consistently applied at the different times it has momentarily appeared in the mainstream debates. The problem is essentially that sociological approaches to the European Union have entered and exited the field according to theoretical – indeed *meta*-theoretical – disputes among political scientists about the core assumptions and approaches of their discipline, not necessarily in relation to what was going on in sociology at the time. The timing and intellectual context of these inconclusive meta-theoretical debates about *ontology* – the objects and elements that make up the political world – and *epistemology* – the methods or forms of reasoning that are appropriate for revealing this world – are specific to internal disciplinary dynamics. The sporadic sociological turns in EU studies thus did not emerge as a result of imperatives emerging out of contemporary sociology and its agendas, but limitations and controversies within political science paradigms.

There is a fascinating history to the peculiar relationship of political science and sociology as seen by political scientists, which is relevant to these misunderstandings. Sociology, as mentioned above, held sway in the 1950s and 60s as the master paradigm discipline for political science, through the influence of Talcott Parsons and functionalist logic. However, from the 1970s onwards political science, particularly in the US, began to realign itself much more with economics as the master discipline, with the rise of methodologies using rational choice and mathematical models. This was a historical paradigm change captured in a famous book by Brian Barry (1971), *Sociologists, Economists and Democracy*. In the following decade, sociological, historical and cultural approaches in political science fell into disrepute. Yet while the mainstream has continued with a 'hard core' economics-led approach, over the years a substantial minority of political scientists continue to be attracted to the alternatives, particularly those working in IR and comparative politics. Specifically, there were two influential works that most characterized the sociological revival in political science: the first in IR, the second in comparative political studies.

Peter Katzenstein, a redoubtable Cornell University professor of German origin, spearheaded the first: a tightly integrated edited collection entitled *The Culture of National Security: Norms and Identity in World Politics* (1996a). Katzenstein, not coincidentally, was a student of Deutsch, a scholar of grand political economy in the post-war world, and was determined to reinvigorate the context-sensitive regional studies of his mentor, and also to put culture back on the menu of an overly rationalist, economics-dominated political science. Rational models alone could not explain variation in the post-war international relations of countries such as Japan in comparison to countries like the US and Germany, as he found in his own related work (1996b); nor could they do historical justice to the situated motivations of actors embedded in cultural, value-laden action or influenced by social norms, as he laid out in the *The Culture of National Security*. When historians study political actors using archives it is natural that the motivation and socialization of such actors must bring culture and social values into explanatory models. Katzenstein also presented his argument in terms of going back to Barry and what he called 'rummaging in the graveyard of sociological studies' (1996a: 1). Sociology, in other words, was in this view already a dead discipline, and the best that could be done with sociology at that point was to go back to the future – to a Parsonian-style functionalist theory, and its emphasis in explanations on the ordering role of collective values, identity and the stabilizing pressure of social norms, in order for political science to advance.

Katzenstein's vision provided an extraordinarily powerful and seductive vision of an alternative political science for the legions of frustrated qualitative and theoretically-minded international relations students resisting what was seen as the hegemony of rationalist intergovernmental IR. A whole new generation of younger authors, many of whom were involved in the original collection, poured in through this door, particularly those emphasizing the influence of norms, ideas and culture – conceived in terms of normative notions such as democracy, freedom, security, or human rights – on political institution building and outcomes (Finnemore 1996; Keck and Sikkink 1998, Risse *et al.* 1999; see Checkel 1998a). The EU, as an unusual form of international organization, became a ripe territory for this kind of work. In one archetypal move by a leading figure, Thomas Risse moved from studying human rights and INGOs to studying the EU as a new source of identity and novel political construction (Risse *et al.* 1999, Cowles *et al.* 2001).

Others in IR sought to take the cultural turn even further, moving debates up to a meta-theoretical level about language and concept construction, to critically question the mainstream discipline and its 'realist' assumptions about the world (Wæver 2003). Rather, locating themselves in the philosophical 'idealist' tradition – that holds that 'reality' is hidden behind the language and ideas through which we perceive the world – they sought their inspiration in other, older, sociological classics, such as Berger and Luckmann (1966) on the social construction of reality through language and concepts, and Erving Goffman (1974) on the notion of conceptual framing. The most spectacular version of what become known as the 'social constructivist' turn it inspired was *Social Theory of International Politics* (1999), a book by Alexander Wendt, an associate of Katzenstein, who also puts to use another sociological favourite of IR theorists, Anthony Giddens' theory of structuration (1984). This set the scene for a fully worked out social constructivist programme on the social construction of the EU, a book which for many defines the sociological approach: Christiansen, Jørgensen and Wiener's *The Social Construction of Europe* (2001), and its continuation in the theoretically-minded works of associates such as Diez (1999), Rosamond (2001) and Checkel (2006). These are all writers who like to stress the influence of language, symbols, discursive formations, culture and norms – understood in the 'normative' ethical or philosophical sense – on EU actors who might otherwise be conceived as acting 'rationally' in terms of pre-defined 'interests'. Rather, social constructivists believe that such political action is determined by the social context and modes of interaction embodied in the collective language and culture shared by particular actors. These authors label their approach as 'sociological', but their intellectual positioning is entirely determined by their hostile relationship with the 'rationalist' or 'realist' political science mainstream, not by any intention to contribute to sociology as a discipline (for another view on these disputes, see Rosamond 2003).

Meanwhile, during the 1990s, comparative politics scholars had come to stake a claim to study the EU, with an alternative approach to international relations and international organizations (Hix 1994). Just as in IR, a battle was raging in comparative politics about dominant 'rationalist' versus alternative models. A focal point for a more qualitative, comparative political science, knitting together the outlying sub-disciplines of political economy, organizational sociology and normative political philosophy, was being provided around this time in the famous synthetic article (1996) by the Harvard political economist Peter Hall and sociologist Rosemary Taylor, which summed up a decade in which political science had been rediscovering institutions and organizations as a key way of understanding political dynamics.

Hall and Taylor's famous three versions of institutionalism identified one strand that uses modified rational actor assumptions; a second called 'historical institutionalism', which brings in a crucial temporal dimension of change in political systems, and a third, 'sociological institutionalism', which points to how political action is not merely explained by utility-maximizing choices but also influenced by 'culture', that is by ceremonial routines, symbols, frames of meaning, or social norms. They were particularly influenced in this reading by scholars in organizational sociology, such as John Meyer (Meyer and Scott 1983) or DiMaggio and Powell (1991), who had re-introduced a more cultural understanding in these terms into bureaucratic and organizational behaviour dominated by more rationalist Weberian theories. As with Katzenstein, this work opened the door for a generation of comparative politics students seeking alternatives to the rational choice mainstream; it became the key foundation for all subsequent institutionalist studies of the EU (Stone Sweet et al. 2001; Parsons 2006; Schmidt 2006). However, there were also unintended effects of identifying the third strand of institutionalism as the definitively 'sociological' one. There is a misperception at work here in identifying sociologists *only* with qualitative-style work on the influence of discourse, meanings, frames, norms, ideas, and so on. In fact, sociologists might be identified in all three strands of institutionalist work: there are also many influential rational choice and historical institutionalist sociologists (for a sample, see Brinton and Nee 1998). Another way of putting this is to note that political scientists tend to equate sociology with the more cultural and holistic Durkheimian form of reasoning – and its distinctively non-individualist and idealist social ontology – while overlooking those parts of sociology more in the rationalist and realist Weberian style, which is grounded in methodological individualism. Both Katzenstein's and Hall and Taylor's definition of sociology underlined the Durkheimian current in sociology, perhaps because the Parsonian sociology being recalled from the 1950s and 60s was itself essentially an updated, highly Americanized, version of Durkheim.

Notwithstanding this point, the rationalist versus anti-rationalist dichotomy – the stylized opposition of rational choice models versus constructivist and sociological institutionalist alternatives – has since the 1990s become a staple feature of theoretical debates in EU studies. There has, of course, been a counter-backlash amongst hard core 'positivist' political scientists against the 'sociological' trend. Thus, when the social constructivist and sociological institutionalist versions of EU studies have been attacked by rationalists, sociology as such gets tarred by the same brush for the fallacies of 'sociological' studies (Pollack 1998; Hix 1998). The rejection of the social constructivist wave is best expressed by the American political scientist Andrew Moravcsik, who is known for his rationalist intergovernmental accounts of the EU. In a quite devastating critique of Christiansen *et al.*'s paradigm-defining book, he argues that if this was the new way of doing 'sociological' studies of the EU – all discourse and language, soft methods, anecdotal evidence, and far too much meta-theory – there was indeed 'something rotten in the state of Denmark' (Denmark, through the Copenhagen school of critical IR, being the place most associated with the social constructivist style of political science). Moravcsik is canny enough in his review to also point out that the absence of much concern with operationalizing meta-theory empirically, or seeking a social grounding in research for the constructivist claims, in fact distanced the whole social constructivist project from what goes on in any American sociology department that he knew.

Despite the critique, the social constructivist wing of EU studies continues to be very active (Schimmelfennig *et al.* 2006; Wiener 2008). Moreover, a further 'sociological' trend in EU studies has emerged with the developing debate on European identity. Based either on Eurobarometer measures (Gabel 1998; Citrin and Sides 2004; McLaren 2006; Green 2007; Fligstein 2008), or alternative empirical strategies (Duchesne and Frognier 2002, 2008; Díez Medrano 2003, 2009; Bruter 2005; White 2010), a range of scholars have convincingly shown how a national identity variable can account for differences in public opinion about the EU, particularly in relation to the much debated breakdown of the 'permissive consensus' (Hooghe and Marks 2004, 2008). Thomas Risse's later work on European identity reads the concept as a question of social psychology (rather than sociology as such), which opens a whole new set of tools (Herrmann *et al.* 2004; Risse 2010). The most recent wave of work has developed ambitious new methodologies for studying the relation between public opinion, European citizenship and identity, via, for example, focus groups with working class and political activist groups (Duchesne *et al.* 2010), new analyses of location and space in identification with the EU (Berezin and Díez Medrano 2008), or elite interviews (Ross 2008). A recent collection brings together some of the best alternative works on European identity across the disciplines (Checkel and Katzenstein 2009).

As the eclectic disciplinary origins of these scholars reveals, identity is not in the end a uniquely sociological concern: it is a stereotype of other disciplines that sociology is particularly preoccupied with this theme. Some of the works on European identity involve sociology and sociologists, others do not. Many sociologists – particularly the variety we present in this volume – would be more comfortable with research that focussed less on attitudes or opinions and more on behaviour, thus treating 'identity' – a notoriously difficult concept to define, and one heavily polluted by its everyday political uses – as an attitudinal black box that needs unpacking in behavioural terms (see Brubaker 2000; Favell 2005). They also often prefer to limit themselves to talking only about self-conscious declarations of actors in terms of 'identification' not 'identity' as such (Duchesne 2010; Díez Medrano 2010). The sociology of the European Union is in fact much more interesting for what it might have to say about this: pushing the public opinion question away from thin measures of identification, in terms of revealed preferences or stylized survey data, towards the development of new methodologies, extensive measures, and new datasets on Europeanized behaviours or practices on the ground. This, we argue, would be a more distinctive and original way for sociologists to engage with the concept of Europeanization, and is the starting point for several chapters in the book.

Comparative sociologies of Europe

In his *Euroclash: The EU, European Identity, and the Future of Europe*, a book sure to become a landmark in the sociology of the European Union, Neil Fligstein (2008) likens EU studies to the study of an iceberg. Political, legal and institutional studies of the EU tend to focus only what is *visible* about the European construction. Yet logically and temporally there has to be something causally that precedes or underlies the building of the European Union as an institutionalized legal–political form, that is, a societal-led process of the European Union as a historical transformation of Europe in space and time, a regional integration perhaps linked to other global and regional processes. This is what lies under the water, as it were, and it is where the sociological shifting of the object of study may be most needed, in moving sociological effort away from studying (only) political and legal processes towards thinking about a European 'society' as perhaps undergirding the legal–political construction above.

As we suggest in the introductory section above, the obvious way to conceptualize this would be to speak of a sociological agenda for studying the Europeanization of European economy and society as both an upstream cause and downstream consequence of processes building the European Union – analogous, perhaps, to ways in which the globalization of societies has been studied, although in this case regionally specific. Sociologists in fact were slow to discover Europeanization in this sense, and the recent emergence of this agenda needs explaining. It is worth noting, though, that by the early 1990s anthropologists had already begun to use the term 'Europeanization' in a similar way, as a broad umbrella for studying the human dimension of European regional integration, whether it be through border interactions, shared sporting competitions, or pan-European regional associations and movements (for a comprehensive literature review see Kearney 1997). Anthropological work was never convincingly recognized by mainstream EU studies, and many anthropologists subsequently lost interest in the EU and moved on to other topics, although a small number of works are well known and became key references in the cultural and constructivist turn in EU studies (Abélès 1992; Bellier and Wilson 2000; Shore 2000; Holmes 2000).

Using 'Europeanization' in a deeper and broader sense, however, became problematic as certain leading EU studies scholars – mainly public policy analysts – started to pin down its meaning to a sense referring much more narrowly to the downstream effects of EU policy implementation on national bureaucratic structures, and the bureaucratic or legal politics linked to this (Héritier et al. 2001; Knill 2001, see also Olsen 2002; Featherstone and Radaelli 2003; Graziano and Vink 2006), often with an argument about avoiding 'concept stretching' (Radaelli 2000). The field has thus come to focus mostly on questions of legal compliance, and the way national policy makers or institutions adapt differentially to EU pressures (Börzel and Risse 2003), rather than what sociologists would propose studying: the societal forces, structures and dynamics that must logically and temporally lie behind or below the EU, moving the iceberg through time and space. The mainstream Europeanization debates, then, do not really grapple with the broader societal processes that might lie behind the EU.

This is why we call for a broader conception of 'Europeanization'. To be clear, this is less a point about the concept itself – which can be easily critiqued as excessively teleological, and potentially too normative in tone – but rather the more substantial object of study to which it should be pointing. As we keep stressing, sociologists would wish to use the concept to evoke a macro-regional scale process – both social and spatial – parallel to the notion of globalization. This would also re-connect the English usage of the word with the way it is used commonly by scholars writing in German and French. To some extent, then, the problem here is a question of expanding the range and ambition of EU studies, both historically and theoretically, so that it recognizes itself again – as it did in the era of Haas and Deutsch – as a form of macro-regional studies. Some sociologists, though, will be equally concerned with the everyday micro-level of these processes, on 'putting a human face' (Smith and Favell 2006) on regional European integration.

Mainstream comparative sociologists, though, have found it difficult to grapple with the question of a European society – often for good historical reasons. In fact, sociology as a discipline is unusually attached to the modern nation-state. A broad section of post-war and contemporary sociology has thus been concerned with the comparative historical study of the making of societies – that is, the making of nation-states. Nation building was the core outcome of the twin processes of modernization and industrialization, first in Europe, then the world; this theme was, if anything, the defining question of the founders of sociology (Giddens 1971). The enormous historical sociological literature, whether in a Marxist, Durkheimian or Weberian tradition, above all showed how *slow* these processes of building (national) societies were. Such sociology focused on the *longue durée*, the tectonic shifts in European history. Social structures rarely change dramatically. It arguably took decades, generations, even centuries for the recognizable nation-state-societies of modern Europe to fully form in their twentieth-century versions. For this reason, there has been an almost inevitable expectation amongst most comparative historical sociologists that whatever the EU is making, it is making it slowly, and that it is unlikely to affect existing European social structures, anchored predominantly in a variety of national forms and 'paths to modernity' (on this, see especially Mann 1993a). Consequently, many such sociologists have been slow to take up the question of the European Union as one on which they might have something to say.

A further reason for the slowness of comparative sociology in grappling with the notion of a society beyond the nation-state lies in the scientific and bureaucratic self-understanding of modern societies. Rooted in the state-centred apparatus of statistical categorization of (bounded) populations, and national historical archiving, this has led to an inbuilt 'methodological nationalism' (Wimmer and Glick-Schiller 2002) in the concepts and data made available by modern societies to the scientists that study them, especially when that science is interlinked, as is often the case, with national policy-making or social engineering. As authors such as Brubaker (1992) have pointed out, there is a characteristically Weberian process at work here: a dual movement, in which borders are strengthened and the inside is differentiated from the outside (through institutions such as citizenship and the welfare state), while an internal order is organized and a national society gradually homogenizes (via culture, education, socialization and so on). No surprise again, then, that comparativists find it hard to see beyond the nation-state, or detect transnational or regional trends at work.

In some sense, these are limitations specific to comparative empirical sociology. Viewed in terms of the more famous grand social theories, it is clear that a large part of contemporary sociology has been directed at the notion of society beyond the nation-state, but towards *globalization* rather than Europeanization on a regional scale. The global transformations evoked by contemporary social theory in terms of metaphors of 'mobilities' (Urry 2007), 'liquid modernity' (Bauman 2000), 'the space of flows' (Castells 1996) or 'reflexive modernisation' (Beck *et al.* 1996; see Cohen and Kennedy 2007 for an overview of contemporary social theories of globalization), tend simply to look past the regional particularities and technical empirical details of the European construction. At best, for them, Europe might affect local inflections on an unstoppable global narrative generalizing much more broadly about the dynamics of (mostly Western) modern and post-modern social forms. This has not always been the case with these so-called 'grand' social theorists, who are certainly the most visible household names of sociology worldwide. Europe – partly because they are mostly European – has sometimes been a congenial playground for their ideas, often overlain with a normative hope that the European construction could one day actually embody some of the highest Enlightenment hopes of a viable and just post-national construction in a post- or late-modern global age. Of the famous names, Jürgen Habermas (2001) and Ulrich Beck (Beck and Grande 2007) have been most suggestive in their engagement with the idea of the EU. Habermas identifies the possibility of the EU as a post-national construction rooted in a new form of 'constitutional patriotism' that will supersede national forms of political community. Beck similarly reads the EU normatively as the expression of a universalist cosmopolitanism which will be able to surmount the national conflicts of the past and the risk-preoccupied global challenges of the future.

The question remains: how to operationalize these often sweeping social theories of change and conceptual innovation into specified and fully operationalized empirical research about post-national, transnational or cosmopolitan society? Clearly, we present a partial and particular vision of what sociology is, and for social theorists who identify themselves as 'post-positivist' our empirical angle may be controversial (see the critique of Favell and Guiraudon in Rumford 2008). We do not cover much here works that have taken direct inspiration in EU studies from Habermas (Eriksen 2005b; Wessler, Peters *et al.* 2008) or Foucault (Barry 2001; Walters and Haahr 2005). Yet a volume on the *social theory* of the European Union would be a rather different book, and we warmly recommend those written by other authors who offer this kind of vision (in particular Delanty and Rumford 2005; see also Manners 2007). We also offer one chapter by Hans-Jörg Trenz (Chapter 9) that links up with this kind of approach.

There are antecedents, though, to the empirical comparative sociology of the European Union that we foreground in this book. It was in fact at the intersection of sociology and political economy that the first ambitious comparative works on Europe started to emerge. These included pioneering studies on trade unions and industrial relations (Crouch and Pizzorno 1978); on neo-corporatism by Streeck and Schmitter (1986); on the origins of the European state by Rokkan (1999) or Tilly (1990); and the early comparative work on the welfare state by Flora (1986) or Korpi (1987), which was later to evolve into the 'varieties' or 'worlds' of welfare capitalism associated respectively with Hall and Soskice (2001) and Gøsta Esping-Andersen (1990, 1999), which we discuss presently. Looking at the output of European sociology as a whole, however, these were quite exceptional efforts – and not even always driven by sociologists. More telling from our point of view is that *none* of these key comparative social structural works mention or give any credence to the impact of the European Union, or look for a underlying Europeanization of European society influenced or structured by the EU. There was, in short, no clear thought about the emergence of a distinctive European society (in the singular), even if some of the work hinted at convergent European social structures. In many ways this dominant perspective on the international comparative tradition comes together in another landmark work, Colin Crouch's *Social Change in Western Europe* (1999), in which he focuses on the political and social compromises forged across Europe after the Second World War and how they in fact gave new vigour to the national welfare stare model. European industrial capitalist societies were organized around the state, its citizens' rights and its institutions – and continued to be so, according to Crouch, even in the face of simultaneous, even dramatic processes of the European Union.

The legacy of the EU's most renowned historian, Alan Milward (1992, 1993), is in fact another key starting point for the sociology we propose. There is an old argument to be reopened about what Milward calls, in a casual but still unjustly neglected piece, the 'social bases' of European integration (Milward 1997). This obscure work is to be found in a maverick volume by historians and sociologists that sought to pose new questions about the EU (Gowan and Anderson 1997). Milward makes the very basic, but fundamental point, that European integration has ultimately been driven by the broad wishes and support of the European middle classes: the same median populations that have determined national political outcomes in the post-war period, ensured the maintenance of the welfare state and pastoral national institutions, and represent the social core of European national societies. To some extent, the sense of an external grounding to the political dynamics of European integration was a hallmark of the original pluralist accounts of the EU, as well as later intergovernmentalist ones (Moravcsik 1998). In these, the 'bases' were often rather crudely aggregated into national political 'interests'. But Milward made a basic point that has been reiterated in Moravcsik's more recent statements (2005) about the EU's democratically legitimate 'constitutional compromise'. The cliché of technocratic EU elites freely manipulating a far-off and hostile mass population is neither a realistic nor viable model of how post-war (democratic) European economy and society has (more or less) stably worked in the last fifty or more years, even if we may now need to ask if the 'permissive consensus' is broken.

To answer such a question about the underlying social structure of the European Union and its relative stability or transformation over time, one comparative strategy would be first to ask: what, if anything, distinguishes the European economy and society from its regional rivals, North America and East Asia? On this point, one key reference stands out. Distinguished social historian Hartmut Kaelble's classic *Auf dem Weg zu einer Europäischen Gesellschaft* (1987), as well as later work (2007), maps out the essential agenda here. Kaelble was the first to define the criteria that might distinguish European society from its non-European rivals, zooming in on key structural features of European society: family structure, educational patterns, the role of women, the welfare state, urbanization models, forms of inequality, the structure of the working population, and shifts in economic modes of industrialization.

Kaelble's original social history of Europe, translated into several languages, was in fact a root text for the broader wave in the 1980s and 90s of comparative macro-sociological projects on the European economy and society discussed above. Yet while these works documented the structural sources (in terms of class relations) and growing convergence (in terms of social models) of European societies, plus certain elements of pan-Europeanization (such as consumer behaviour or cultural practices, or the evolving differentiation of the European model from the rest of the world), they rarely if ever mentioned the European Union as a factor in this. Kaelble, however, suggested to a much greater extent that there was indeed a European society in the making. A French scholar, Henri Mendras, was working along parallel lines in collaboration with Vincent Wright, Arnaldo Bagnasco, Patrick Le Galès and Anand Menon (Mendras 1997), in an international project based at the University of Poitiers called the *Observatoire du Changement en Europe Occidentale*. With hindsight now, we can see Kaelble, Mendras, and their associates' efforts as a cornerstone of the regional sociology of European integration. They are reflected strongly in another landmark synthetic work by Göran Therborn (1995); in further work on the diversity of capitalism (Crouch and Streeck 1997); and in a whole series of other inter-related works that developed a long-term research programme about sociological Europeanization of different dimensions of European politics, economy and society (Suleiman and Mendras 1995; Bagnasco and Le Galès 2000; Cavalli and Galland 1997; della Porta and Mény 1997). In the last few years a number of good integrated textbook sociologies of Europe have appeared, adapting theories of modernity or comparative welfare states to a more specific European terrain (Outhwaite 2008; Rumford 2009; Roche 2010; Immerfall and Therborn 2010). There has also been a second generation of scholars in German sociology – also mainly working in German – who are less committed to nation-by-nation comparison and much more alive to the transnational dimensions of the Europeanization processes (Bach, Lahusen and Vobruba 2006; Gerhards 2007, 2010; Münch 2008; Haller 2008; Mau et al. 2008; Mau and Verwiebe 2009; Mau 2010). Connections back to history can also be made to contemporary EU historians – who have now gone well beyond the restrictions of nation-centred diplomatic studies. As well as the more well-known grand synthetic works about post-war European and EU history (Mazower 2000; Judt 2005; Anderson 2009), there are also those building empirically on the Milward legacy, yet with a more transnational account of

European integration, alive to its specific political and legal dynamics and its social rootedness (Kaiser 2008; Kaiser *et al.* 2008; Knudsen 2009).

On the whole, though, we are still quite far from a true convergence of interests between the comparative or comparative historical sociologists of Europe seeking a distinctly Europeanized model of economy and society, and the overt study of political, legal or institutional processes building the European Union, even when they are filtered through a sociological lens.

There are some exceptions to this lack of development within the field. One young American sociologist, Beckfield (2006), has opened an agenda for comparative quantitative studies on stratification with his work using the Luxembourg Income Study on how regional integration in Europe has over several decades led to a rise in income inequality in West European countries. The key question here is sorting out what is caused by regional integration, and what is caused by globalization, a central question of the quantitative tests on European market effects carried out by Fligstein and Mérand (2002). In subsequent studies, Beckfield and associates have enlarged this to look at comparative regional effects of globalization on trade, economic integration and inequality, comparing Western Europe with the US and Japan, as did Crouch (Brady *et al.* 2007). These studies do indeed suggest there are distinctive dimensions to the European model. However, their survey of the relevant literature also makes clear how rare it is for any study in global political economy to even mention the EU amidst vast data sets focused exclusively on cross-national comparisons.

More familiar to the mainstream of EU studies, the Sapir report (2004) on the future of the EU model in the light of the visionary Lisbon agenda of 2000 gave an extremely prominent place to ideas of 'flexicurity' in Europe – that is, the structural feature of (some) European welfare states that allow a liberal economy and labour market to be combined with strong social and employment benefits that enable retraining and rapid re-employment. This echoes the warnings of familiar faces to the EU mainstream, such as Alberta Sbragia and Brigid Laffan, about how EU politics must respond to struggles and contestation over European social models. Most obviously, the Sapir report called up as a key reference the later work of Esping-Andersen (1999), which compares alternative models of welfare capitalism in Europe, and defends a Scandinavian variety as the potential European future. Esping-Andersen himself, however, almost never mentions the EU in his models, and is focused resolutely on cross-national comparison within Europe.

Bizarrely, just as the comparative sociologists hardly ever mention the EU in their studies, there is little or no trace of such comparative political economy in the widely discussed theories of integration that are supposed to conceive of European integration in the broadest and most ambitious terms in EU studies (in textbooks such as Rosamond 2000 or Wiener and Diez 2003). While these authors are certainly sympathetic to a 'sociological' agenda in EU studies, it is perhaps symptomatic that they do not factor into this vision the kind of core works in comparative sociology or international political economy that have most effectively spelt out the structure of the post-industrial society and welfare state in Europe, and which are slowly beginning to recognize its linkages to the regional process of European Union. On both sides, then, the linkages need to be made. In the contributions to the first half of this volume, we thus present a variety of ways that connections can be built between comparative macro-sociology, international political economy and EU studies, using examples of contemporary sociological research on the EU.

The political sociology of EU politics

If Part I of this volume focuses on Europeanizing behaviour, practices or social structures, and the possible emergence of a European society and Europeans who might populate it, Part II focuses on the political production of specifically European, that is, EU decisions, that affect social practices across the continent from work to study, care to leisure. It is thus aligned with the mainstream's understandings of the topic of Europeanization, while offering a quite alternative toolbox of concepts and methods.

The second half of the book again presents work that may be less familiar to most mainstream EU scholars, largely because it is being led by scholars working in French. We are very conscious in this volume of the need sometimes to break out of the hegemony of English language-only EU studies – as we have seen, much of the most important comparative sociology of Europe has over the years been first developed in Germany. Over the last ten to fifteen years, the burgeoning of EU studies in France has led to what we describe here as a 'new political sociology' of the EU. Of course, much of what has been presented in earlier parts of the book could well also be described as 'political sociology', some of it coming more out of political science, some of it more from sociology. Defining political sociology is a complicated business: while still strong if not dominant in some national traditions of political science (France being a good example), it is almost entirely absent in others (the US especially), where all political sociology essentially goes on in sociology departments. A central handbook on Anglo-American political science (Goodin and Klingemann 1996) relegates sociology to a peripheral role in chapters on political behaviour or political economy; an international handbook on political sociology, meanwhile, which covers a vast array of big and central political topics, is mostly compiled of sociologists (Nash and Scott 2001). Yet, whatever the disciplinary division of labour, there are persistent common questions, in particular when it comes to the study of power, political legitimacy, civil society, public opinion or citizenship, as examined in the context of nation- and state-building, and traditions of democratic theory. What we thus propose here is to apply to EU politics and policies some rather old questions that date back to the classics of the political sociology canon, such as Ferguson on civil society or de Tocqueville on democracy. Yet the new political sociology of the EU puts into action a rather distinct approach to other political sociologists, mixing strong ideas about the theoretical construction of their object of study with in-depth empirical research using new methods on the EU terrain.

What does this view bring? We may feel we already know the European Union as an object of study. The institutions are a familiar constellation to any students of the EU. The EU enlarges and deepens. Yet another treaty comes into force. The European Commission routinely issues proposals, the European Council of Ministers and the European Parliament approve legislation, the European Court of Justice rules on cases, and, once in a while, European citizens vote 'No' to a referendum on a new EU treaty, or demonstrators gather enough momentum to gain media attention and make headlines denouncing the European construction. Numerous EU textbooks cover the subject in this sense (Dinan 2005; Hix 2005; Cini 2007). Yet just as in Balzac's and Thackeray's novels, we want to know more, from a 'sociological' viewpoint: who exactly are the 'upstarts' in Brussels and Bucharest, learning and applying EU-specific resources and skills, what are they in fact doing and why? We also wonder how ordinary Europeans – but also citizens of candidate countries and resident 'third country nationals' – view, experience, debate, and contest the European integration process. It is thus precisely the increasing complexity of the European Union as a field over and beyond formal politics and law itself, that requires us to study the very people – the actors – that are building Europe, at both the core and the periphery of the Union, in the capital and at the margins. Rejecting a stratospheric view of the EU, typical of the institutions-focused mainstream (*'une vue trop aérienne'*, in the words of Smith 1999, or the 'birds' eye view', as Guiraudon 2006 puts it), is there a way we can focus in on these actors' behaviour, their social characteristics, and their distinctive views of Europe? As people, with a human face, they surely have much to tell us about EU political dynamics.

Others may wonder why we need to study Europeans sociologically in order to understand European integration. The sociological view, however, is not entirely absent from recognizable names in the field of EU studies. Sidney Tarrow (2001) and Stefano Bartolini (2005) have noted an analogy between European integration and historian Wayne te Brake's notion of 'composite polity' in early modern European history. As te Brake says: 'it was often in the interstices and on the margins of these early modern state formations that ordinary people enjoyed the greatest political opportunities' (1998: 14–15). The analogy suggests that EU scholars should be asking how the emerging EU institutional complex changes or does not change the sources of social power and its distribution among live European actors. It is a clearly a key question for political sociology (Mann 1993b), but it also matters for disciplines such as political science and law interested in shifts in what they would call 'the attribution of competences'. In other words, there is a call for new kinds of empirical studies on the actors that take part in what mainstream EU studies has typically called the 'institutionalisation of Europe' (Stone Sweet et al. 2001).

In the 1990s, a range of political sociologists took up this agenda. They have developed new ways of studying mobilization in relation to the EU, by studying the actions of what might be called 'EU professionals', in both institutional settings and beyond. Thus the careers and social profiles of politicians, bureaucrats and judges have come to be documented and analyzed in-depth, as well as others orbiting EU institutions – such as lobbyists, collective actors such as associations, trade unions and social movement organizations that position themselves in relation to European integration, even the media professionals that cover all this as news. Political sociologists re-discovered Europe as an object of study in the early 1990s, after the *relance de l'Europe* (relaunch of Europe), the single market completion 1992 deadline, and the Maastricht Treaty of 1993. While the development of a new political sociology of the EU has been much more advanced in France, there were signs of this renaissance in the mainstream Anglo-American literature. As well as the work of Tarrow and Bartolini mentioned above, a key example was political sociologist George Ross's account as an observer within the Delors cabinet (Ross 1994). This also reflected a period when a handful of anthropologists, mentioned above, first became intrigued by the EU and Europeanization (Abélès 1992; Bellier 1994). In 1993, one team issued a notorious report based on the first extensive insider ethnography of the Commission and Parliament (Abélès et al. 1993). For those anthropologists who joined in the rush to study the EU, the EU was not so much an object of study as a laboratory or (as the French love to say) a terrain, a location for field work.

What sociologists and anthropologists shared is a view that political and other actors implicated in the EU are always also socially embedded in worlds outside politics *per se*. They can thus be observed as more than just political actors, by a variety of methods, including ethnography and comparative datasets. They can be observed in terms of the social resources that individuals taking part in EU politics can draw on and build up over time to improve their position in society at large; the way that they incarnate a role that might have been carved out of nothing or constructed over time; and the extent to which these resources and roles differ from typical political elites and activists in national or international contexts. Different kinds of professionals can be considered: whether they are sitting MEPs, *fonctionnaires* at the Commission, advocate generals at the European Court of Justice, NGO and think tank personnel, or EU media correspondents. As we will see, this focus on such actors in context can lead to a rather different view of the EU, which seeks explanations for familiar European institutions and policies, not within the dynamics of politics as such, but outside – in the social positions and trajectories of such actors and their symbolic conflicts about meaning, legitimacy and social power in wider society.

In France, a variety of studies along these lines has developed, often under the theoretical and methodological influence of the sociologist Pierre Bourdieu. They seek to understand the formation of a distinct European *field* of political action, specify the specific types of 'capital' thus valorized, and the 'habitus' they incarnate (for good introductions to the French political sociology of the EU, see Kauppi 2003; Irondelle 2006; Georgakakis 2008; Weisbein 2008). A field here denotes the unclearly defined and ever-shifting political space in which different political actors define themselves in relation to others, and struggle over dominance and influence over each other. To do this, they call up a variety of different resources – forms of capital – that actors can use to position themselves with social power and domination over others. These can range from straightforward economic resources to cultural credentials, social know-how and other forms of prestige. Habitus, meanwhile, here refers to the habits and automatic reflexes that specialist professionals develop through their socialization into different roles and social positions. The pioneering work in this vein by Didier Bigo (1996) on the transnational field of security professionals and Niilo Kauppi (1996b) on MEPs and European Parliament campaigns, both explicitly adapt Bourdieu's notion of field to capture what are always emergent and protean dynamics.

A first set of studies has sought to contribute to this new socio-history of the EU by re-examining what had become unquestioned common sense in political science studies of the same subjects. This is particularly the case in research on the importance of legal expertise and the European Court of Justice in European integration (Jettinghoff and Schepel, 2005; Rask Madsen, 2005; Cohen and Vauchez, 2007a). They focus on the human face of law by looking at the social means by which legal professionals consecrate their own circles and legitimate the supremacy of European law. They seek to explain what we take as an explanation – integration through law – by situating the Court in its broader social context, in which European lawyers are struggling for social power in relation to their peer group(s) back home, as well as other EU professionals in the EU institutional environment. The legal field is in fact rather porous and lawyers or persons trained in law are everywhere to be seen both inside and outside EU institutions.

Other sets of studies focus on the careers of different EU professionals. With roots in the political anthropology of the EU mentioned above, these more recent political sociologies have used ethnographic methods to go inside EU institutions, immersing themselves in the *loci* of power: whether following debates over Europe and institutional reform (de Lassalle and Georgakakis 2007; Cohen and Vauchez 2007b); focusing on policy developments (Guiraudon 2003; Smith 2004a; Mérand 2008); studying places where 'Europe' is taught, such as Bruges (Schnabel 1996) or training schools in European affairs (Michel 2006); and immersing oneself in the world of Brussels journalists and their social networks (Baisnée 2007a). Still others have created personalized databases of individual careers within EU institutions, gathering as much information on the socio-demographic characteristics of EU officials and tracing their educational and professional trajectories (Dorandeu and Georgakakis 2002). The study of the Commission (de Lassalle and Georgakakis 2007), for example, shows the increasing specialization of personnel over time with the development of particular profiles: transversal/political posts for Commission top managers with international and EU experience versus technical/sectoral posts for national civil servants. Studying who people *are* and what they *do* highlights processes of distinction over time. Work on the European Parliament is telling in this respect as one sees over time the institutionalization of the MEP function, with its emphasis on expertise and the professionalization of 'unlikely' politicians, such as women, celebrities and minority parties' members, such as the Greens and Right-wing populists (Kauppi 2005; Beauvallet and Michon 2010). This work dialogues with theories developed in other streams of political science. In a recent study based on a biographical database, Willy Beauvallet and Sébastien Michon (2008) seek to explain why there are many women in the European Parliament (around 30 per cent in the 2004–9 legislature), going beyond the main hypotheses that focus on the electoral system (proportional voting) and focusing rather on political recruitment strategies, political resources and strategies. Given that women have made up around 40 per cent of French MEPs and only 10 per cent of the national parliament in the last decade, they code and compare the biographies of male and female MEPs to establish how women are less endowed with social and political capital (in terms of education and career trajectory). They also show how this then influences the strategies and behaviour of women once they are elected: the positions that they occupy as MEPs and the role that they construct for themselves.

Studies that flesh out EU institutions show power struggles between insiders and outsiders, lines of cleavages, and rules of entry and interaction. In brief, they show how fields are institutionalized, and roles are scripted there rather than institutions being taken for granted (Guiraudon 2006). They help understand practices and their social significance within institutions, for example the broader meaning of a vote in the European Parliament (see Kauppi, Chapter 7 in this volume). And finally, they show that that true power holders in EU fields are those that are multi-positioned in both national and EU fields and can thus act as brokers and gatekeepers (Favell 1998; Guiraudon 2000; Ruzza and Bozzini 2008).

Meanwhile, quantitative studies all point to a steady increase in mobilization targeting the EU and in the discussion of the EU in the media since the 1990s and the advent of the single market (Imig and Tarrow 2000). There has been much debate about the emergence of a European 'public sphere' and its importance in making the EU a political community that people could identify with. Normative Habermasian approaches are one way to consider this (Trenz and Eder 2004; Eriksen 2005b). Comparative studies of news items, editorials and public claims made by political actors in national newspapers have followed (Fossum and Schlesinger, 2007; Wessler *et al.* 2008; Díez Medrano 2009; Koopmans and Statham 2010). Drawing on original databases, they demonstrate the remaining differences in the domestication of EU developments by national media and actors.

As the variety and range of the works cited above suggests, there is a whole new field of work emerging in EU studies that takes a distinct political sociology angle on the field. This new political sociology of the EU has struggled for recognition in the mainstream, although it is now beginning to receive attention from advocates and critics, sceptics and sympathizers alike (Favell 2006; Guiraudon 2006; Dezalay *et al.* 2007; Adler-Nissen 2008; Menon 2008, Saurugger 2008, 2009; Mérand and Saurugger 2010, Rumford 2008; Parsons 2010). Our sample here in this volume offers a further taste of a mode of analysis of the EU that is likely to grow in importance in the coming years, as sociological tools and methods are adopted by the mainstream.

How to do a sociology of the European Union

In the light of the three surveys in this chapter of what are currently understood as sociological approaches to the European Union, what might a new sociology of the European Union look like? In the chapters that follow this introduction, we present a series of distinct but complementary visions of how this question might be operationalized in empirical work. Split into two halves which cover Social Foundations and Politics and Policies, we introduce each section with a brief summary of each author's contribution and their relevance to current concerns in EU studies. The book thus opens with themes from the central agenda of sociology – addressing questions of class, identity and mobilities, culture, social stratification and economic organization – to assess the emergence of a 'European society'. Later chapters then move into applying theories and modes of analysis in sociology to revisit the core issues of EU studies: addressing the political sociology of the EU and various dimensions of democracy, representation, mobilization and policy in the EU.

At the end of this journey, we hope that the contribution of the sociology of the European Union will be clear. We do not present this manifesto as a turf war exercise. This would only reify a discipline-centred view of the field in a fluid age where all scholars might need to be inter- if not post-disciplinary in some aspect of their work. But past and present relations between the disciplines need clarifying, and we do argue for an appreciation of what a distinctive new empirical sociology – not yet fully recognized – might bring to EU studies. While joining our agenda, most of the contributors to this volume think of themselves as thoroughly interdisciplinary scholars. Their involvement in an inherently interdisciplinary field such as EU studies puts them at the margins of their own discipline and is sometimes worn as a mark of their own frustration with it. Nevertheless, we believe the key to true interdisciplinarity is the ability to understand the differences between disciplines, both in terms of how they look from the outside and how they operate from the inside. Law, history, economics, anthropology and political science all have their distinctive *modus operandi* in relation to studying the EU; so does sociology. We hope here to have presented a clear overview of how sociology can be positioned in relation to other disciplines' work on the EU, and of what kind of new empirical contributions it can bring to the field.

PART I:
Social Foundations

The European Union has evolved from a customs union into a single market and political union with a common currency and institutions that cover a whole range of policy areas. From the point of view of many sociologists, the key question in the study of Europeanization is: what impact has this transformation had on everyday European citizens' lives and experiences? They thus seek to look beyond the more usual and more limited focus in mainstream EU studies on Europeanization on institutional effects, legal cases or policy implementation. Moreover, their interest points to a prior question in the historical emergence of the European Union. What kind of social foundations underlie the political and legal construction on which regional integration in Europe has been built?

In a range of works during the last decade, **Juan Díez Medrano** has been developing an empirical sociology of European Union that might begin to answer these questions systematically. In particular, his landmark book *Framing Europe: Attitudes to European Integration in Germany, Spain, and the United Kingdom* (2003), used a systematic frame analysis of post-1945 editorials, attitudinal surveys and extensive interviews in three member states to get at the question of European identity and its variation across the continent. Here, building on his 2006 Einaudi lecture at Cornell University, he explores whether European integration has affected Europe's underlying social structures. As he points out, several authors have argued that the 'social bases' to the European project must reflect the interests of a European middle class (Therborn 1995; Milward 1997). But this is by no means an easy question to operationalize. The challenging question here supposes that one can find indicators that might reveal the existence of European social classes, with characteristics similar to those that are traditionally associated with the national social classes that emerged with the formation of European nation-states. Based on the sociology of class and social stratification, Díez Medrano thus operationalizes the study of putative European social classes, in terms of identity measures, social ties, and political mobilization, putting into action a distinctly Weberian (as opposed to Marxist) approach. While Díez Medrano concludes that existing indicators suggest that one cannot yet speak of 'European social classes', he diagnoses the main obstacles that stand in the way of their emergence. He also argues, however, that we may find clear evidence of Europeanization (of Europeans) well before we find evidence for the emergence of such classes.

In the next chapter, **Adrian Favell** and **Ettore Recchi** complement Díez Medrano's analysis of social stratification and identification by taking on the issue of intra-EU migration encouraged by the free movement rights of workers/persons within the European Union. They pose the question: does such spatial mobility lead to improved chances of social mobility for migrant EU citizens, and what might be the consequences for the European project? They build upon the PIONEUR project, a unique telephone-based survey directed by Recchi that was designed to measure Europeanization through the lives and experiences of flesh-and-blood European citizens: five thousand 'movers' – EU citizens living abroad – who were compared to the majority population of 'stayers' surveyed by instruments such as Eurobarometer and European Social Survey (Recchi and Favell 2009). They also draw on Favell's investigative ethnography *Eurostars and Eurocities: Free Movement and Mobility in an Integrating Europe* (2008) which portrays the foreign European populations in three major hubs of European mobility: Amsterdam, London, Brussels. Whereas structurally little evidence can be found to show upward social mobility among EU free movers, Favell and Recchi go on to offer examples of individual narratives to show how EU mobility laws and policies have facilitated extraordinary success and experiences for a small self-selecting population of pioneers.

Also addressing the relationship between European Union and social structures is the chapter co-authored by **Alberta Andreotti** and **Patrick Le Galès**. Building on extensive work about European cities (Le Galès 2002), they present research on the broader mobility strategies of European middle classes, which do not necessarily include international migration as such, but which are enabling elites and upper-middle classes to dominate opportunities opened by European integration. Their analysis presents findings from an original network survey developed in several major European cities. How are the more affluent members of European society using the emergence of a European space to change the way they behave financially outside national tax regimes, develop personal networks beyond borders, arrange schooling and educational advantages for children abroad, or engage in new forms of international consumption or property acquisition? The main research question is whether European integration offers urban elites and/or upper-middle classes the possibility of 'exiting' their own nation-state or national society: in terms of job trajectory, networks, consumption, education, property ownership and so on. This may also extend to their expression of social and political values (for example, opting out of local public schools and services) without ever actually physically exiting (that is, moving abroad). The chapter considers the question of whether these exit options are particularly European in nature, or rather are only a local manifestation of the rise of a global capitalist class. They set out a new agenda for prospective sociological students of the EU by showing how the European Union cannot be overlooked in debates in urban studies and political economy.

In turn, economic sociology – one of the best established and most influential fields in sociology – can shed light on European Union. **Neil Fligstein**, the most distinguished American sociologist to have developed work on the EU, here develops the part of his broad agenda in his aforementioned book *Euroclash* (2008), concerning the EU's distinctive construction as a market beyond the nation-state. Focusing mainly on the behaviour of firms within the market-making project – that is at the core of the European Union as a legal construction – he reminds us of the importance of economic structure and material interests in understanding adhesion to the European project and policy dynamics. Here, drawing on tools and methods familiar in economic sociology, Fligstein uses available data to show how the European economy has been Europeanized rather than globalized. To illustrate the strategic responses of large firms to market integration, Fligstein introduces a sectoral example: a case study of the re-organization of the telecommunications industry. Fligstein shows how the political project of the EU has deliberately constructed a particular version of the liberal market – with a distinctive range of property rights, governance structures, rules of exchange and conceptions of corporate control – that both distinguishes Europe from its American and Asian regional rivals, and is institutionalized in a range of policy domains. The EU's Single Market and other market opening projects have profoundly affected the European economy by creating new Europe-wide markets and increased trade. Firms have taken advantage of these common rules to expand their activities across national borders, thereby making economic integration not just a political project but an economic reality.

CHAPTER 2

Social Class and Identity

Juan Díez Medrano

> **Key concepts:** operationalization, class, social structure, social stratification, identity, social ties, mobilization, Europeanization, nation-states, transnational social groups, distinction, nation building, social transactions, socialization
>
> **Key references:** Esping-Andersen, Crouch, Marx, Weber, Bourdieu, Deutsch, Gellner, Lawler

One of the key objectives of an empirical sociology of European Union would be to explore the ways in which the single European market and EU legislation, policies and institutions have impacted on European society as a whole. The timing of this call for sociology in EU studies is not an accident. The reason why it makes sense now and not in, say, the 1960s, is that since the late 1980s what we now call the European Union has transformed itself from a customs union into a single market with a common currency and institutions that cover a whole range of economic, social and political policy areas. The new European Union has a tremendous impact on European citizens' lives. It is thus worth exploring what impact these dramatic institutional transformations have had on Europe's underlying social structures, rather than focusing exclusively, as political scientists have done so far, on the institutional impact of EU policies and legislation on European nation-states.

To speak of social structure immediately raises the question of *social class* in European society. To what extent can we speak today of the existence of *European* social classes, with similar characteristics to those that traditionally characterized national social classes? Authors such as Alan Milward (1997) or Göran Therborn (1995, Chapter 10) have argued that there must be a definite social base to the European project that reflects the interests of a European middle class, or those of populations that have gained most from regional integration (such as populations closer to European borders). The proposition looks plausible on the face of it, but it is by no means an easy question to operationalize. In this chapter, then, I first offer a brief introduction to the sociology of class and social stratification, in terms of both existing studies of Europe, and its roots in classical social theory. Using this, I then offer an empirical operationalization of the study of putative European social classes, in terms of identity, social ties and political mobilization. On all of these indicators, I argue, it is too soon to speak of the existence of such classes. Seeking to explain why such phenomena have yet to emerge, I then go on to analyze the main obstacles that stand in the way of the emergence of European social classes – and hence, implicitly, a fully-fledged European society – by drawing an analogy between the making of European Union and the historical emergence of the nation-state.

Social groups and classes in the sociology of Europe

Most of what we know about social classes comes from research on Western societies. This literature is mainly grouped under the heading of *social stratification*, the study of the distribution of individuals in society according to different social positions linked to income, education or power. This literature is also centrally concerned with the question of *social mobility*, which is dealt with elsewhere in this volume (Chapter 3).

There is an abundant literature on class stratification and social mobility in West European states (Müller 2004; Wright 1996; Goldthorpe and Erikson 1992; Breen 2004). The major questions that this literature has addressed since the mid-1950s have been the existence of processes of convergence or divergence between European stratification systems, the contrasting role of education in the stratification process of different European societies, and the emergence of the new middle class linked to its political power to determine elections and its economic power as consumers.

In the mid-1980s, Gøsta Esping-Andersen's pioneering work shifted the focus of social stratification research from description and documentation to the institutional explanation of stratification patterns in terms of the varieties of welfare state systems in Europe (Esping-Andersen 1990, 1999). He argued for the existence of three major welfare regimes, which he labels Liberal, Conservative-corporatist, and Social Democratic. This classification was initially based on the extent to which labour is decommodified and on stratification patterns. His most recent work maintains the 'three worlds of welfare capitalism' distinction, but pays more attention to how the characteristics of families and women's roles in different societies introduces distinctions within each type of welfare regime. Finally, Colin Crouch's *Social Change in Western Societies* (1999) brought together both strands of work to produce a synthesis of class stratification systems in Europe and their institutional foundation, in a study which, like Esping-Andersen, stresses the varieties of capitalism and the social models that have been built in Europe. The end of the Cold War and the transition to capitalism in Central and Eastern Europe has also seen a shift of focus in stratification research from the West to the East. Work by Eyal *et al.* (2002), Róna-Tas (1994), and Domànski (1996) analyzed the transformation of the stratification system in Eastern Europe, with particular attention to transitions from social positions under communism and social positions under capitalism and to winners and losers in the process. Other authors (for example, Haller 1993) addressed traditional stratification questions, this time including both Western and Eastern European states.

Seen from this chapter's perspective, three features characterize this literature. First, there is the taken for granted assumption of the nation-state as the basic unit of analysis for the study of stratification in Europe (Breen and Rottman 1998; Berger and Weiss 2008). Second, there is an understanding of class only as a particular location in the stratification system. There is no attempt to discuss the interaction between social groups or the distinctive lifestyles that each group adopts, something central to the work of Pierre Bourdieu about class *distinction* (for example, 1984 on France), or in historical work such as Kocka's and Mitchell's study (1993) of nineteenth-century European bourgeoisies and Michael Mann on the rise of nation-states and social classes (Mann 1993). Finally, stratification scholars, with the lone exception of Jason Beckfield (2006), have yet to investigate the impact of the European Union on the stratification systems of its members and on the development of pan-European social classes. Beckfield's pioneering study does this and finds that European integration has been responsible for half of the rise in social inequalities in Western European countries as the Union has progressed.

Class, social structure and Europeanization

Empirically speaking, is it possible to talk about class formation beyond the nation-state? On this question, it is possible to analytically distinguish two processes that follow from the acceleration of European integration in the past twenty years: Europeanization and European class formation. Definitions of Europeanization in the literature generally refer to the European Union's institutional impact on domestic politics and national economies. As with other contributions to this book (see Chapter 1), I depart from this narrow political science definition and propose an alternative that bears strong similarities to how the sociological literature defines the process of globalization. Europeanization of national societies can be conceived as the widening of the geographical scope of the national citizens' lives and economic and political activities on a European scale, just as globalization would conceive this on a global scale.

The Europeanization of European national societies, in terms of behaviour, attitudes or even the identity (or self-perceptions) of European citizens would be one thing. My chapter, however, looks beyond this to the wider question of the emergence of European social classes: that is, of groups of people who, as well as identifying primarily as Europeans, share similar social positions, interact with one another, and (potentially) mobilize politically as one group. To understand the distinction I make between the parallel processes of Europeanization and European class formation, we have to go back to the different meanings that the concept of *social structure* has had for sociologists in the past. Sociologists have understood the concept of social structure as:

1   a set of interrelated normative expectations about how people in different social positions should behave (an *institutional* definition);
2   a pattern of social interaction between people, structured in particular ways (a *network* definition);
3   shared subjective meanings within a group about the world and about how to behave (a *cultural* definition); or
4   a set of objective social positions and the distribution of people along these positions (a *stratification* definition).

Whereas the sociological study of the Europeanization of national societies tends to prioritize a network conceptualization of the social structure, with a focus on the network's geographic scope, the study of European class formation should also refer to both objective stratification and cultural conceptualizations of the social structure people find themselves in. The focus of the topic of European class formation then would be on the emergence of fully distinguishable European social groups: that is, *transnational* groups of European citizens whose behaviour and consciousness denote solidarities that transcend national and sub-national affiliations.

To conceive class in this way combines elements borrowed from both Marx and Weber on social class. These classical sociologists remain key to understanding the question of class and stratification in modern societies. As in Marxian perspectives, I distinguish between the concepts of 'class in itself' and 'class for itself' and focus on the identity/consciousness dimension of class. A class in itself, such as the working class, is a group of individuals who share the same economic and political interests because of being located in a similar position in the economic production structure of society. Individuals may not be aware, however, of these shared interests and therefore fail to mobilize politically as members of the same social group. This is the reason why Marxists introduced the aforementioned distinction between 'class in itself' and 'class for itself'. The latter is a class in itself whose members have acquired consciousness of belonging to the same group and thus can mobilize politically as a group.

I go on, though, to also incorporate a Weberian perspective on class. Weber argued that social group formation need not be reductively linked only to the economic structure of production, but could include actors' ability to mobilize around other group definitions such as culture and beliefs. So, in my approach, as with Weber, I distinguish between the concepts of class position and social class, focusing on the interactive dimension of the latter. Weber's concept of class position bears some similarity to the concept of 'class in itself', but whereas Marxism derives classes primarily from people's position in the production structure, Weber derives classes from people's objective opportunities in the market. For Weber, people in a class position become a class when they interact frequently and intensely with each other, often because of common culture or beliefs.

Using Marxian and Weberian concepts in this way points towards a particular synthesis in the study of class. In many ways, Pierre Bourdieu effects this synthesis of Marx and Weber in his work on social class in France (1984). He adds to the conceptualization of social class a dimension of interactive *distinction* which refers to the way members of a social class distinguish themselves from other social groups by upholding certain tastes or practices which can be broadly defined as consumption patterns. Taking these conceptualizations together, then, identification with a group, intermarriage, joint political action, and distinct consumption patterns can be seen as some of the empirical dimensions one would need to explore when studying European class formation. This is how the study of European social classes can effectively be operationalized.

Europeanization or European social classes?

Logically speaking, we would expect Europeanization to proceed faster than European class formation, since the former is a precondition of the latter. Europeanization changes the behaviour of firms, and brings tourists, exchange students, migrant workers, retirees and political claimants from different countries into contact with one another. Without these contacts, the solidarities that constitute social groups could not develop.

Since 1986, the European Union has made tremendous strides toward the development of a single market space, through the elimination of the numerous non-tariff barriers that existed to the free movement of goods, capital and people. Formal tariffs, meanwhile, had already been virtually abolished by 1968 (Rodríguez-Pose 2002). Parallel to this transformation, there has been a Europeanization of trade and investment (see Fligstein, Chapter 5 in this volume). Moreover, during the 1990s, there was a significant increase in the number of EU qualified workers and professionals who chose to work in other European Union countries (see Favell and Recchi, Chapter3). The EU has developed a conception of European citizenship, as well as policies to substantiate this concept. The Erasmus programme and the Schengen Treaty, in particular, have contributed decisively to the Europeanization of the European Union citizens' travel and cultural experiences. More indirectly, liberalization measures in the air transport industry, which have favoured a significant lowering of travel costs around Europe, and financial support for the improvement of the European land transport network have also contributed to this Europeanization of experience.

The European Union has considerably expanded its range of competences and the budgetary resources at its disposal since the early 1990s. It now legislates on a wide variety of policy areas and has budgets that it can use to fund a wide array of projects and activities that redistribute resources from richer to poorer regions and sectors. Furthermore, in the last twenty years the concept of the primacy of European Union law over national law has been firmly established. As the European Union has broadened its legislation and policy-making capacity, and as its budget has increased and diversified, a growing number of social groups in the European Union states have developed stakes in the decisions of the European Union. The significant increase in the political scope of the European Union has meant that interest groups and social movements might increasingly address their grievances to the European Union (see Imig and Tarrow 2001; Guiraudon, Chapter 6 in this volume).

In sum, there is a clear relationship between the strengthening of the European Union's economic and political institutions since the late 1980s and the Europeanization of national societies, whether we think of exchanges, experiences or political mobilization. But still, Europeanization of this kind does not necessarily involve the emergence of European social classes. When people exchange goods and invest capital in other European countries, when they sit on the boards of directors of firms from different European countries, when they visit other European countries as tourists or exchange students, when they move to other European countries in order to work, when they join Europe-wide associations, or when they address claims to the European Union institutions, they do not necessarily do it yet as members of an emergent European society. Nothing prevents them from doing it as Spanish, Danish, Czech, or Maltese citizens. Indeed, as the section below shows, few in fact do so as members of a European class or group. While Europeanization is a first step toward the emergence of a European society, the latter will not necessarily follow from a further intensification of the Europeanization process. Further changes would be necessary for a new, European society, with a distinctive transnational class structure, to emerge, as I will argue.

To this end, is there a stronger way of looking at Europeanization? The European society that would interest Marx and Weber is not the one examined by an author such as Crouch: that is, a model of European society constructed merely on the basis of an aggregation of nation-by-nation statistics on occupational and sectoral distributions of the European labour force, as related to distinctive welfare state institutions across Europe. A fully-fledged notion of European society would stand a level above this statistical construction: as a European social structure built on a distinctive order of Europeanized social class or classes. The notion of a European social class must also go beyond a network or territorially based notion of Europeanized behaviour or interaction. Consequently, to operationalize Marxian or Weberian understandings of class demands a focus on three constitutive dimensions of a European social group. Examining the evidence for these three dimensions will allow us to draw conclusions about the existence or not of European social classes.

These dimensions are represented in Figure 2.1. One of them is the consciousness of being part of the same social group. Social scientists speak of this in terms of the concept of *identity*. Indeed, the Marxian and Weberian conceptions of social groups implicitly see *identity* as the core constitutive element of social class. Empirically speaking, this would demand from potential members of a European social class that at the very least they self-identify as Europeans. A second dimension that characterizes social classes is the existence of *strong ties* between those who identify as European. Measurements that can identify such strong ties would need to find good empirical proxies for this concept. In the study of the upper classes, intermarriage has generally been considered the ultimate indicator of such strong ties, not only because of the emotional element involved but also because it generally represents a form of capital merger, at least from the heirs' perspective. 'Cold' joint ownership of capital, that is, co-ownership without a deep emotional component, is another good indicator of strong ties. A key third element in establishing a social class as defined here is joint purpose: this could be conceived as joint political action. Here I will measure this in terms of transnational *mobilization* by social movements.

Figure 2.1 leaves out a fourth element of social groups that might also be used to operationalize the notion of class: *consumption*. This is because consumption patterns do not so much define class as generally follow from it. To define class, we might thus look for the development among members of a social group of shared consumption practices as they compete for symbolic capital with other social groups. This kind of study of class consumption patterns is

Social Class and Identity

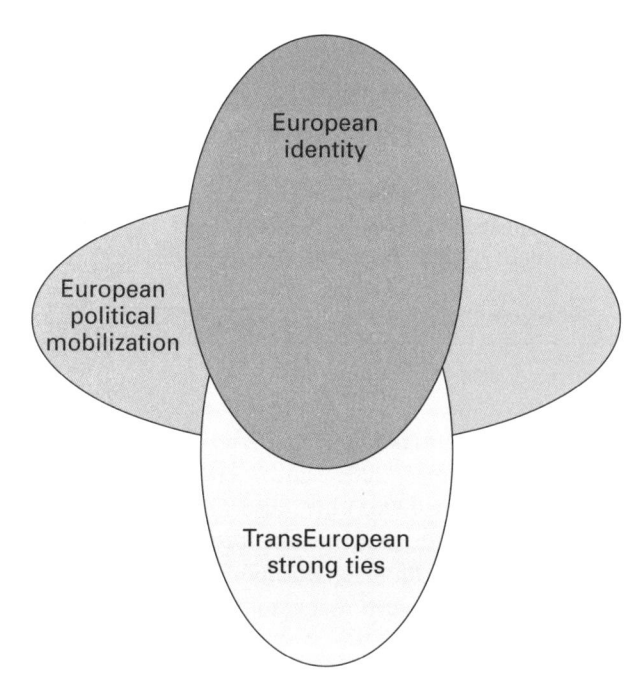

Figure 2.1 Dimensions of European social groups

most strongly influenced by Weber's conception of social class, and is reflected especially in the work of Bourdieu (1984). A sociology of European society would certainly need to focus on this dimension of class behaviour too, but we leave that to a later chapter (dimensions of this question in urban contexts are addressed by Andreotti and Le Galès in Chapter 4).

Identity

Undoubtedly, of all the criteria that an aggregate of individuals needs to fulfil to be considered a social class, the most important one is that people in the same social position consider themselves members of the same group. There is abundant survey information measuring the prevalence of a sense of identification with Europe among the population (see Eurobarometer; also Duchesne and Frognier 1995; Sinnott 1995; Díez Medrano and Gutiérrez 2001; Herrnstein, Risse et al. 2004; Fligstein 2008). Although survey data is more meaningful when complemented by ethnographic information on the depth, situational character and meaning of identification with Europe, it does provide good information on aggregate trends. There is, of course, a developing literature on European identity of relevance here. Among the most important contributions

Table 2.1 Trends in relative identification in the EU (1992–2004) (% of population)

	1992	1996	2000	2004	2005
Nationality only	40.0	53.3	39.5	41.4	41.0
Nationality and European	47.3	35.4	47.5	46.9	48.0
European and nationality	6.1	5.5	6.3	6.9	7.0
European only	3.2	3.5	3.4	3.1	2.0
Don't know	3.4	2.3	3.2	1.8	2.0

Source: Eurobarometer (European Commission).

to this are Hewstone's *Understanding Attitudes to European Integration* (1986), Díez Medrano's *Framing Europe* (2003), and Menéndez-Alarcón's *The Cultural Realm of European Integration* (2005) (see also Duchesne et al. 2010; Bücker 2008). All of these studies argue that the extent to which individuals see themselves as Europeans depends on how Europe has been constructed in their respective countries, which reverts back to national political cultures and historical developments.

The percentages displayed in Table 2.1 show in fact that citizens do not identify any more with Europe today than they have over the last two decades. 1992 is a relevant starting point in that this was when the institutional transformations of the European Union were beginning to gain momentum. Yet the Europeanization of economy, law and political behaviour, and the expected Europeanization of the behaviour and experience of citizens, have thus far failed to translate into a commensurate emergence of a shared sense of identification with Europe. Consistently less than 10 per cent strongly identify as 'European'. At the same time, however, we should not dismiss the finding that about 57 per cent of the respondents in the 2005 Eurobarometer survey express *some* form of identification with Europe.

Since national identification varies across Europe and sometimes competes with sub-national and even local identifications, we get a better sense of the prevalence of identification with Europe if we compare data from these surveys with data on national identification in plurinational countries such as Spain and Switzerland. International Social Survey Programme (ISSP) data collected in 2003 for these two countries show that in Spain 97 per cent express some form of identification with Spain, with only 24 per cent of them identifying as 'only Spaniard' or as 'more Spaniard than member of their region'. In Switzerland, 84.4 per cent express some form of identification as Swiss, with 52 per cent of the population identifying as 'only Swiss' or as 'more Swiss than member of their region'.

The data thus show a vast contrast between levels of identification with Europe and levels of identification with the state in *even* the most plurinational states in Europe. Nonetheless, the fact that more than half of Europeans express some form of identification with Europe, even if usually secondary to the national or regional identifications, reveals the early development of a proto-European society layered over national and sub-national societies. Whether it actualizes as a fully-fledged society or not remains to be seen. The 10 per cent or so of citizens who identify more with Europe than with their nation are the core of this society. In his recent book, Neil Fligstein (2008: 123–65) measures the sociological core of 'Europeans' produced by European integration in terms of these numbers, which he argues identify the elite and highly mobile populations who have most benefitted from European Union. Ten per cent is probably the upper boundary of EU citizens who can be called 'Europeans' in this way. The literature has indeed shown that younger, more educated citizens, and the upper echelons of the salaried workforce are more prone to identify as Europeans than the rest of the citizens. These social distinctions are important if we want to move from conceiving Europe as a community to conceiving Europe as a fully fledged, socially stratified society. When one disaggregates by level of education – typically a fairly reliable indicator of class position – one finds that among people with university education the percentage of the population that identifies as 'more European than national' or as 'only European' is double the one observed for those with little or no education. Indeed, among the former, the percentage of people who identify as European more than as national is around 13 per cent, whereas among the latter the percentage goes down to about 6–7 per cent.

Theoretical perspectives on identification might expect the European middle classes to represent the forerunners of European society (see Andreotti and Le Galès, Chapter 4 in this volume), just as the middle classes were the first ones to develop a sense of identification with the nation back in the late nineteenth century. The empirical evidence clearly suggests that it is too early to speak of a European middle class in this sense. Thirteen per cent of the highly educated in a population includes a lot of people, but this percentage pales in comparison with the 80 per cent or more that still identify primarily with the nation-state. Even more sobering is the fact that despite all the transformations that have occurred in Europe in the last twenty years, the percentage of people who identify as Europeans has hardly changed during this time period.

Social ties

What about other, more behavioural, measures of a putative European social class? Certainly, debates on Europeanization have pointed out that the way

Europeans consciously think about themselves does not always reflect their aggregate behaviour (Favell 2005). The British always figure among nationalities with the lowest identification with Europe, yet in terms of their holiday choices, retirement abroad, or their willingness to consider buying property elsewhere in the EU, they are among the most enthusiastic users of their European citizenship rights. Still, this kind of behaviour surely falls short of constituting a class. These kind of choices do not imply a lessening of national identification, and can be highly individualistic in their patterns. To imagine something stronger in terms of social ties, we need to consider other measurements.

Social ties are a vital concept in contemporary sociology. They are often at the heart of sociological claims that something structural is needed to fully account for the successful functioning of an economy or political system. Authors such as Mark Granovetter (1985) and Robert Putnam (1993) have established that all economic activity is socially embedded, that is, that it takes place within networks of social relationships, which explain things such as the diffusion of information, collective mobilization, and trust. The strongest ties of this kind are, of course, those embedded in family relationships. The prevalence of love partnerships between nationals of different EU members would thus be one suitable indicator of the strength of group ties. Researchers who study national cohesion in multi-ethnic states have often used this measurement (Sekulic *et al.* 1994; Botev 1994). The possibility of a new generation of cross-national children from mixed nationality marriages is obviously one potentially striking consequence of these patterns. The intermarriage rate between members of different EU states is also of interest because of the contribution that intermarriage can make to the transcendence of local identifications and the development of a sense of belonging to Europe.

Unfortunately, there are very few studies on intermarriage between Europeans and those that exist lack a comparative or Europe-wide dimension (see, however, Schroedter 2004; Gaspar 2009; Braun and Recchi 2008). One empirical illustration can provide a rough idea, however, of the numbers that we might be dealing with. Data for Spain for 1996 and 2007 reveal that the percentage of inter-European marriages out of the total number of marriages involving Europeans – leaving out marriages in which one of the partners is non-European – has risen from 1.8 to 4.4 per cent during this period. If one focuses only on marriages involving at least one Spaniard, one also sees that the percentage of marriages between a Spaniard and a person with another European nationality has increased from 1.8 to 3.8 per cent. These numbers prompt two remarks. First of all, the percentage of inter-European marriages remains extremely low. Considering the porousness of borders with freedom of movement, the apparent ubiquity of international travel, shopping and education nowadays, and the functional intermingling of many border regions, it is still remarkable how few cross-national marriages there are. Second, the percentage has certainly increased proportionally in the space of eleven years. Statistically, this is a quite striking and possibly highly significant change. In fact, the odds that a Spaniard will marry another European have doubled or more in this period.

A systematic explanation of the change described above for Spain is beyond the scope of this chapter. Such an explanation would require that one address the methodological complexity involved in disentangling marriage market effects from changes in the propensity to marry people from other nationalities. This in turn would require that one collect accurate demographic information on the pool of marriageable people from different nationalities. The composition of these intermarriages by nationality, however, provides some clues as to the relative roles of the two potential explanatory variables, for it shows a relatively high proportion of Spanish–Irish and Spanish–British marriages. Since Britons and Irish are among the largest communities of non-Spanish Europeans and since nothing suggests that Spaniards would prefer to marry British and Irish citizens rather than people from other nationalities, the most plausible conclusion one can draw is that an increase in the availability of non-Spanish Europeans accounts for the trend observed in Spain.

There is no reason to believe that the factors impacting on intermarriage rates are different in the rest of Europe from Spain. Therefore intermarriage rates are surely higher in countries where the presence of citizens from other European countries is greater than in Spain. These points relate to the issue of intra-European migration and spatial mobility (see Chapter 3). There has of course been substantial south to north migration in the past – notably the 1950s and 60s – and post enlargement East Europeans are now moving west in large numbers. Yet despite this, intra-European migration rates are generally low, and the percentage of Europeans who settle permanently in European countries other than their own is also in single figures (see Recchi and Favell 2009). What this means is that intermarriage rates between Europeans are necessarily low everywhere in Europe. For intermarriage to express pan-European class cohesion and to cement this cohesion, more geographic mobility would be needed.

Another indicator of social group cohesion might be data on co-ownership of firms. Willingness to embark on risky investments with other business people and the design of common investment strategies demands a minimum level of trust between self-interested actors, with trust expressing group cohesion. This, again, is a key theme in the sociology of economic behaviour. In the past, research on the interlocking directorates of firms has been used to measure both the boundaries and fractions of the capitalist class, as well as cohesion and control strategies by members of this capitalist class (see Burris 2005; Mizruchi 1992, 1982; Zeitlin and Ratcliff 1988). Research on the topic of pan-national ownership, or what we could call 'global capitalism', is also very scarce, however, and often encompasses the world rather than Europe as a bounded region. This is partly due to the problems involved in getting reliable information on who really owns a firm. The scant research available suggests that we are still far from the existence of a 'European' business community (Kentor and Jank, 2004; Cárdenas 2008).

One study using a network analysis of ownership data for the companies with the largest capitalization in the biggest stock markets in the European Union shows indeed that investment strategies tend to have a national or extra-EU character but not a European one (Rodríguez *et al.* 2006). These data in fact argue for a quite different conclusion to the one drawn by Neil Fligstein later in this book (see Chapter 5). Rodríguez *et al.* show, for instance, that some top Spanish companies invest in the same companies as top US companies and that top Italian companies invest in the same European companies as other top Italian companies. The only evidence they present for the existence of something akin to a 'European' cluster of companies coordinating their investment strategies are the investment patterns of a group of four German and Belgian companies (Deutsche Bank, Allianz, Fortis and Gevaert) in the financial sector. These findings do suggest that a European capitalist class is emerging in the densely populated and capital-rich areas at the intersection of Germany and the Low Countries. In fact, the finding is not surprising since it is precisely in this region where citizens identify most frequently as Europeans. Indeed, in terms of the questions presented in Table 2.1, whereas about 17 per cent and 16 per cent of Belgian and West German citizens respectively identify primarily as European, about 10 per cent of European Union citizens do so as a whole.

Mobilization

The previous discussion, although based on only preliminary research, does not yet offer much evidence of the existence of social groups that one could describe as 'European'. Our third possibility might be to look for patterns of political mobilization in Europe. In the Marxian tradition, this is the litmus test for the existence of a class: the very reason Marx and Engels wrote the *Communist Manifesto* was to awaken the revolutionary conscience of the working class after they had identified it structurally as a prediction of their objective class analysis. Joint political mobilization would be revealing of the existence of a consciousness among people from different EU countries that they share common interests.

Work by Imig and Tarrow (2001), though, demonstrates that cross-national solidarity at the EU level is still weak, something that has also been confirmed more recently in the large-scale EUROPUB project that considers the emergence and breakdown of European 'claims making' across a variety of European policy sectors (Koopmans and Statham 2010; see also Guiraudon, Chapter 6). Again, what can be observed is more a question of Europeanization than class formation. There has certainly been a process of Europeanization of mobilization, as farmers, fisherman and other occupational groups have began to address their grievances to European Union institutions. There has been a slight increase in coordinated mobilization on the part of workers across Europe, with the latest example being protest against the planned Bolkestein directive for the liberalization of the provision of services across the European Union. As Imig points out, however, despite the simultaneous character of mobilization, and despite the similarity in the tactics employed, many instances of coordinated mobilization simply reflect the juxtaposition of domestic national interests rather than European interests proper (Imig 2004). The kinds of actors who mobilize in this fashion actually represent the citizens who least identify with Europe in the European Union: that is, farmers and workers. Chapter 7 in this book will explore the question of mobilization and social movements in more depth.

Taking these three empirical tests together, it should be clear by now that it is still too early to speak of European social groups in the strong sense we were seeking. If they are emerging, the place to find them would be the core regions of the European Union, but even if one finds them there they cannot represent more than a tiny fraction of the 10 per cent of the population who primarily identify as European. Thus, given the emergent character of this European middle class, it might be useful to approach the topic of the development of a European society in a less ambitious way, one that focuses less on the existence of European classes 'for itself' and more on what one could call a European middle class 'in itself', something more consistent with a sociological conception of Europeanization rather than European class formation as such. This is, for example, what Adrian Favell asserts in his study on the 'Eurostars' (2008), when he asks us to focus on the behaviour of free-movers in order to determine the characteristics of this European middle class. In fact, seizing upon the opportunities of the new single market and settling in cosmopolitan cities like Amsterdam, London or Brussels is for him the defining trait of this highly Europeanized social group.

Perhaps this is a way of rescuing the notion of a European social class. Once we abandon the level of consciousness and self-identification as European in order to define the new European social classes by attitudes, and focus on behaviour as the key indicator, then we can even go beyond Favell's stress on intra-European mobility. We may then want to focus on other behavioural indicators that act as a signal for the emergence of European class fractions within national stratification systems. It may indeed be the case that a segmented European bourgeoisie is emerging across Europe, as national bourgeoisies split into local and European fractions, distinguished by their consumer patterns and their outlook on life. Willingness to move to another country might be just one indicator of this emerging split. These European segments of the national bourgeoisies may first develop as 'imagined communities', to borrow Benedict Anderson's famous phrase, before they start coming into substantive contact. Driven by common tastes, and through travel, student exchanges, work, or residence abroad, these interactions begin to coalesce into a European class 'for itself'. A sociological agenda on European integration must therefore include the investigation of the extent to which this split between local and European segments of national bourgeoisies is indeed taking place, a theme that will be picked up again by Andreotti and Le Galès in Chapter 4.

Why is there no European society (yet)?

How do we explain the sluggishness in the development of a European society relative to the rapid Europeanization of behaviour and experience? One way of answering this question might be to draw a historical analogy of the emergence of Europe and the historical emergence of nation-states. Here, we can draw on a rich historical sociological literature on nationalism and nation building, which has sought to identify theoretically the key elements in the formation of national societies. From this literature, I draw three theoretical conceptions that have been deemed necessary to this process: *social transactions, socialization,* and *security*.

Social transactions

A key reference in the sociology of nationalism and the sociology of European alike is the scholar Karl Deutsch (Deutsch [1957] 1969; Deutsch *et al.* 1967). His approach to the question of society formation has been labelled *transactionalism*, and it is one of the rare sociological contributions widely recognized and discussed in mainstream EU studies. Neil Fligstein, for example, makes extensive use of Deutsch as a theoretical starting point in his *Euroclash* (2008) (see also Rosamond 2000). Deutsch predicts that a common societal identity will result from the intensification of contact, communication, and transactions among Europeans – provided this intensification proceeds faster at the European than at the national or other sub-national levels. The argument is appealing because such Europeanization – again, defined as a transnational widening of the geographic scope of people's experiences and activities – is an essential precondition for contact and thus for the development of a European society. Theoretical considerations and empirical data, however, are likely to question whether it plays the central role. In other words, it is unlikely that in the next generation the Europeanization of economic and political behaviour and of experiences, such as travel and studying, will lead to the emergence of large social groups that one could call 'European' in these terms.

From an empirical perspective, we have already seen that Europeanization in the past twenty years has had a negligible impact on the proportion of citizens who identify themselves as European. In fact, data show that Swiss and Norwegians (both outside the European Union!), express the same level of identification with Europe as the average EU citizen. The Deutsch hypothesis is vulnerable to exactly the same empirical evidence used to rule out the emergence of European social classes. On these terms, we can go no further than Fligstein in his recent attempt to test the Deutschian hypothesis using all available data on an emerging European society. To go further and develop a sense of what would be needed for the emergence of large European social groups, we thus need to draw on additional theoretical and empirical contributions to the study of nation building processes.

Socialization

Other inspiration can be found in the historical sociology of nation building. Scholars in this vein have demonstrated, for example, that nation building was generally more a top-down process than a bottom-up one (Gellner 1983, Weber 1981; Breuilly 1986; Hobsbawm 1989). Perhaps the most famous version of this thesis is the one developed by Ernest Gellner. Gellner argues that the elites driving the modernization and industrialization used the promotion of national popular cultures, and the centralization of national education and bureaucratic systems to cement the form of the modern nation-state society in Europe. While networks of communication and other forms of interaction contributed to the development of a vague feeling of membership in an 'imagined community' among the literate – the contribution to the literature associated with Benedict Anderson – it was institutions created by an expanding state in late nineteenth-century and early twentieth-century Europe that really began to integrate the average man and woman into these national imagined communities. The most important institutions were the school and the army. As Eugen Weber (1976) puts it, it was the universalization of primary education and of conscription that turned peasants into Frenchmen. Needless to say, in the contemporary world, the school and the army have lost some of their socialization potential in much of Europe. Instead, political messages transmitted by the electronic and written media are the main vehicle for the transmission of national identities, and the ones on which one ought to focus empirically in order to determine to what extent they contribute to the development of European group solidarities.

When one uses this perspective to examine the European Union, one begins to understand why, despite the dramatic intensification of transactions in the last couple of decades, there has been little change in the degree to which citizens identify with Europe. Essentially, national states and national political elites are still in direct or indirect control of the main socialization agencies: very little of this has been Europeanized.

Education remains a national or regional competence and, consequently, the geography and history curricula in most countries are still predominantly national ones. My own examination of British, German, and Spanish secondary school history textbooks since the 1940s (Díez Medrano 2003) demonstrates this, showing that when these textbooks concentrate on extra-national geographical areas, these tend to be former colonies, as in Spain or Great Britain (a contrasting view, however, is offered by Schissler and Soysal 2004). Furthermore, in many countries recent trends have gone in the direction of emphasizing sub-national history or geography rather than European trends. True, there is one bottom-up process under way, the Bologna process toward homogenizing systems of higher education. This homogenization has more to do, however, with the duration and credit requirements of the undergraduate and graduate curricula than with the homogenization of curricula.

The second classical institution, the military, has become a much less significant agent of socialization. As the work of Frédéric Mérand in Chapter 8 here and elsewhere (2006) shows, different national military figures have different national representations of what they are defending, although there has been some Europeanization of practices. For the mass public and media, though, armies remain the most proudly nationalizing image of solidarity and national unity, although it must be said that the elimination of compulsory military service in some countries has made them irrelevant as socialization agencies in the countries concerned (Schnapper 1994).

Finally, the media, the most powerful socialization agency in contemporary societies, remain national media, which give privileged access to national political actors keen on reproducing national identities over European Union actors (Schlesinger 1999). Again, the recently completed EUROPUB project offers a very useful distinction here on the potential Europeanization of media in Europe, distinguishing between horizontal and vertical dimensions of European integration (Koopmans and Statham 2010). Europeanization can be built by national actors reporting events about, or making claims upwards to, the European institutions (a vertical relationship); but it can also be a result of increased cross-national media or mobilization references to what is going on in other member states (a horizontal relationship). See also the discussion on mobilization and the media by Guiraudon, Chapter 6 in this volume.

Security

Recently, scholars sensitive to the fact that people can have several identities simultaneously, some of them nested in one another like a Russian doll, have complemented the top-down perspective on nationalism pioneered by Gellner, Eugen Weber and other scholars. In 1992 the social psychologist Edward Lawler made a very powerful argument to the effect that people identify most with those units on which individuals depend the most for their material and physical security. Decentralization processes, whether in industry or in polities, do not enhance people's attachment to the broader identity; on the contrary, they strengthen the local or narrower identities around which the decentralization processes are built, because they increase the individuals' dependence on the security provided by those narrower units.

Thus, when we focus on the sources of material security for European Union citizens, we see that the national state and, sometimes, the regions are still the social units primarily responsible. It is the national state, if not the region, which provides public education, unemployment benefits, pensions, health insurance, housing allowances, and so on. The European population as a whole in fact opposes the transfer of these functions to the European Union, thus preventing European institutions from gaining control over the other major mechanism for the creation of a European identity. Evidence has been presented, though, that suggests citizens are sometimes more willing to transfer these functions than are their national elites (see Hooghe 2003). The European Union has certainly increased its role in the provision of security to European citizens, mainly through the structural and cohesion funds at regional level in poorer parts of the EU. A recent article in fact demonstrates that these structural and cohesion funds are associated with strong support for European integration in Spain, Greece, Portugal, and Ireland (Berezin and Díez Medrano 2008). In the 1990s, Ireland moved from being one of the poorest states in Europe to becoming one of the wealthiest. Simultaneously, its citizens moved from being among those opposing European integration the most to becoming enthusiastic supporters. Berezin and Díez Medrano's analysis shows, however, that fund transfers have had no impact on the level of attachment to Europe, not even in Ireland. One could interpret these results as indicative that the funds are not generous enough to offset the sense of security that citizens derive from the state to which they belong. After all, in a context that has received the most in structural funds, namely Spain, they have still represented only a tiny percentage of the GDP.

The enduring salience of the national

The first half of my chapter focused on testing the evidence for whether sociological Europeanization or the formation of European social classes can be said to be taking place. The answer was positive in some respects for the former, largely negative for the latter. In the second half, I seek to explain why there is no European society yet, by drawing out the analogy with the comparative historical literature on nation building. The discussion here suggests that the lack of development of a European group identity in the European Union is consistent with theoretical predictions and supports the top-down approach to identity formation more than the bottom-up, transactionalist one.

In many ways, though, it is perhaps wrong to contrast the European Union with ongoing nation building and nation reproducing processes. We could add, in fact, that the entire European Union edifice is often dedicated to the preservation of national identities, an argument consistent with Alan Milward's famous argument about the European rescue of the nation-state (1992). Although the role of the European Parliament in the process of European integration has dramatically increased in significance over the last fifteen years, the Council of Ministers, which represents the member states' interests, remains the most powerful institution. In fact, the recently signed – and not yet ratified – Treaty of Lisbon further stabilizes the role of states by allowing for greater control by national parliaments over the European Union's legislative process. Furthermore, most policies in the European Union follow a territorial principle.

The territorial principle applies as much to rules for the recruitment of civil servants in the European Union, as to policies such as the structural and cohesion funds or research and development policies. One of the main requirements for the acceptance of proposals here is that they consist of networks of researchers from the different members of the European Union. While this approach contributes to equity in the allocation of European Union resources, it also has the effect of strengthening the salience of national identity – even when the main goal is the internationalization of national researchers. This is again a consistent finding in the literature on identities. Identifications bear a direct relation to the extent of their institutionalization in government policies. For instance, a decision to classify the population into ethnic or racial categories, regardless of how justified this decision is, contributes to increasing the salience of these categories as the focus of identifications, something that is a long-standing theme in studies on immigration, race and ethnicity (Alba 1992; Waters 1990).

Autonomous developments outside the institutional context of the European Union also contribute to the strengthening of national identity.

Prima facie examples of Europeanization such as the football Champions' League or the Eurovision Song Contest, to name just two popular ones, rather than contributing to the development of a European group identity, intensify national sentiment by pitting one state against another. Regions such as Catalonia feel so strongly about this, that they often demand to have a Catalan football team of their own. Eurovision, or European football are of course welcome examples of the civilization of war between European countries, consistent with the kind of view of history established by classic authors such as Norbert Elias. Nothing hints toward the formation of European teams to compete in the Olympics, football competitions, or other types of contest. The Ryder Cup in golf is the only instance where a European team has been created, with the public cheering on the Europeans against the Americans (all from the US). Sports, probably the most popular form of entertainment and the most significant popular cultural element in the development of identities, remain organized as battles between national teams (see, however, Fligstein 2008 for a contrasting view in an analysis of the diffusion of European pop music across borders). Banal nationalism, as pointed out by Michael Billig (1995), still rules in Europe today.

Perhaps, though, we should not create false expectations about what needs to happen for a European group identity to develop. Sociological theory predicts that a stronger European Union, the attribution of welfare state competences to the European Union, and a more de-territorialized form of government would favour a shift of identifications from the states and regions to the European Union. The theories discussed in the above section, however, are incomplete. The static character of Lawler's theory of nested identities prevents us from distinguishing between processes of decentralization and processes of centralization of rule. While there is strong evidence to the effect that decentralization erodes identification with the whole, the evidence that centralization of rule leads to greater identification with broader identities is more ambiguous, partly because of the resistance the process generates among the political units that lose sovereignty. Meanwhile, Eugen Weber's study of the state's role in the creation of national identities focuses on France, a state that had in fact already been successfully centralized during Napoleon's rule. The historical record shows, however, that nation building processes have been relatively unsuccessful in states where sub-national imagined communities had developed *before* the state-led nation building processes began. Scotland and Catalonia are prime examples of the resilience of identities that endured despite the respective national states' relentless efforts to assimilate them to the dominant nationality. Many other sub-national identities centred on culturally distinctive traits were actually invented just as states were implementing homogenizing and nation building policies. In sum, if states, despite the extensive power they were able to garner, failed to erase pre-existing identities and replace them with stronger national identities, how can we expect that these national and sub-national identities, much stronger than any known imagined community in nineteenth-century Europe, would be superseded by a European identity? The European Union needs to offer much more to the citizens than it currently does for a durable shift in identities to take place.

Conclusion: the prospect for European classes

The Europe that is unfolding is not and will not be in the foreseeable future a European society in the strong sense. Nor, to allude to two famous sceptical articles about European and globalization by Michael Mann (1998, 1999), has it ended the rise and ongoing building of European national societies. Europe, however, will continue to Europeanize and a European class distinguished by its lifestyle may develop, although popular identities and culture will remain anchored at the national and sub-national levels. Europe will remain a multi-tiered polity with a segmented social structure, corresponding to the national and sometimes sub-national levels. If we compare this situation with that prevailing in late nineteenth-century European societies, the most significant development that we can perhaps expect is the gradual emergence of a cosmopolitan European middle or upper middle class that would join the old European aristocracy in constituting an actual European social group. The European bourgeoisie is still, however, in its infancy, with subjective European identifications not yet complemented by strong cross-national social ties or expressed in European political mobilization.

This chapter suggests future directions for a sociologically informed and original approach to stratification in Europe. I have shown that we know too little about intermarriage patterns, intra-European migration and pan-European business strategies, even though these are clearly the kinds of empirical issues that need exploring to answer our questions. Similarly, research has only scratched the surface of what it means to identify with Europe. Yet not 'all is quiet on the Western front'. Gradual changes are taking place in all four dimensions of social group formation suggested here: identity, social ties, mobilization and consumption. Analyzing these processes will tell us something about emerging social groups in Europe, about the possibility that these social groups may differ from the rest of society in their cultural and political outlook, and how they might lead Europe in new directions. It is not the first time that social scientists are ahead of the changes that they are describing, looking for processes that can not yet be clearly observed. When Marx and Engels wrote their *Communist Manifesto*, mainly addressed to the

French proletariat, there was no French proletariat worth its name. Yet their analysis of class structure and conflict in capitalist societies not only inspired generations of social scientists but also anticipated and contributed to the social transformations that so dramatically unfolded in the late nineteenth and early twentieth centuries.

CHAPTER 3

Social Mobility and Spatial Mobility

Adrian Favell and Ettore Recchi

> **Key concepts:** social mobility, spatial mobility, stratification, operationalization, methodological nationalism, quantitative and qualitative strategies, social structure, process, rational action, occupational status, social spiralism, locals and cosmopolitans, norms, variation, bell curve, structural functionalism, path dependency, ideal types, habitus, field, scale
>
> **Key references:** Erikson and Goldthorpe, Treiman, Breen, Lamont, Merton, Gouldner, Abbott, Wimmer and Glick-Schiller, Borjas, Parsons, Durkheim, Weber, Bertaux, Bourdieu

There is no subject more central to sociology than *social mobility*.[1] The degree to which modern industrialized societies enable talented, ambitious or lucky individuals to move up in status, or conversely the extent to which they reproduce inherited inequalities or social hierarchies from one generation to the next, are questions that still dominate much of the empirical mainstream of the discipline under the general rubric of *stratification*. Some of the most longstanding and detailed debates in the mainstream have centred on attempts to measure and distinguish the patterns of social mobility of European societies in comparison with others (Ganzeboom *et al.* 1989; Erikson and Goldthorpe 1992; Treiman and Ganzeboom 2000; Breen 2004). In particular, Europe is generally

---

[1] This chapter was conceived jointly by the two authors. Ettore Recchi was the principal author of 'Operationalization 1' section and Adrian Favell the principal author of 'Operationalization 2'. All other sections were written equally together.

taken to be less fluid than America: the stereotype of the old world of ingrained privilege, tradition, and slow moving social change, set against the new world of opportunity, achievement and flux. Yet the emergence of a European society built largely on legal and institutional structures that facilitate free movement – that is, the *spatial mobility* of capital, goods, services and people – poses an interesting question for a sociology of the European Union. Has the spatial mobility enabled by the breaking down of barriers to movement and the notion of European citizenship – the establishment of a borderless labour market, sustained by the norm of non-discrimination to foreign nationals – also done something to the likelihood of social mobility within the European population? To put this in other terms: can people now move *out* of their own country in order to move *up* socially in relation to where they come from, and if so, who is moving and where are they moving to? It is not hard to see that operationalizing this question might be one of the most direct and fruitful ways of conceiving of an empirical sociology of the European Union. Such a sociology might bring new facts and phenomena to EU studies, but also engage in debate with the mainstream of the sociology discipline, which has hitherto largely ignored the European Union as a subject of interest.

In this chapter, we offer a guide to *how* the question of social and spatial mobility can be posed as part of a new sociology of the European Union. Doing empirical sociology is all about issues of operationalization. One of the interesting aspects of studying social and spatial mobility in the EU lies in the necessary complementarity of *quantitative* and *qualitative* strategies of research. Designing a study that can genuinely work across national borders in Europe also highlights some of the great methodological problems in avoiding the pervasive *methodological nationalism* of cross-national comparative work. In our chapter, after a brief review of the relevant literature and theoretical concerns, we thus present first a quantitative then a qualitative take on the subject, both based on original empirical research. A constructed survey on social and spatial mobility in the EU reveals both that Europeans do not move much spatially, and that there is not much social mobility associated with the building of a borderless Europe. Quantitative evidence in fact underlines the *structural* marginality of mobility in Europe today despite its visibility and apparent ubiquity. On the other hand, qualitative strategies, that home in on ideal-type cases of mobility in Europe, reveal a different picture of Europe: of European Union as a *process*, in which hidden populations and crucial pathways to social mobility can be revealed, and in which marginal or improbable behaviour (in statistical terms) can have a much larger *symbolic* impact on the continent as a whole than its structural size would suggest. Both structure and process, and structure and symbolism, are a necessary part of the empirical sociology we propose.

Social and spatial mobility in Europe

Mobility and immobility in Western societies

Europe is not famous for its social mobility. Unlike the US, which is widely seen as a society that enables anyone to become an American, make money, and claw their way up the social ladder, European societies have traditionally been preoccupied by subtle and not so subtle struggles over the *reproduction* of class privileges and distinctions: how one generation manages to transmit to its children (or grandchildren) status and class assets, and the social identities that go with these. On the structural side, ample evidence shows that Europeans, predominantly, are more fixed than Americans into their parents' status ranks and class positions, with Sweden being the only significant exception. Such a finding is corroborated by research carried out with different theoretical and methodological approaches (see Treiman and Ganzeboom 2000, or Breen and Luijkx 2004a, 49–50, for a guide to this). The story of upper-class children attaining upper-class lives and working-class children getting working-class jobs is still very common. Maybe even more relevant is the transatlantic difference in cultural terms – that is, in the solidity and capacity of class cultures to reproduce themselves across generations. This capacity has been explored in comparative cultural sociology by Michèle Lamont who shows how class (in the US and France, in her studies) is cemented by distinct sets of values, morality and sense of community among different classes and social groups in each country (Lamont 1992, 2000; see also Willis 1981).

Likewise, spatial mobility. The US is seen as a country where working, middle and upper classes routinely move around the country from job to job, often changing states and major cities of residence several times over a lifetime. Rates of cross-state mobility are historically set at around 3 per cent of all Americans per year (Theodos 2006); moreover, the dynamism of mobile talent, especially among the more educated, is seen as a crucial historical engine of the American economy. In Europe, if we may take it for a moment as a 'United States of Europe', rates of such mobility (across states, in this case nation-states) are dramatically lower – at 0.3 per cent of the population per year (Herm 2008), and Europeans move less *even* from region to region inside nation-states (at 1 per cent per year) than Americans across states (Ester and Krieger 2008: 2).

These at least are the conclusions one would draw from standardized definitions of class, occupational and residential mobility in the two continents. Social mobility in Europe has occurred but at rates typically lower than in the US or other settler countries. Some of the most recent studies on this have added that in so far as mobility is growing in Europe, it is likely to be due to its immigrant populations (Breen and Luijkx 2004b, 401–2). This is an as yet untested, but intriguing, thought for linking social and spatial mobility in Europe. Human geographers meanwhile have, since the more marked social flux of the 1950s and 60s, observed very interesting couplings between internal migration and social occupational mobility (Fielding 1995). Typically, the move of younger citizens from the rural or provincial location they grew up in to the metropolitan city is accompanied by an *escalator* effect: it is a spatial move linked to a social mobility outcome, like stepping on a moving escalator that sweeps you along and upwards faster than your peers. Talented and ambitious individuals have historically always moved out of the local worlds they live in, in order to move up: this was a key dynamic of industrialization and the formation of the nation-state in the modern world (Weber 1976; Moch 2003), and it continues today – although arguably less now than in the more meritocratic and egalitarian era of *les trente glorieuses*, that is, the post-war boom years of continental European economies.

Reflection on this subject links back to classic distinctions in the structural functionalist literature – associated with Robert K. Merton (1957: 387–420) and Alvin Gouldner (1957) – between 'locals' and 'cosmopolitans'. According to this model, one of the key dynamics of modernizing societies is *social spiralism* (Watson 1964) as a way of moving up in society. Talented or educated people from provincial places and social locations might feel blocked in their career aspirations if they stay local to where they come from: the social mobility ladder may be fixed, or only reproduce existing status hierarchies. To get on, then, they may choose to move out, spiralling up through society by taking a detour away from their place of origin. Residents in cities used as destinations for spiralist ambitions thus often display a tension between the ambitions of 'insider' *locals* – to move up through existing work structures that reward incumbency and patience – and those of 'outsider' *cosmopolitans* ready always to exit and move elsewhere if their efforts are not rewarded. This tension is a familiar feature of all kinds of locations under conditions of globalization or regionalization where (local) natives compete with (cosmopolitan) newcomers. In an apparently ever more mobile world, ingrained structures are often being swept away by the forces of change represented by those who moved. On the other hand, there is also a tension between the obviously visible examples furnished by qualitative studies that focus on movers, migrants, transnationals, cosmopolitans, and so on, and the change they bring, and aggregate structural studies that often arrive at sceptical conclusions on the overall impact of the mobile minority on the broader established social order. Sadly, preferences in the debate and the conclusions that are drawn are often tied dogmatically to the methodological option that is chosen to study it, but it may be possible that both observations are truthful – in the manner of Schroedinger's famous cat in Quantum physics

– if one approach is viewed as a snapshot of an emergent process, and the other a depiction of temporal background stability.

Analyzing social mobility data

The mainstream sociology of social mobility tends to be carried out on a grand cross-national comparative scale. Variations in rates of mobility are thus studied across different national societal units, each assumed to be a more or less bounded, single systems coterminous with individual nations. This approach is driven by the available statistics and modes of generating data internationally which are typically linked to national state techniques of counting, measuring and classifying resident populations (in terms of income, occupation, education level, etc.). As a simple example, Table 3.1 presents the basic information on intergenerational class mobility in the five largest national societies of the EU15 (EU member states up to 2004). These tables are based on the European Social Survey, one of the largest-scale independent representative surveys of the European population.

When examining a social mobility table, diagonal cells are the first to be inspected as they include those individuals who stay put in their parents' class. Overall, this corresponds to about one third of respondents in every country. The totals on the rows and the columns represent the overall class structure of each society, before and after generational change respectively. We can thus quickly note how, across the board, in each country there are now higher percentages in upper and middle class categories, and lower percentage in the working class. This change has been found to be principally driven by the structural transformation of the occupational structure of Western societies over the past decades, which has enlarged the size of middle and upper classes and reduced that of the bottom of the pyramid. Because of these structural changes, upwardly mobile people are in larger numbers than people moving the other way around. As a matter of fact, in all countries there are higher proportions of working class kids who make it to the bourgeoisie than offspring of the upper class in working class occupations. This is especially the case in Southern Europe, where the transformation of the occupational structure has been more marked in the late twentieth century. In Spain, for instance, 25.6 per cent of the bourgeoisie is made up of the offspring of the working class, while only 2.8 per cent of the non-qualified working class stems from upper-class families. In other words, sons and daughters of the working class are 'more than sufficient', so to speak, to fill in the ranks of manual occupations in post-industrial societies. This leaves out the question of immigrants, who are, symptomatically, not included in these tables – an issue to which we will turn in a moment.

Table 3.1 Intergenerational social mobility in the five largest countries of EU15 (inflows, column %)

Germany	Class of destination					
	I–II	III	IV	V–VI	VII	Total
Class of origin						
Bourgeoisie (I–II)	29.3	13.6	20.2	9.3	11.4	*17.3*
Routine non-manual (III)	28.2	31.0	22.7	25.1	19.4	*26.3*
Petty bourgeoisie (IV)	11.6	12.5	28.6	8.3	11.8	*12.8*
High-skilled manual (V–VI)	16.5	21.8	15.3	28.8	25.5	*21.7*
Low/non-skilled manual (VII)	14.4	21.2	13.3	28.6	31.9	*22.0*
Total	*27.6*	*27.3*	*8.6*	*17.0*	*19.5*	

N=2350

France	Class of destination					
	I–II	III	IV	V–VI	VII	Total
Class of origin						
Bourgeoisie (I–II)	31.8	9.9	12.9	11.0	7.0	*16.2*
Routine non-manual (III)	18.0	17.4	11.2	13.6	9.8	*14.9*
Petty bourgeoisie (IV)	20.2	19.5	41.4	10.7	20.5	*20.0*
High-skilled manual (V–VI)	10.8	20.1	6.0	19.5	11.6	*14.5*
Low/non-skilled manual (VII)	19.3	33.1	28.4	45.2	51.2	*34.4*
Total	*28.8*	*23.3*	*9.2*	*21.6*	*17.1*	

N=1258

UK	Class of destination					
	I–II	III	IV	V–VI	VII	Total
Class of origin						
Bourgeoisie (I–II)	30.7	20.6	21.9	10.6	11.9	*20.7*
Routine non-manual (III)	18.7	20.0	15.6	15.9	10.3	*16.5*
Petty bourgeoisie (IV)	15.5	11.6	24.4	11.2	12.8	*14,2*
High-skilled manual (V–VI)	16.8	20.6	18.1	27.1	22.1	*20.2*
Low/non-skilled manual (VII)	18.3	27.1	20.1	35.3	42.9	*28.3*
Total	*30.1*	*27.7*	*8.9*	*9.4*	*23.8*	

N=1799

Table 3.1 continued overleaf

Table 3.1 *continued*

Italy	Class of destination					
	I–II	III	IV	V–VI	VII	Total
Class of origin						
Bourgeoisie (I–II)	20.5	9.3	7.2	7.0	0.9	8.5
Routine non-manual (III)	26.3	20.9	11.1	14.1	10.2	16.1
Petty bourgeoisie (IV)	27.6	34.6	47.3	33.8	32.6	35.9
High-skilled manual (V–VI)	10.3	10.4	6.3	9.9	10.7	9.4
Low/non-skilled manual (VII)	15.4	24.7	28.0	35.2	45.6	30.1
Total	18.8	21.9	24.9	8.5	25.9	

N=831

Spain	Class of destination					
	I–II	III	IV	V–VI	VII	Total
Class of origin						
Bourgeoisie (I–II)	22.8	7.9	4.9	2.5	2.8	7.8
Routine non-manual (III)	17.3	14.3	4.4	3.1	4.7	8.2
Petty bourgeoisie (IV)	23.2	24.3	51.7	33.1	22.7	29.2
High-skilled manual (V–VI)	11.0	12.9	6.3	14.4	9.9	10.4
Low/non-skilled manual (VII)	25.6	40.7	32.7	46.9	60.0	44.4
Total	20.7	11.4	16.7	13.1	38.1	

N=1226

Source: European Social Survey (2004) *ESS Round 2: European Social Survey Round 2 Data*. Data file edition 3.1. Norwegian Social Science Data Services, Norway – Data Archive and distributor of ESS data.

The highest rate of social immobility is found among low/non-skilled workers: in France and Spain, where more than half of them (51.2 and 60 per cent respectively) perpetuate the social class position of their family of origin. That about one third of Europeans are intergenerationally immobile is also shown in a larger-scale comparative study on social mobility in Europe (Breen and Luijkx 2004a). This study also reveals that the percentage of upwardly and downwardly mobile individuals has remained substantially the same in the last three decades of the twentieth century, with the exceptions of Ireland and Poland, where it increased substantially, and Hungary, where in fact it declined. Overall, however, there are two widespread long-term tendencies in the social mobility regimes of European national societies, that counter to some degree the perception that there is limited social mobility in Europe: first, towards higher levels of social fluidity – that is, a reduced association between parents' and children's social class (Breen and Lujikx 2004a: 73); second, to a 'high degree of similarity among countries ... in all the measures of mobility' (ibid.: 49). Such a convergence in patterns of social mobility is rather unique to Europe, making national boundaries less significant both substantially and analytically. Nevertheless, on all these measures, it can be shown that there is substantially more mobility overall in the US than Europe (ibid.).

One of the problems with such analyses is, fairly obviously, that they assume closed social systems of mobility and class structure, congruent with the idea of a bounded nation-state-society. Immigrants' mobility can only be measured *within* the system – by comparing, say, the first with second and third generation. This says nothing about how the family is doing relative to the country where they came from – which might be a far more salient issue for them, particularly subjectively. It is now routine in other research areas to question the bounded form of the nation-state-society as a given closed social order. Globalization is all the rage in social theory, and transnationalism beyond the nation-state a dominant focus of attention, in most European sociology at least. Furthermore, we would never dream of arguing that economies and the multiple transactions that sustain them end at national borders – even if it is true that nearly all international measurements of aggregate societal outputs – of the kind, for example, produced by organizations such as the OECD – are still measured in stylized, bounded nation-by-nation GDP terms. But what of cross-border mobility, hence mobility compared *across* societies and *across* categories of individuals moving in and out of stable national boxes? Nation-by-nation data itself reproduces the fiction of there being bounded national societal systems; only what lies within the national box makes sense, the rest is noise; people who move across borders by definition mess these units up (Joppke 1998).

The problem of methodological nationalism

This problem lies under the general heading of the pervasive *methodological nationalism* found in the social sciences, in particular in empirical studies that rely on state-derived technologies of counting populations necessarily bounded by conventional politically defined territories. Some leading scholars such as the anthropologists Andreas Wimmer and Nina Glick-Schiller (2002), or the social theorist Ulrich Beck (2000), have recognized this problem and proposed programmatic solutions. However, the question of social mobility is not one they pose. Meanwhile, the discussion on this point in sociology has been mostly theoretical, reducing it to a conceptual issue and neglecting concerns on how to deal with it empirically (exceptions being Breen and Rottman 1998; Berger and

Weiß 2008). The anthropologists' case studies and the social theorists' metaphors and problematizations are not enough. What is really needed are some empirical analyses that work through ideas of how to operationalize a genuinely transnational approach to social and spatial mobility.

Spatially mobile Europeans form a clear test to the usual cross-national comparative findings on social mobility in Europe. There are two reasons. One is the structural possibility that spatial mobility will alter the relatively stable patterns of social mobility and social reproduction in the Europe of national societies. The second has to do with the transformation of the categories with which units of society (that is, classes) are recognized and rendered comparable. Formal comparative work often misses this aspect of temporal and categorical change, a point that has been emphatically developed in the work of Chicago sociologist Andrew Abbott (2001). In moving across societies, spatially mobile Europeans might also be rendering ambiguous the clear units of migrants, natives, residents, workers and classes by which other comparative assessments are made: mobility may lead to categories changing, emerging or disappearing. So, if we could somehow compare a subset of European 'movers' (EU citizens who have chosen to live and work abroad in another EU member state) with the majority of 'stayers' (the average national population sampled by conventional social surveys), we might be able to ask new questions about flux and mobility in Europe, both structurally *and* conceptually. There is good reason to think that mobile Europeans are having a substantial impact on the continent, even when statistics suggest they may number as little as one in fifty of the population. In fact, official figures on intra-European migration suggest that only 2 per cent of European nationals live in another EU member state, and only about 4 per cent have had experience of living abroad (Vandenbrande *et al.* 2006: 14). As Table 3.2 shows, numbers of EU citizens in different countries range from highs of almost 10 per cent in Ireland, 6.4 per cent in Belgium or 4 per cent in Austria or Sweden, to barely 1 per cent in Italy, Netherlands or Denmark, and less than 1 per cent in Greece, Hungary and Poland (for an elaboration, see Zaiceva and Zimmermann 2008). Moreover, EU-born foreign residents (intra-EU migrants) invariably number between about a third and a quarter of the total of non-EU born residents (traditionally perceived as immigrants).

Yet the small minority of international mobile Europeans lies at the heart of conceptualizations and idealizations of European citizenship. They are highly symbolic of some of the ideas of a unified Europe conceived by the founding fathers of European integration. More concretely, economic theories of European integration – particularly policy-driven analyses of how a more fluid and dynamic European economy can be built in the wake of the EU's 2000 Lisbon Agenda (Sapir *et al.* 2004) – suggest that more mobility is likely to be a good thing for Europe as a whole, both in (re)deploying workforces where and

Social Mobility and Spatial Mobility

Table 3.2 Proportion of foreign-born residents in EU member states (% of total population, end of 2006)

	Born in the EU	Born outside the EU	Total
EU15			
Austria	3.8	7.5	11.3
Belgium	6.4	6.3	12.7
Denmark	1.5	3.7	5.2
Finland	1.1	1.7	2.8
France	2.7	6.8	10.3
Germany*	2.1	4.5	6.6
Greece	0.7	4.4	5.1
Ireland	9.6	0.7	10.3
Italy*	1.1	3.1	4.2
Luxembourg	23.8	4.3	28.1
Netherlands	1.7	6.3	8.0
Portugal	1.0	3.5	4.5
Spain	1.0	4.5	5.5
Sweden	4.3	7.9	12.2
UK	2.7	6.3	9.0
EU12			
Bulgaria	0.1	0.2	0.3
Cyprus	4.9	8.6	13.5
Czech Republic	1.4	0.6	2.0
Estonia	0.6	11.0	11.6
Hungary	0.3	1.1	1.4
Latvia	1.1	11.0	12.1
Lithuania	0.3	3.8	4.1
Malta	–	–	–
Poland	0.4	0.8	1.2
Romania	0.0	0.0	0.1
Slovakia	0.7	0.1	0.8
Slovenia	0.6	6.0	6.6

* Proportion of foreign citizens
Source: Office for National Statistics (2006) *Labour Force Survey: Employment Status by Occupation and Sex, April–June 2006*. Reproduced under Crown Copyright.

when they are needed within a single market, and in politically helping people identify more with the idea of Europe. Thought of as rational actors, people who chose to make the big move abroad might well be expected to be selected for their frustration at home, hence be talented individuals looking for more opportunities, and more willing to take risks. This *positive selection* is often postulated under pure economic conditions of the kind that the removal of barriers to free movement in Europe was supposed to ensure: the basic economic models for this selection process under 'free' labour market conditions, as theorized particularly by the Harvard economist George Borjas (Borjas 1989). If they are the folkloric 'brightest and best', they are more likely to be a population that would kickstart again social mobility effects in Europe or at least be a potential vector for economic growth (see Borjas 1999 for an application of his theory to an integrating Europe).

Hypotheses about social and spatial mobility in Europe

From these kinds of considerations, we can now move to formulating empirical hypotheses that could assess the impact of EU free movement opportunities on spatial and social mobility within Europe. In particular, we elaborate on the *class position* and the *patterns of social mobility* of movers in a context of free movement opportunities.

Firstly, we might expect spatial mobility to be class insensitive (Hypothesis 1). That is, the likelihood of moving from one country to another within Europe should not be influenced by individuals' social class. This is because open and universal EU freedom of movement laws (for EU citizens) should have levelled the playing field, evening out the kind of bias of mobility towards elites supposed to be a feature of more general global mobility – in effect *democratizing* intra-EU migrant opportunities. It would therefore be creating the kind of ideal conditions under which the social spiralists – talented and dynamic movers who self-select as the 'brightest and best' – might be able to use spatial mobility as a social mobility strategy regardless of class background.

Secondly, EU movers are expected to experience no discrimination in their occupational opportunities (Hypothesis 2). They are not like traditional immigrants who face discrimination or glass ceilings according to their 'ethnic' non-European origins. Rather they enjoy European citizen status, on a legal par with natives in the labour market; moreover, they are ethnically and culturally proximate, and often relatively invisible as migrants. Downward career mobility – which is in fact frequent among immigrants from less developed countries – should be quite exceptional among EU movers taking jobs abroad in the Union. Given the converging levels of salaries in Western Europe, moreover, possible downward class movements at migration are not justified, on average, by significantly higher monetary returns in the host country. At the very least, EU movers should be able to preserve their pre-existing class positions, if not do better – otherwise there would be no economic or symbolic rationale to their mobility.

The analyses that follow will control to what extent these *ex ante* suppositions, predicated on a rational choice view of spatial movements driven by the maximization of socioeconomic benefits in an open, pan-European free labour market, describe the real trajectories of class mobility of intra-EU migrants. The dataset used in this chapter merges two similar sources: the European Internal Migrants Social Survey, an original survey (EIMSS) for movers, and the well-known European Social Survey (ESS) for stayers, with data for Britain, Germany, France, Italy and Spain (see Recchi and Favell 2009, in particular appendix A, on this methodological strategy and the data sources used). However, as the focus of this chapter is on social mobility achieved through occupations in a foreign country, EU movers without any job experience in the host country, such as students, non-working spouses and pensioners, are not included in the analysis.

Operationalization 1: a quantitative approach

How might we control these hypotheses? An obvious move would be to construct data that can be directly related to the kinds of data sets being crunched on social mobility in cross-national comparative terms. The required data have to describe the class and/or occupational status of movers before and after their international move(s).

To answer these questions, an original survey was needed. Survey data always has to be found or generated. In this case, nation-by-nation statistics and studies were not much use. Studies on foreign and migrant populations are often not comparable across nations, due to the very different way of classifying, counting and observing foreigners, immigrants and minorities in different countries. A classic example is the difference between the data produced on these populations in Britain and France. In Britain, many immigrants are classified according to racial and ethnic self-classifications; in France such a process has always been a taboo, and migrants disappear into the statistical mass as soon as they are citizens or reach majority (see Favell 2001). Even if the issue is limited to foreign residents clearly distinguishable by nationality of origin, a second problem arises with foreign European nationals, in that as populations they are generally far too small to generate adequate sample sizes from the largest-scale national surveys that are made. Even national Labour Force Surveys – the widest existing surveys in the continent – have sample sizes that are too small to fill the cells with enough foreign European residents from even the largest neighbouring countries. Generally a minimal number of cases – a good rule of thumb would be 1,000 – would be needed for reliable samples. If EU movers are 2 per cent of the population we would need a random sample of 500,000 residents to find 1,000 of them. These kinds of sample sizes are far beyond the capacity of even the biggest national survey operations. Some surveys at this point give up on the criterion of representativeness and start generating cases by non-random means, such as snowballing or hunting down foreigners through networks or localities with known concentrations (see, for example, the methods used in Tribalat et al. 1996 or Modood et al. 1997, two of the most widely discussed immigrant surveys on France and Britain respectively). Others content themselves with generalizations about immigrant groups from very small numbers.

The PIONEUR project (Recchi and Favell 2009) adopted a different and original strategy, generating an original survey called the European Internal Movers Social Survey (EIMSS). EIMSS turned out to be one of the largest ever original comparative surveys made on immigrants. How was this data collection achieved? The PIONEUR project in fact developed an innovative procedure based on the probability of finding foreign national residents in the host country through their first and family names. It thus collected information on the rankings of the most popular first and family names from each country – for example, in Spain, Pedro, Carlos, Ramon, Lopez, Hernandez, Garcia, and so on – discarding names also likely to be found amongst nationals of the other nations in the study. It then sampled these 'most likely' names in publicly available telephone directories, to find the requisite number of Spanish in the UK, Germans in France, and so on, generating lists of telephone numbers for the survey operators. Despite some obvious problems, such as the heterogeneity of immigrant origins in countries such as France (where there are many Italian names among French citizens), or problematic frequencies in border regions (where cross-national mixed backgrounds are common), the method in fact worked in terms of the high proportion of telephone answers made by people who were indeed foreigners of the nationality targeted. A total of 5,000 30-minutes telephone interviews across the five countries – Britain, Germany, France, Italy and Spain – were thus completed using a battery of questions about class background, migration motivations, cultural adaptation, identification with Europe, political behaviour, media consumption, and so on. At the core of the interviews lay the spatial/social mobility question as perhaps the key sociological issue tied to the process of European integration. Data from EIMSS provides some structural answers to the hypotheses posed above (see p. 60).

The short answer to the two hypotheses posed is that neither of them – sound as they may seem in rational choice or economic theory terms – are borne out by the systematic evidence, with only the second being partially fulfilled. In relation to Hypothesis 1, in terms of class positions before leaving their country of origin, upper-class individuals are over-represented and members of the working class are under-represented among EU movers (Table 3.3). Across the

Table 3.3 Class position of EU stayers and movers (before their movement) by country of residence and nationality (column %)

					Nationality						
			German					British			
COR	DE	GB	FR	IT	ES		GB	DE	FR	IT	ES
Bourgeoisie (I–II)	27.6	57.7	41.9	44.4	30.9		30.1	38.3	53.1	46.1	33.5
Routine non-manual (III)	27.3	28.8	32.4	35.9	38.8		27.7	30.2	24.5	36.8	27.1
Petty bourgeoisie (IV)	8.6	2.5	5.4	8.6	9.7		8.9	3.2	7.5	4.8	6.8
High-skilled manual (V–VI)	17.0	8.0	14.9	6.1	14.5		9.4	19.8	9.5	6.1	16.3
Low/non-skilled manual (VII)	19.5	3.1	5.4	5.1	6.1		23.8	8.6	5.4	6.1	16.3

			French					Italian			
COR	FR	GB	DE	IT	ES		IT	GB	DE	FR	ES
Bourgeoisie (I–II)	28.8	37.2	34.3	45.4	41.1		18.8	29.7	2.9	35.9	25.0
Routine non-manual (III)	23.3	42.4	39.5	35.1	29.2		21.9	31.2	14.5	18.2	25.0
Petty bourgeoisie (IV)	9.2	2.3	4.7	3.9	9.4		24.9	6.9	5.8	6.1	15.8
High-skilled manual (V–VI)	21.6	7.6	13.4	5.9	13.5		8.5	7.9	21.0	16.7	16.8
Low/non-skilled manual (VII)	17.1	10.5	8.1	9.8	6.8		25.9	24.3	23.2	23.2	17.3

			Spanish			
COR	ES	GB	FR	IT	DE	
Bourgeoisie (I–II)	20.7	28.6	39.9	31.1	19.5	
Routine non-manual (III)	11.4	31.3	20.8	34.4	18.3	
Petty bourgeoisie (IV)	16.7	1.8	6.6	4.6	3.0	
High-skilled manual (V–VI)	13.1	9.8	12.6	10.6	16.5	
Low/non-skilled manual (VII)	38.1	28.6	20.2	19.2	42.7	

Notes: 'Stayers' data in italics; (COR = Country of residence)
Source: European Social Survey (2004) *ESS Round 2: European Social Survey Round 2 Data*. Data file edition 3.1. Norwegian Social Science Data Services, Norway – Data Archive and distributor of ESS data.

board, the figures for residents in social class category I–II (bourgeoisie) are higher for resident migrants than natives of the country (the left hand figure in italics). Upper- and upper middle-class movers reach their highest number in Italy: around 45 per cent of British, French and Germans in Italy are drawn from class I–II. Only Italians and Spanish in Germany (about 45 and 60 per cent respectively from class V–VII) are exceptions to this rule, fitting in larger numbers with the traditional immigrant profile as low-skilled or manual workers. High-skilled workers leaving their home country are particularly unusual, although there are cases: Italians (in France, Germany and Spain), Spanish (in Germany), and British (in Germany, where some go as posted workers, and Spain, where they rather move as retirees). Overall, though, the free movement regime appears to widen the opportunities of social reproduction of the higher social strata rather than creating a comparable avenue of social mobility for all. Intra-EU migration is thus not notably democratized by the removal of borders or the economic convergence of Western Europe.

Regarding Hypothesis 2, looking at patterns of career mobility when changing country of settlement – here considering only respondents who had a job before and after moving – a similarly cautious set of conclusions emerges. Overall, with little variation by nationality and country of residence, more than two-thirds of EU movers (71.3 per cent) did not change social class when taking up their first job after migration (Table 3.4). Moreover, four out of five (80.7 per cent) held the same class position in the transition between first and current job in the host country. Contrary to our hypothesis, though, the work-with-migration transition (Transition 1 in Table 3.4) is in fact associated with some risk of downward mobility. This is the case for 14.3 per cent of respondents, while 8.5 per cent are upwardly mobile. However, in line with the

Table 3.4 Patterns of intragenerational class mobility of EU movers (%)

		Transition 2 (from first to current job in host country)				
		Immobile	Non-vertically mobile	Upwardly mobile	Downwardly mobile	Total
Transition 1 (from last job in home country to first job in host country)	Immobile	62.1	1.8	5.8	1.7	*71.3*
	NV mobile	4.2	0.9	0.6	0.1	*5.8*
	UP mobile	6.7	0.5	0.2	1.1	*8.5*
	DOWN mobile	7.7	0.4	6.1	0.1	*14.3*
	Total	*80.7*	*3.6*	*12.8*	*3.0*	*100.0*

Note: Reference to social classes and forms of class mobility as defined in Erikson and Goldthorpe (1992).
Source: European Internal Movers Social Survey, N=2180.

hypothesis, the subsequent career in the host country is much more likely to be on the upside (12.8 per cent) than on the downside (3 per cent). Apart from this, the overwhelming majority of occupational shifts for intra-EU migrants occur within the classes to which they belong, qualifying these shifts as either progress within an already class-tracked career or fine-grained changes that hardly alter the overall class structure in which they occur.

Interestingly, though, elsewhere in our analysis an escalator effect does emerge for one national destination for younger migrants, the UK, which, given the disproportionate importance of the capital in terms of migrant destination in this country, corroborates what is frequently claimed about London as a 'Eurocity' enabling a new kind of mobility for ambitious young European movers (Favell 2004). This is an aggregate finding that would be worth further exploring with qualitative case study data – a classic methodological rationale for the quantitative-then-qualitative strategy being presented here.

Overall, then, the picture we get from the quantitative survey is one of little change. European Union appears not to be having significant mobility effects, with one or two unsurprising exceptions. Indeed, it appears to be having a reverse effect to the one that might be hoped for by the builders of the EU: enabling *more* not less elite social reproduction in the continent. Advocates of migration and mobility here might find the results rather gloomy. We cannot presuppose the dynamizing of the European economy, or the beneficial selection effects of migration if in fact the integration of the continent is only benefitting the most privileged (on this, see Haller 2008). If we stop here with the study, we might well conclude that the well known social theoretical claims about globalization and mobility – that the ability to be globally mobile increasingly indexes social inequality (Bauman 1998) – is in fact unproblematically true. This would be an empirically substantiated finding that would go well beyond the speculative rhetoric that has mostly sustained this particular critique of the globalizing and regionalizing world.

Operationalization 2: a qualitative approach

A quantitative approach can tell us a lot about the structural background and aggregate effects of Europe in change. It allows us to question appearances and determine what is and what is not statistically meaningful in a range of behaviour or values that may or may not be changing with European integration. As we can see with the example above, it invariably takes a sceptical line towards hypotheses that might otherwise be hastily reached as conclusions through untested theorizing. This, at least, gives us a reason as to why an empirical sociology of the European Union is likely to look quite different to the outpouring of social theory of Europe and European integration that has become quite visible in EU studies in recent years. Empirical methods and operationalization here can make all the difference.

Aggregate structural analysis also typically reveals *norms*: that is, statistical averages which indicate the most probable and hence most stable forms of social behaviour or values in a given society. Variation from norms is measured from the statistical mid-point, and typically lessens the further one moves in any given distribution from the norm. Societies whose vital statistics are pictured this way have fat 'bell curve' shaped structures that point to how society reproduces itself through attracting behaviour or inculcating values that conform to the 'fat' average part of the distribution (that is, what the mainstream does or thinks), rather than the much more scarcely populated extremes. Visualizing society, as conventional statistics does, in terms of a 'bell curve' distribution – something which technically is inevitably produced when variation is enumerated, as it is conventionally done, in terms of non-scalar degrees of variation from the statistical norm – thus links norms to an explanation of how societies work. A certain bell-shaped distribution of values, behaviour, or social positions, locking in upper limits (variation) on mobility can, as the next step, then be seen as the *cause* of the stable functioning of the society in question. One might describe such a society as 'well integrated': this kind of pattern becomes a definition of societal integration. Wild or disruptive deviations from these norms, which are normally only statistically marginal behaviours, threaten disintegration or revolution. Mostly, then, societies by this account function well when everything is 'in its right place'. The most significant instance is the division of labour, leading to class division and stratification, as an invariable functional necessity of a modern industrialized society. Building a theory on top of the aggregate of statistical norms and probabilities as the core *modus operandi* of empirical sociology thus led, in classic sociological theory, to the doctrine of 'structural functionalism', associated above all with Talcott Parsons, but present already in the sociology of Emile Durkheim. As well as being an inherently conservative vision of society, there is also clearly a blind spot in this form of theory about radical possibility of change to the system – the possible impact of populations that are located at the margins or tail end of the bell curve distributions.

Structural functionalism, which had a massive impact on the social sciences during their most confident modernist, developmentalist phase in the 1950s and 60s, is thought to be a largely redundant theoretical doctrine nowadays. Its logic, though, is inescapable in any structural analysis that posits some kind of stable reproduction of social structure through aggregates such as 'culture', 'institutions', 'norms' or 'ideology', and it has thus crept back into much recent social and political science under the heading of 'new institutionalism', particularly the fashion for explanations using the term 'path dependency'. Path dependent analyses that stay close to the concepts origins in institutional economics (North 1981; Pierson 2004) are not necessarily functionalist in their logic. The lock-in effect of social reproduction in the accounts of these pioneering authors is specified, in actor-centred terms, in the discrepancy between long- and short-term pay-offs to actors thinking about changing course. Yet as the term has been used more and more metaphorically by others, referring to 'self-reproducing' forces such as norms, ideologies or discourses that cannot think and act, it often takes on a functionalist character (see Barry 1971 or Coleman 1990: ch. 1, for classic critiques of 'sociological' logic in these terms). In EU studies today, popular institutionalist and constructivist arguments claiming to be 'sociological' thus often use implicitly functionalist logics.

There are obvious problems here. An analysis based on norms and statistical significance is clearly important in an account of stable structures and reproduction, but it is not well equipped to detect change, process or flux. In looking only at the aggregate distributions of mobility or occupations in intra-EU movement, we may, in short, be missing a lot of the most interesting stories. Critiques of mainstream bell-curve statistics often point to the disproportionate impact in reality of marginal actors or events – the 'black swans' that cannot be predicted by aggregate statistical methods (Taleb 2008). This can be related to the analysis of marginal international movement in Europe *vis-à-vis* the dominant patterns of staying put in national locations of origin. Actors stepping away from dominant norms – particularly those associated with stable nationalized patterns of, say, educational and career attainment, or family life – may embody the process of a different Europe in the making, and be pointing towards a ferment of change not detectable in the aggregate analysis. Plus, as in many studies dependent on problematic statistical information, there is a great 'hidden population' problem associated with spatial and social mobility across borders. In part this is a category problem (Abbott 2001) of the target population moving in and out of the groupings – the usual stable, nation-by-nation categories – with which statistical comparisons might be made. Yet, look on the streets of major European cities, and we seem to be able to see in abundant numbers the people we think embody the new European social and spatial mobility. Official numbers and surveys of foreign populations, particularly relatively invisible ones such as mobile Europeans, who are ethnically and culturally proximate, and able to come and go as they please, might thus be missing in some if not most of the data. Another possibility is that it is precisely the marginality of the movers in the 'long tail' (Anderson 2008) of the European population distribution that has given them unique social powers to succeed in a Europe in flux. As pioneers they may find rich and unique pay-offs precisely in being and doing differently to the mainstream norms, although as their numbers rise, there will be a threshold effect and hence diminishing returns relative to the mainstream.

As suggested by our Hypothesis 2 above, EU free movers are interesting as a case of international migration which *prima facie* has nearly all the inbuilt disadvantages of typical migration processes taken out. With political and legal barriers down, and cultural or ethnic disadvantage and exclusion at a minimum, they should in theory be avatars of a Europeanized economic selection process that is undistorted by these other (typical) factors in the workings of the international labour market – a perfect market, so to speak. That we do not necessarily find this in the quantitative analysis might be a question of their marginal numbers, rather than a problem with the theory as such. Their quantitative marginality suggests rather a qualitative 'ideal type'-based approach. What if we were to empirically go out and look one by one for *prototypes* of the ideal European mobility proposed in theory, and then assess these different exceptional cases in relation to the mainstream European norms (of dominant national values, immobility, stable class positions, etc.)? The ideal type approach to empirical work has its own venerable tradition in Weberian sociology. The theoretical construction of such cases can also be used profitably with the logic of counterfactual analysis – that is, searching precisely for what might be the outcomes under theoretical conditions explicitly different to the actual dominant situation as established by empirical statistical analysis (Hawthorn 1991).

This was precisely the methodological logic put to use in the ethnographic and documentary research for the book *Eurostars and Eurocities* (2008) by Adrian Favell, a study that ran in parallel to the PIONEUR project. We know that free movers in Europe are numerically scarce, yet their theoretical and symbolic valence in thinking about the sociological impact of European Union is undeniable. Moreover, go to any of the major cosmopolitan centres of Europe, and we find them in quite large concentrations – a whole new generation of mostly young, mobile, ambitious or adventurous Europeans using their free movement rights to live and work abroad, regardless of whether they are showing up in official statistics or surveys. *Eurostars and Eurocities* thus eschewed a conventional quantitative approach and sought rather to construct its empirical sample by actively seeking out the most likely individuals who might embody the propositions about spatial and social mobility in Europe, and its social spiralism and transformative effects on a possible new European society. It went looking, in other words, for the most likely 'highly Europeanized' Europeans in the most likely 'highly Europeanized' places, eventually settling on the foreign EU populations in three of the major hubs of internal European migration in Western Europe: Amsterdam, London, and Brussels. Each of these cities can lay claim to being a 'capital' of Europe: in cultural, economic, and political terms, respectively. *Eurostars and Eurocities* sought to put flesh and blood on the theoretical construct of an ideal type European 'free mover', among a population that ranged from the young, freely mobile, individual movers in their twenties, through to older people in their thirties and forties who might now be settling into cosmopolitan single or family lives in the three cities.

The study used a variety of snowball and networks-based sampling techniques to find this population, varying interviews by age, gender, nationality, marital and professional status. Given the fact that so many of these foreign residents are missed in the official possible 'sampling frames', such as national survey statistics or foreign consulate registries, it also sought to juxtapose the cases found with studies of populations made by commercial organizations interested in selling products or services to this target population of foreigners: for example, magazines or websites for expatriates. Through this variety of statistical sources on the population, a broader picture of the overall moving Europeans emerged, from which particular under-represented categories of individuals in each city was then sought in a second wave of interviews. This method, for example, allows the correction of stereotypes of the European foreign population in any given city, a case in point being the conception that all the foreign European residents in Brussels are EU employed 'eurocrats' or corporate 'expats'. The technique follows a distinctly francophone current in social research that emphasizes 'constructing the object of research' as a key empirical step, and never taking the empirical object as 'given' or immediately 'readable' from given preconceptions (Bourdieu *et al.* 1968; Lenoir *et al.* 1996). It is nevertheless an eminently empirical, rather than purely social theoretical strategy.

By thus constructing the object of research, a total of sixty primary interviews was completed in the three cities, alongside over five of years of intermittent participant observation, numerous secondary interviews and extensive documentary research about the foreign EU population in the three cities. The small n of interview cases could, by the constructivist methodology by which the sample was made, claim a certain kind of representativeness of this elusive population. Moreover, the long interviews were conducted using a narrative life history approach – asking questions in the manner of an oral history – which has been promoted by maverick social stratification scholars such as Daniel Bertaux (Bertaux and Thompson 1997), precisely as a way of capturing process and flux in social mobility structures that are missed by the dominant quantitative approaches. *Eurostars and Eurocities* also foregrounds a 'phenomenological' or 'grounded' technique of research, that is, allowing actors to speak for themselves in order to inductively reveal their everyday *habitus*, the kinds of everyday social practices and habits they embody as Europeans today (Glaser and Strauss 1967). Indeed the book simply reproduces many of the *in situ* interviews, to offer a direct window into the lives and experiences of these prototypical free movers.

The study thus discovers phenomena that remain largely undetected in the quantitative survey. It also puts flesh and blood on those exceptional currents in spatial/social mobility that were found in the broader aggregate data. The prototypical rational, individualistic, social spiralist EU movers emerge qualitatively as young, ambitious, career minded, highly educated career women from the south of Europe, who have deliberately moved to the North-west of the continent as part of a planned international career mobility. They sought to differentiate themselves from their peer group back home, opting out of more reliable, mainstream, but heavily gendered national career and marriage paths, that would lead to professional and family stability much more quickly had they stayed. In describing her reasons for moving, Nicole, a mid-twenties IT programmer, who moved to London from the north of France, speaks for many of these women:

> There was a big sense of frustration about the personal development thing. The Latin countries are absolutely not flexible on the work market. I can do anything I want there but it's not going to change my situation. You are just young, so your opinion doesn't count. They say you don't have any experience – even though you have! – and I was working crazy hours, and being paid peanuts, no rewards. And still you live in Paris and it is very expensive. At the end of the day I didn't study five or six years for that.

Following the perfect logic of an economist's theory of European integration, where the brightest and best of young EU citizens would just 'get on their bike' to go and look for work and a better life across national borders, Nicole also speaks for the droves of young French people, in particular, who abandoned an economically depressed France during the mid to late 1990s to go to the global Eurocity of choice, London, in search of fame and fortune. London's role as an escalator region is thus also corroborated in the qualitative findings, which are able to personify structural trends that showed up in the quantitative analysis.

Beyond this data, though, we begin to find things not in the quantitative survey. Social spiralism *is* found to be a feature of many of these younger movers to the three cities. Many have come from relatively obscure provincial regional origins, choosing a path out of their own country as an alternative to the well trodden elite national path through their own national capitals. Frustration at home can be the motivation for a chancy move abroad, that gives new impetus and, eventually, mobility through the liberating effect of what can thus be called a *de-nationalizing* experience. European free movement has effectively created a new kind of regional freedom in the world, uniquely available in terms of European citizenship status rather than elite privilege. European movers discover themselves as individuals, learn to free themselves from norms they learned as nationals, to play around and instrumentalize their identities, try out new social pathways. This perhaps accounts for why among the most unique movers there is an important selection effect that accentuates talented people able to think differently or take risks, as the economic theory of European integration predicts. Franz from Germany, now a highly successful banker in London, with experience also working in France and Spain, pinpoints how this works:

> Why are people moving? My first move was from Frankfurt to Paris. I was looking for a job in Paris, because it would mean I am not number 15,907 of Germans in Frankfurt looking for a job as a banker ... I think I was quite unique there, to say, listen, I quit my job now, I take my little car, I go away and see what I can do.

Their difference is valued in the new location, as long as they are relatively scarce. Moreover, with all these moves an important element is that they are moves between relatively close and easily accessible locations. Many of the Eurostars also emphasize that a key to their European move is the ability to go home at weekends – perhaps to catch up with a doctor or dentist's appointment, if not sometimes to take some washing back to mum. Cross-national commuting and split households also become a possibility. This points to a new, Europeanized mode of social and family organization, enabled by ease of mobility on a regional scale, particularly through new high-speed train links and abundant low cost intra-European airlines.

A further self-selection operates with people using mobility to opt out of the standardized mainstream values that impose themselves on lives lived only on a local scale. Family life is changed irrevocably by mobility and distance. For some, the choice of a third international city becomes the way that couples of different nationalities reconcile their difficult to balance private and professional lives across borders. Their children will necessarily grow up as cosmopolitans outside of familiar national structures, with new forms of social capital, but also perhaps disadvantages relative to traditional nationalized elites. For others, mobility is associated with an individual move out of conventional family norms. Hence the high prevalence in my sample of childless couples, gay people and singles, particularly women. Amsterdam, London and Brussels all have lively gay sub-cultures that provide a home for mobile individualists adrift from family and social norms – and pressures – that would have been felt that much stronger if they were still living in their home countries. Amsterdam, not an easy place for foreigners to settle in many ways, has functioned as a comfortable capital in this sense, precisely because it is easier to identify with the city and Dutch culture as a progressive identity if you are gay. The internationally mobile, career-minded attitude becomes a justification for the choices single women have made to live their lives away from typical family norms. Helen, a very successful logistics manager, who has constructed a happy life in Brussels and then Amsterdam away from her native Northern Ireland, puts it this way:

> I'm a very lucky person in life, I've just been a cat landing on its feet ... I don't need anybody around me that much. On the one hand you do want to move on, it's what you like doing. On the other hand, it's a big emotional upheaval. You are not married, so you are in it by yourself ... But I wouldn't have it any other way. This is what I want.

These Eurostars are, in short, pioneers. Not statistically significant enough maybe to alter aggregate social mobility charts, but symbolically the very emblem of the new, de-nationalized Europe that the European Union has enabled. They embody the process, flux and change that the European Union has released, albeit around the edges of European society. On both counts, they are statistical 'black swans' whose impact extends well beyond their structural location in the margins. Moreover, their unusual lives and experience cast sharp light on the background norms and patterns that continue to hold much of Europe in place. Indeed, many of them could never have succeeded in their lives if those norms were not there, and they were not rather unique statistical exceptions. Their category-crossing experience – which is neither conventional migration, nor conventional social mobility – also points to elements of flux and change in Europe linked to urban–periphery distinctions, growing individualism, and new forms of spatial-temporal organization across borders. All of this would have been undetectable 'noise' in the conventional quantitative approach. Social theorists have been quick to point to the transformative effects of highly 'mobile' (John Urry), 'liquid' (Zygmunt Bauman) or 'reflexive' societies (Anthony Giddens, Ulrich Beck). The new Europe might be what they have in mind. But they have not investigated these claims empirically. When all we have otherwise to assert these transformative social currents is speculative social theory, the ethnographic/documentary approach detailed here is revealed as an essential empirical complement to the quantitative mainstream approach, a vital part of the apparatus needed for a true sociology of the European Union.

Conclusion: a European field of mobility

When Caterina moved to Brussels from Northern Italy to work as a medical administrator she was already in her 30s. A wholly individual choice, it was a rather speculative move, given she had no specific interest in or connection to Brussels, and had never previously visited. She just thought it was a good 'somewhere' to find work, and give the international life a try, to 'see how it was' and 'look for something else'. 'I wanted to challenge myself in a different environment, discover things and enrich my life', she says – a prototypical Eurostar reasoning. Although a relatively adventurous move compared to her peers back home, the fact that the *scale* was European made all the difference. European citizenship meant formal barriers were down, yet it was still close enough to home in Italy. She would not have moved otherwise. Now nearly 40, she left behind a cosy and stable life in her native Italy, to which she still dreams of returning – maybe to 'go in a hole', she laughs, someday when she gets old.

This is the pioneer attitude, typical of so many EU movers: the EU as a new European *field* of mobility on a regional scale, picking up on the conceptualization of structure and action proposed in the sociology of Pierre Bourdieu. This is not a defined metric of rational choices with a clear, easy to assess pay-off, but an open, undefined, protean horizon beyond the nation, a place for self-discovery and adventure as much as possible opportunity and advancement, that works because of its relatively bounded scope. As the PIONEUR project also finds quantitatively, it is often not rational economic motives that caused people to move, so much as ideas about adventure, quality of life, or – a big factor in the post-Erasmus student Europe – romance with a European of another nationality. These factors perhaps account for why the strictly rationalist models on which economic theories and structural hypotheses about mobility and European integration are built do not work so well in practice. They do not measure the qualitative dimension of mobility and change, let alone the symbolic and cultural energies unleashed. The de-nationalized European freedoms enabled by the freedom of movement are, in many ways, not yet a recognized currency. This may be the EU's most precious invention: a new sense of regionalized freedom – since it is wrapped up in very European virtues of security, welfare, quality of life, and lived out on a European scale – but freedom nonetheless. And indeed 'the freedom to travel, work and study anywhere in the EU' is what the majority of Europeans constantly cite as the most important benefit of EU membership, according to Eurobarometer data. Free movement *is* the EU in Europeans' minds. Much of this freedom is experienced by those that try it as a shot in the dark: there is no clear feedback to others who might want to try, the rational calculation is unclear if not obscure, and there are clearly diminishing returns if too many free thinking, de-nationalizing individuals start moving. A shift in too many people upsetting national norms and patterns might undermine much upon which European social structure – ultimately its distinctive balance of economy and society – is built. The one in fifty who move are likely to remain a marginal niche, statistical exceptions, albeit individuals who point to how Europe has changed the most.

Some of the effects of this movement may be inherently temporary. The mid- to long-term evaluation of the European move of the Eurostars is often not so encouraging. Long-term settlement, in even the most cosmopolitan of cities such as London and Amsterdam, often proves elusive. Home countries of origin and foreign countries of residence alike have their way of re-asserting their norms, value systems and social hierarchies over the lives of these pioneers. They see their experiences and opportunities being *re-*nationalized by the weight of mainstream lives lived in national structures; they are often caught out on a limb in their life choice, out of time and place in terms of both the peers they left back home, and the natives living and working around them. Structures outside the standard nationalized society for things like child care, education, welfare, and pensions – issues that increasingly form the terrain of struggle for middle classes seeking better quality of life in urban settings (Butler and Robson 2003) – are often very vulnerable. But the few that do dare to move are perhaps a symbol of a better, brighter Europe as was hoped for by the founders of the European Union.

The marginal mobility of the Eurostars points to how social mobility opportunities have been extended to a far wider range of European citizens than clichéd images of European elites allow. When enumerated one by one, mobile Europeans are often provincial, upwardly mobile, middle- and lower middle-class individuals with high education. The aggregate structural evidence about European mobility, though, continues to suggest that spatial mobility opportunities are still dominantly monopolized by upper and upper middle classes in Europe. The symbolic and structural potential of the EU thus co-exist: European Union enhances both social fluidity and social reproduction.

However, the relation may shift once the question is extended to the economic integration and social changes associated with the new East-West movers, now able to enjoy free movement rights in the EU after the twin accessions of new East European members to the EU in 2004 and 2007. While these forms of migration cannot be directly assimilated to the free movement of West Europeans prior to 2004 – despite theoretical arguments about the integration of the European labour market which suggest this may one day be the case – there is strong evidence for the Poles, Lithuanians, Romanians and others moving Westwards of distinct social mobility, income improvement, and return development effects relative to their countries of origin, even when in status terms the move West is a move down the occupational hierarchy. In a few short years, a marked effect of EU enlargement and integration on new member states has been visible via the new intra-EU mobility it has enabled. Studies of Western Europe may not conclusively provide a sociological base for claims about European integration and spatial or social mobility. But to put a face on the very visible and striking social structural impact of European Union on the continent, we may need only to think of these new highly mobile East-West workers – a very real spatial and social mobility that may prove the most significant demographic change in the continent since the end of the Second World War.

CHAPTER 4

Elites, Middle Classes and Cities[1]

Alberta Andreotti and Patrick Le Galès

> **Key concepts:** mobilities, social class, elites, middle classes, service class, cities, exit and voice, transnationalism, capitalism, europeanization or globalization, scale, place, territory, social differentiation, operationalization
>
> **Key references:** Urry, Mann, Crouch, Bartolini, Rokkan, Giddens, Appadurai, Tilly, Weber, Lagroye, Pinçon and Pinçon-Charlot, Savage, Butler, Hirschman, Lockwood, Wagner, Goldthorpe, Préteceille

Year after year, the European Commission faces a major disappointment. Despite all its efforts to promote the free movement of EU citizens as part of the single market for capital, goods, services and people, the statistics keep showing that Europeans do not move that much. Even EU citizens who might declare themselves enthusiastic Europeans in other types of measurement do not seem to avail themselves of the thing that is most frequently cited as the most important benefit of European citizenship: the right to freely live and work in another EU member state. As Favell and Recchi show in this volume (Chapter 3),

---

[1] The research reported on here was coordinated by Patrick Le Galès and Alberta Andreotti, and financed by PUCA, le Ministère de l'Equipement and the RTN-UrbEurope project (see our website: http://www.urban-europe.net/). Other researchers include Francisco Javier Moreno Fuentes, coordinating the Spanish case, François Bonnet, Brigitte Fouilland, Julie Pollard, Charlotte Halpern, Barbara Da Roit, Stefania Sabatinelli, Chiara Respi. We thank all colleagues involved in the project.

mobility conceived this way seems to be a marginal feature of the European society in the making.

But perhaps this is only one way to look at 'mobility'. Some social theorists, notably John Urry (2000), have suggested – not without controversy – reconceptualizing sociology beyond the traditional conceptions of *spatial mobility* (that is, migration) and *social mobility* (as Favell and Recchi set out), but in terms of a much broader range of 'mobilities' that characterize late modern societies under increasingly globalized conditions. Urry suggests that the old idea of the nation-state-society is dead, and sociology should, by this account, start focusing on movement, mobilities, contingency and flux in particular. He aims at reinventing 'sociology beyond societies', the title of his book, in terms of these mobilities, to escape from the national territory bias of sociology. It is possible that these multiple mobilities might indeed be a growing feature of the everyday lives of European citizens without their needing to physically move residence or live and work in another country. These ideas are interesting avenues for empirical research. However, instead of focusing solely on mobility, we argue that in order to assess social change related to mobility, it is necessary to study both the dynamics of mobility *and* the dynamics of rootedness. In this way, we hope to contribute towards an empirical sociology of European Union by showing how these ideas might be operationalized in cities-based research.

Our chapter presents the preliminary results of exploratory research considering the making of a European society as the building of new social networks and practices among European higher social status groups – in particular upper-middle and middle classes – taking place in the interconnection of some European cities. The hypothesis at the core of the research is whether European integration is offering these *urban elites* the opportunity of 'exit' from their own nation-state or national society: in terms of job trajectory, social networks, cultural consumption practices (such as holidays and travel), media use, property ownership, education for children, or their expression of social and political values. The possibility of exit can also characterize their relation to the local urban *public sphere*: for example in their choices to opt out of public urban services, such as schools, to withdraw from public networks and associations, or frequent public spaces. This has indeed been claimed as a part of the growing inequalities of some Western societies in urban contexts, seen, for example, in the rise of 'gated communities' (Blakely and Snyder 1999; Atkinson and Bridge 2005). In this research we thus cross-reference the possible exit strategies from national society with such urban exit strategies. Within this framework, the chapter considers the question of whether these exit options are particularly European in cause or effect, or rather are only a local manifestation of a new *global* ordering of elites, the rise of a *transnational capitalist class* that is leading and most benefiting from the expansive direction of *globalization*.

The chapter is organized in four parts. The first discusses the theoretical background to these issues, in terms of the idea of society beyond the nation-state, and the social theory of globalization and transnational elites, leading to two hypotheses that will guide our research. The second presents some existing empirical studies on the dynamics of urban middle classes between rootedness and mobility. The third discusses the methodological considerations behind the operationalization of these questions in our own research. Finally, in the fourth section we present our results. These enable us to draw some preliminary conclusions about the changing patterns of elite and middle class practices and social organization under the twin effects of Europeanization and globalization.

Social theory, nation building and globalization

As this volume has stressed throughout, sociologists have often found it difficult to grapple with the concept of European society. There are good reasons for this. The nation building process of making distinctly *national* modern industrial societies was the very question that drove the founding fathers of sociology, such as Marx, Tocqueville, Weber and Durkheim. Most historical sociology research has underlined the slow making of societies as nations and national societies progressively governed by a state, for example, the Weberian account of the rise of nations and social classes in the work of Michael Mann (1993). The concept of society is taken to refer to three ideas: a certain intensity of relations between individuals and groups; the idea of capacity and autonomy expressed through collective action or political institutions, and finally, the idea of a bounded territory.

Within Western Europe, each national society had followed its own trajectory and undergone its own form of development, contrasting with others. The different elements of national societies have been more or less in place since the late nineteenth century in most European countries – and in some cases, much longer. Differences of language, social structure, and culture were simply reinforced by the strengthening of the nation-state throughout the twentieth century. In his comparative study on the sociology of Europe, Colin Crouch (1999) stresses how the social compromises forged after the Second World War – despite the European integration process also begun then – gave a new vigour to this model, a position that emphasizes the *varieties* of European economy and society (see Crouch and Streeck 1997). European industrial capitalist societies were organized around the state, its citizens' rights, and its institutions, and remained heavily nationalized, despite international relations and international commerce. This was a distinctively Weberian process: the dual movement in which borders are strengthened and the inside is differentiated from outside, while the internal order is organized and gradually homogenizes as a national society – a dynamic central to the Stein Rokkan-inspired political sociology of Europe developed by, for example, Stefano Bartolini (1998, 2005).

Comparative sociology is deeply embedded in the historically specific notion of the modern nation-state-society dealing with social, religious and political cleavages (Rokkan 1999). Not surprisingly, then, many sociologists think that the social structure of European societies is not changing dramatically because of the making of the EU, and even if it does, it will not be the case for decades. For others, European societies are changing dramatically, but under the general processes of globalization, not of Europeanization. These authors have moved their thinking both beyond the old nation-state-society unit, but also beyond the European Union. Anthony Giddens and Arjun Appaduraï, for instance, suggest the making of a global society without considering the notion of a distinct Europe. In other words, these global theorists emphasize that flows, transactions, and the strategies of individuals or collective actors are being reshaped directly on a global *scale*, according to globalizing processes. Social systems with absolutely no linkages to the nation-state context are on a trajectory of formation, but the European scale is not particularly part of their picture. Cultural practices, images and representations, social movements (especially global movements such as environmental and human rights movements), and of course capitalism itself – or at least the vanguard forces of these processes – are said to become more and more disembedded from the nation-state. To these authors, the global scale becomes a new level for structuring major cultural and social conflicts of interest. Appaduraï (1996), from a cultural point of view, forecasts the advent of a 'postnational global cultural economy'. Giddens (1994), in his article on 'post-traditional society', explains that the traditional institutions of the nation-state have been disembedded, and that they have been replaced by institutions that follow the dictates of globalized communication and interactions.

This raises important questions in terms of social class formation, in parallel to the questions raised by Díez Medrano in Chapter 2. Leslie Sklair, starting from a more Marxist perspective analyzing the impact of global capitalism, has explored the globalization of what he calls the *transnational capitalist class*. He suggests that the globalization of the economy has led to the emergence of a new social class: a highly mobile global elite, which can move countries, organize itself across and around borders, and thus avoid the constraints of life and work in national societies. He defines it as 'an international bourgeoisie: a socially comprehensive category, encompassing the entrepreneurial elite, managers of firms, senior state functionaries, leading politicians, members of the learned professions ... plus the [leaders of] media, culture, consumption' (1995: 62, 2001). This new global elite speaks English, and has mastered the codes that operate within Anglo-American firms, universities and consultancies. It is developing a common global culture and particular consumption practices. Their global society is apparently organized less on the basis of major conflicts and more on the basis of professional networks, with norms and models of excellence driven from within the professions – by consultants, legal specialists, managers, university academics, doctors, accountants, bankers, and advertising executives. Within this framework, international bodies – from professional associations to the World Bank – would give their 'good practice' seal of approval or else shoot barbed remarks at those who do not play according to the new rules. Their discourse on globalization and its benefits is central to the legitimating of these processes and to their global domination as a social group. To put it more accurately, Sklair argues that the discourse on globalization establishes the hegemony of this new social class, which is principally a transatlantic bourgeoisie linking Europe and North America.

Yet, despite all important transformations linked to globalization, this global society is, as yet, still more potential, more virtual than real, more a stage on which these actors interact than a defined system. Moreover, in terms of empirical research, it has been rather more theorized about than investigated. Furthermore, it remains a possibility that a regional European society might be more advanced than the global one when looked at in the same terms. European societies which share some common and distinctive features might be more Europeanized than globalized in terms of the social organization and behaviour of their elites and middle classes.

The reason for this is Europe's distinctiveness as a region. In his historical social theory of Europe, Göran Therborn (1985), for example, stresses the distinctive European trajectory towards modernity based upon industrialization, a strong working class and the welfare state. Moreover, the territorialization of European societies differs globally for two main reasons: the tradition of stable peasants on their land (Mendras 1997), and the long history of medium-size cities, two elements that have been historically important in the understanding of the particularities of European society within wider global processes (Bagnasco and Le Galès 2000). The distinctiveness of European cities has thus been central to the history of the continent since the Middle Ages (Kaelble 1987). Max Weber's famous analysis of the occidental city already highlighted this point quite well and it has been used by numerous historians to demonstrate the long term stability of European urban structure, interconnecting cities across the continent through trade and interaction. They underline the importance of its numerous middle-size cities, particularly those running through the north-to-south heartland of the continent from the Low Countries to northern Italy, a structure still important today (see Dunford *et al.* 2002; Le Galès 2002; Kazepov 2005). The order of modern Europe has thus largely emerged out of the developing relationship of this longer-standing structure of cities with the later emergent nation-state territorial units, a process famously studied by Charles Tilly (1990). In this history, cities have always retained a certain independence from nation-states, a historical feature of Europe that might be returning in a world where nation-states are, at least partly, eroding.

The second element is the role of longstanding urbanized *bourgeoisies*, and their strong influence in these same cities. Historically, upper- and middle-class dynamics have proved quite essential to the understanding of European societies: the rise of cities was also the story of the rise of the bourgeoisie in European cities. Against the feudal order, *burghers* – merchants, bankers, artisans, shopkeepers and lawyers – were the new actors of modern European urban expansion and of cities' autonomy from the old order. This bourgeoisie of early mercantile capitalism gradually invented itself as a social class and status group with its own interests, but also with its own ways of life, consumption behaviours, values, ideas, and organizations. It put in place distinctive ideas of law, used strategic marriages, and saw the formation of clans and rivalries between great families trying to monopolize power, prestige and wealth. As Max Weber famously argued, social hierarchies were established through reversals of fortune, alliances with overlords or the acquisition of positions of power within the guild or the commune.

A change of scale in the making of society usually leads to social differentiation. Studying the making of nation-states, and writing about processes of social differentiation within Europe, Jacques Lagroye suggests that the nationalization of society goes hand in hand with 'the appearance of social groups with new resources, tending because of these to organize and to promote their own interests in order to assert their ambitions in relation to the traditional (national) power-holding elites, and thus able to act as support and stimulant for 'modernizing' activity by, for example, those in authority' (Lagroye 1997:100).

Is something similar going on now in Europe or beyond Europe? Is a new European elite or middle class in the course of forming, which could gain influence in cities and to some extent reinforce the discontinuity between territories, perhaps giving birth to a new Europe of cities? These research questions are behind the empirical research presented in this chapter and can be reformulated as the following two hypotheses:

- The rise of transnational mobilities and/or transactions may produce *social differentiation processes* and may play a role in re-structuring the social order and social hierarchies within national societies. As urban upper-middle classes have more resources than others in the city – in terms of prestige, income, or status – they are most likely to take advantage of this process. Can we find a strata of upper or middle classes in European cities that take

advantage of these mobilities, putting into practice strategies of exit or partial exit from the nation-state?
- If so, is there a distinctive European (as opposed to global) *scale* to these exit options? Could a new European elite across European cities be in the making in relation to European integration processes?

Between rootedness in urban life and international mobility: the dynamics of middle class formation

An existing literature on sociology and human geography at the national level has addressed these questions in terms of the dynamics of upper and middle classes in cities. Historically, the upper and middle classes in Europe have had a strong capacity to choose where they live. More than a century ago, for example, English middle classes left urban industrial centres to live in residential suburbs. Pinçon and Pinçon-Charlot's work on France, meanwhile (1989; 2000) – which conceptualizes the notion of 'elites' more narrowly than us – have identified the 'spatial stamp' of the bourgeoisie: a way of building and organizing 'good districts' in cities, especially the largest ones. They focus on the very high bourgeoisie (mainly Parisian), and hence the most important families of Paris. The mutual reinforcement in spatial terms enables this particular social class to deploy effective inheritance and reproduction strategies. As Pinçon and Pinçon-Charlot write: 'Spatial segregation, pushed to the extreme, is in fact an aggregation, the choice of a social group, of a class, through which it is expressing its awareness of the group's deep community of interests' (2000: 54). This point is also reinforced in Mike Savage and Tim Butler's research on the British middle classes (2003), which will be discussed further below, particularly in relation to schooling and educational choices for children (see also Zunz *et al.* 2002; Bagnasco 2008).

Again, European cities differ significantly from other world regions, particularly the US, on this point. Historically, because of the special role of the city centre in European cities, the most privileged social strata – that is, the cultural, political, and economic elites – have in many countries remained living in city centres, with the general exception of the UK which historically has the most pronounced *suburbanization* (or 'exurban') processes. They have maintained and reproduced their presence, and they have accumulated economic, social, cultural and political capital using this spatial centrality. New groups of managers and professionals – upper-middle classes – have followed the same logic, but they have settled less systematically in the centre, also moving to residential suburbs. European cities are rarely distinguished by urban crisis in the city centre, except in nineteenth-century industrial cities, ports and some special cases such as Brussels or Frankfurt. On the contrary, the bourgeoisie of most European cities were historically active and well placed enough to push the building of factories and social housing out towards the periphery.

European elites and middle classes have thus not systematically deserted the centres of old European cities (as they did historically in the US), and their urban presence has indeed become more pronounced again since the 1980s, as is shown in the booming literature on gentrification (Butler 2005). Comparative studies of social mobility show higher rates of upper-class segregation in European cities, and not merely in the larger metropolises (Burtenshaw *et al.* 1991). However, some sections of the upper- and middle-class strata have gradually settled in the peripheries of cities. In most European cities, it is easy to distinguish those suburban local authorities where there are concentrations of well-off households, including the richest. In northern cities (for example, in Scandinavia) or southern cities (in other words, in Italy) the phenomenon was initially limited, but it is now gaining momentum. It is more common in Germany and France. Areas of suburban houses or peri-urban developments and small, ethnically and socially homogeneous residential towns, largely of owner-occupiers, have developed on the periphery of cities everywhere. These benefit from the two movements of urban growth and dispersal. Horizontal dispersal has gradually affected European cities but has not generally led to the decline of city centres. Good districts and residential suburbs are also visible in the biggest cities because there are more socially powerful households there – particularly in capital cities, close to government and the organs of media and national culture – but most European cities continue to display this trait (Pinol 2002).

In the European context, then, we now see at the same time parallel dynamics in cities: of continuous *embourgeoisement*, the renewed investment by upper- and upper-middle classes in historical bourgeois neighbourhoods close to city centres, in connection with new financial and corporate districts; of *gentrification*, as middle classes push the working class out in central neighbourhoods; and (to some degree) of *suburbanization*, the making of more or less segregated upper- and middle-class communities, including even 'gated communities' of the kind now common in the US. Making sense of those different dynamics, identifying what David Lockwood used to call 'the urban seeking' versus the 'urban fleeing' middle classes (1995), seems to us a particularly fruitful way of understanding shifting inequalities and processes of social differentiation.

The distinctive contribution here is to bring an urban and spatial dimension into mainstream sociology's understanding of social class. On reflection, this ought to be essential given how territorialized European societies in fact are. In various works the English sociologist Mike Savage following earlier work by urban sociologists Ray Pahl or Herbert Gans identified what he called the 'missing spatial dimension' of class analysis in the UK, in particular in the social stratification literature described above by Favell and Recchi. In other words, in the UK, aggregate national class analysis misses the crucial urban/rural dimension in society, together with the particular role of London in the social mobility of middle classes. Within the urban sociology field or research, numerous studies on gentrification and suburbanization – in the UK, US and Australia in particular – have gone on to identify socio-spatial dynamics of social mobility, social exclusion or inequalities in these terms (Atkinson and Bridge 2005). In France, the dynamics of middle and lower-middle classes working in the public sector were also shown to be deeply rooted with particular types of regions and cities (OCS 1987) The local analysis of class is also relatively well rooted in the Italian tradition (Bagnasco and Negri 1994; Bagnasco 2008).

We argue that this well-studied urban dimension should be combined with the issue of mobility on an international scale (see Figure 4.1). The rising number and various types of mobility options – which the theoretical literature presented above assumes are now available for many elite and middle-class people – are still not widely used by *all* social groups. It is likely that the upper strata of society are more at the forefront of these dynamics, as they have more resources to rely on. But we might also argue, as was the case during the rise of the nation-state and the rise of capitalism that, as part of the current new phase of capitalism and its economic and political organization, new urban social groups within upper- or upper-middle classes may mobilize to challenge existing national elites, to push for different modernization projects and to promote their own ambitions. A new process of social

	Transnational Exit +	**Transnational Exit −**
Urban Exit +	Nomads/Barbarians	Immobile/national urban opt-out/ secession
Urban Exit −	Urban and transnational	Urban and immobile/ national

Figure 4.1 Urban options for European elites and middle classes

differentiation would be in the making, and it might be that this process has distinct European features.

One way that some upper and middle classes might promote their interests and challenge the existing elite is to put into practice 'exit' or 'partial exit' strategies. This conceptualization refers to the classic distinction drawn in purposive social action by Albert Hirschman, between strategies of 'voice' (democratic participation) and 'exit' (opting out of the public realm). One way individuals can choose to exit from their nation-state is to physically migrate, but this remains a rare and extreme option as an exit strategy, involving many costs – even in a Europe with all the barriers to free movement down – as Favell explains in his study *Eurostars and Eurocities* (2008). As an alternative, they can choose to partially exit in a variety of ways: in terms of consumption, friends, jobs, housing, children, or financial investment offshore. Furthermore, these individuals can choose to exit from one of these dimensions and not from another one, creating a complex mix of choices which has to be analyzed on different *scales*: local/urban, national, European, or transnational/global. For instance individuals belonging to these social groups can choose to send their children to an international school or university (an exit option), but they can also choose to engage in the local neighbourhood association (voice). The opportunity for partial exit thus allows them to (re)negotiate their own position within the national social structure, for example, to concurrently protest against or escape high level of taxes, locate property or income outside the nation-state, and actively campaign for a reform of the educational system. This need not only apply to individuals: large firms, religious organizations or environmental groups may also have the capacity to mobilize and invest resources at different levels, allowing them to put pressure on national structures. The very same individuals can therefore combine international exit options with elements of fixity and rootedness in their national or local contexts. The research presented in this chapter thus aims to understand whether, when, how and to what extent these multiple mobilities in the social organization of individual strategies become a viable option.

The point here is similar to what the sociologist Mike Savage has argued about the rise of 'elective belonging' in social class formation and dynamics (2005). With other colleagues, he has argued that the differentiation and overlapping of various scales of interaction for individuals beyond national frontiers has opened up room for manoeuvre in terms of their choice of residence, of social practices, of identity claiming and of investment of different resources (including time and social capital) in different territories. One of the possible consequences is to blur settled national logics of stratification and social distinction. Commenting on Savage's work, Tim Butler (2005) notes that the argument about 'elective belonging' – following a long tradition in sociology

(Goldthorpe, Lockwood *et al.* 1969) – points to the fact that as societies become more complex and mobile, individuals become more privatized in their strategies and choices.

These exit or partial exit strategies in the different dimensions of leisure, work, sociability or education for children cross-reference to residential space choices. Savage *et al.* in fact claim (2005:207) that 'residential space is a key arena in which individuals define their social position' and they note that residence has the greatest fixity in relation to the other dimensions – such as patterns of leisure, work, sociability, and most crucially, schooling – in terms of defining one's sense of 'social location'. Indeed, it is this fixity that often allows access to other dimensions that might be mobile. This insight is particularly important in allowing us to go beyond the classic opposition – still used by Favell and Recchi, Chapter 3 in this volume – between rooted 'locals' and mobile 'cosmopolitans' (Merton 1957). In her review of transnational elites, Wagner (2007) also stresses the need not to oppose those two dimensions but by contrast to study the links between national resources used for mobility and the resources which can be used from the transnational experience within the local or national context.

It is therefore essential to bring together the dynamics of partial exit within the urban fabric on the one hand (the internal dimension) and partial exit from national society (external dimension) to understand dynamics of social change and class formation. The point we want to make is that, for most people, focusing on physical mobility alone is not enough and not very fruitful. Mobility of various other kinds may be instrumentalized to actually reinforce one's rooted position within the city and within society.

Operationalization: a comparison of upper-middle classes in European cities

Social categories and selection of interviewees

The research focuses on the upper-middle classes as the key group at the core of the social/spatial class dynamic identified above. Within this category, different social groups coexist in terms of economic, financial, human and social capital, and thus in terms of status and prestige. This variety is to be found both within countries and across them. Classic sociological research centred on the work of John Goldthorpe has identified some of these groups as those which rose massively in Western societies from the 1960s onwards: professionals, managers, engineers, and so on, with the debate focusing on whether they can be grouped together as a so-called *service class* or not

(Goldthorpe 1982; Esping Andersen 1993; see also Butler and Savage (1995) or Martin (1998) for an excellent discussion of this in terms of the British middle class).

Existing comparative data provide some figures about the weight of the service class of managers and professionals, etc. in the different European countries (see Table 4.1).

When undertaking comparative research, certain compromises and simplifications have to be made in order to identify comparable populations, even when the sample is not statistically representative. Two steps were thus followed in our research: 1) identifying a social and statistical category which referred to the same position within the labour market structure in the three countries chosen for study (in this project, France, Italy and Spain) and 2) within these national categories, identifying some further, more strictly defined criteria.

In the French context, the upper-middle class mainly comprises the social (and statistical) category of *cadres supérieurs*. A well-known literature exists in France about *cadres* (Boltanski 1982; Groux 1982; Bouffartigues 2001), though much less on *cadres supérieurs*. From a sociological point of view *cadres* are not

Table 4.1 Number and percentage of legislators and managers plus professionals in Europe, 2002

Country	Employees	Managers and professionals (ISCO 1 & 2)	%
Belgium	3427	878	25.6
Denmark	2497	468	18.7
Germany	32252	5111	15.8
Greece	2377	417	17.5
Spain	13095	2012	15.4
France	21312	3391	15.9
Italy	15785	1987	12.6
Netherlands	7220	1801	24.9
Austria	3232	491	15.2
Portugal	3733	364	9.8
Finland	2097	493	23.5
Sweden	3883	849	21.9
UK	24978	6523	26.1
Total EU Countries (EU 15)	137501	25214	18.3

Source: EUROSTAT Labour Force Survey 2002.

defined only by their education or job, but rather by a status: they have a separate trade union that negotiates their wages and labour conditions, and their pension is managed by specific organizations distinct from other workers. From the statistical point of view, INSEE *(Institut National de la Statistique et des Etudes Economiques)* classifies *cadres supérieurs* in the *professions intellectuelles supérieures*, which includes both *cadres* and professionals (consultants, lawyers, doctors, etc.). In the Italian and Spanish contexts, the profile of *cadres supérieurs* or *service class* as referred to, respectively, in France or Britain does not have the same social meaning. In Italy, the concept is closer to the social and statistical category of *dirigenti* (Ricciardi 2004), as they have their own association, trade union organization and pension fund, exactly as in France. In Spain, the word *cadres* was brought in under the pressure of multinational companies (*cuadros* and *ejecutivos*) during the last two decades, but there is no exact equivalent statistical category.

Given the inconsistencies of these social and statistical categories, we narrowed our research to two subgroups identified as particularly meaningful comparatively: managers and engineers working as employees. The second step consisted in identifying some stricter, common criteria for these two chosen subgroups. Three criteria were retained: (1) level of education, selecting individuals with at least a university degree, most often at master's level; (2) autonomy at work, meaning the capacity to manage time, and the contents of work; (3) responsibility at work, for example, coordinating a team or deciding upon the careers and salaries of other workers. All interviews carried out in this research were with individuals who fulfilled these criteria.

Selection of cities and local contexts

In order to explore the question of multiple mobilities, and the articulation of lifestyle strategies at different territorial levels in Europe, dynamic metropolitan urban regions were the most appropriate locations for the research. In line with the literature on globalization and global cities, Paris and London seemed obvious, indeed unavoidable, choices as European global cities. Given the existing studies, discussed above, of Tim Butler and colleagues in London, we could focus the attention of new work on Paris, drawing on their published London material to contrast our results (Butler and Robson 2003). Meanwhile, Lyon, Milan and Madrid in our selection represent dynamic, relatively large and international European cities, although they do not display quite the same global features as Paris and London. Our selection thus contributes to understanding whether there is any difference between the largest urban regions such as London and Paris and other European cities, something which has been emphasized by the globalization literature, for example the Globalization and World Cities project at the University of Loughborough (http://www.lboro.ac.uk/gawc).

Within each city, research was planned in four neighbourhoods, with thirty interviews for each neighbourhood. The choice of neighbourhoods was based on two criteria: location and social structure. One basic puzzle of our research is the extent to which respondents prefer to live within or outside the city, that is, the extent to which we can identify the 'urban seeking' versus 'urban fleeing' profiles. The classic centre–suburbs dichotomy discussed in the literature raises the question of whether there are differences or similarities in respondents' strategies *vis-à-vis* their adoption of exit or partial exit strategies in the two cases. For this reason, two neighbourhoods within the limits of the city and two outside the city in the residential suburbs were selected. The other variable orienting the selection of the neighbourhoods was social structure, as always discussed in the urban sociology literature. In each metropolitan context, we thus identified two neighbourhoods with the highest concentration of managers and engineers, and two neighbourhoods with a mixed social composition, one each in the city centre and the suburbs respectively. The selection of neighbourhoods in Paris, for example, was based on the remarkably precise analysis and classification carried out by Edmond Préteceille (2006) of the social composition of the small statistical units comprising neighbourhoods in the city. In the Milan case, the selection was based on the ecological analysis of Jonathan Pratschke (2007). For each metropolitan city, then, we have a table with four cases: one highly homogeneous neighbourhood in the city centre and one highly homogeneous in the suburbs; one neighbourhood with mixed population in the city centre and one with mixed population in the suburbs.

Construction of questionnaire

The hypotheses and related questions elaborated in the previous sections of this chapter cannot be examined through existing data sets for two main reasons. Firstly, existing data do not include indicators of exit or voice and have thus not identified information about potential European social classes in formation. Also, they do not point to possible mechanisms of change. Secondly, these data sets, given the way they are produced, do not provide information about the motivations, strategies and interactions of individuals in specific situations and places. One distinctive feature of our research is precisely the importance of *place*, represented here by the urban dimension in each location. Our study thus adopts a micro-level perspective, looking at the individual experiences, strategies, motivations, values and narratives of managers and engineers living in the four locations. The approach is predominantly qualitative and the sample is not intended to be strictly representative of any population of managers and engineers of the four cities. Yet through this sample clear and revealing behavioural patterns can be identified.

A total of 120 semi-structured in-depth interviews were carried out in each city; we are therefore working with a data base of 480 interviews. Although not statistically representative, the figures provided by the data are quite large and we were therefore able to make quantitative measurements which give an idea of the importance of the phenomena examined. The interviews were based on a long semi-structured questionnaire which included both closed questions with multiple choice answer and open questions allowing interviewees to express their ideas on specific issues. Even in multiple choice answers, interviewees always had the possibility of explaining the meaning of their answers or the reasons for their choice. This means that interviews were quite long by questionnaire standards, lasting on average an hour and a half.

The methodology used in this research, face to face questionnaires in the selected neighbourhood, is therefore comparable to the studies of Butler and Robson in London (2003) and that of Savage and his colleagues in Manchester (2005). In our research the interview grid is more rigid, with the issues already defined although questions are inspired by all the previous studies mentioned. Our questionnaire was structured around the following five themes: 1) working career, 2) residential career, 3) formal and informal social relations, 4) daily practices (such as use of city and neighbourhood services and neighbourhood, cultural consumption practices, frequency of going out, where and with whom, etc.) and 5) representations, attitudes and values using the classical survey questions of the European Social Survey and Eurobarometer.

It is worth detailing how questions were constructed for all five themes. Concerning respondents' *working career*, the information collected was rather limited – this was not the core of the research. Attention was focused, however, on three elements: the structural characteristics of the company the managers belonged to (public or private, national, foreign or multinational, sector, size), the working conditions of the managers (working hours, the concrete functions carried out during a working day, the foreign partners or clients they dealt with, the possession of a company car), and finally the most important steps in the respondents' working career with a special focus on experience abroad. Despite the common economic criteria used to select interviewees, heterogeneity in working experiences and conditions is still relatively high within our sample – not only among different European cities, but even within the same European cities. Much depends on the size of the company and its kind of property. Managers working for large multinational companies are more likely to have similar paths with experience of working abroad, even though for different lengths of time. This relative homogeneity is particularly obvious for the younger generation (under thirty-five) which shares comparable foreign experiences either as students or as managers – most often both.

To investigate *residential career*, attention was focused on the following issues: the reasons for the choice of the neighbourhood or village where interviewees lived, where they used to live before, feelings about their neighbourhood or village, and feelings about the metropolitan area they live in. The information collected provides indicators to understand and test the hypothesis of exit or partial exit.

Examining *networks* of friends and families and where these are located is crucial to understanding the dynamics of internationalization – and Europeanization in particular – considering both the extent to which these networks remain national and local, and the extent to which they are transnational. This information clearly brings new material to test Hypotheses 1 and 2. The more interviewees have interconnected European social networks and homogeneous relations in terms of economic, educational and social characteristics, the more there might be evidence of the formation of a European class – or at least a class in itself, to use Marxist terminology (see also the discussion in Chapter 2). Furthermore, the more the interviewees have a European and international social network, the more they are likely to organize their life on different scales and can put into practice exit or partial exit strategies. To investigate relational networks, four elements were considered in the questionnaire: friendship, neighbourhood relations, the hierarchical positions present in the respondents' network, and finally relations and exchanges within families. The information collected does not allow for a full profile of the respondents' social networks, but it does provide an idea of the sociability of the respondents and their degree of embeddedness or disembeddedness from the local context (Savage *et al.* 2005), bringing further elements to the partial exit hypothesis. The networks-based questions also take into consideration effective participation in local, national, European or transnational associations and political parties, initiatives and public services. The answers to these questions further contribute to an understanding of the strategies of exit or partial exit. For instance, a disinvestment in national policy and disengagement from political parties or associations can bring some elements towards the exit strategy hypothesis.

The analysis of *daily practices* adds other important pieces of information. Special attention was paid to the European or international dimension of consumption (such as watching foreign TV channels, listening to foreign radio, reading foreign newspapers) and travel practices (for example, how many times the respondent flies per month, where and for how long; how many journeys abroad in the last year for professional and non-professional reasons, where and for how long, etc.). Within this section, attention was also paid to educational strategies for children, for example reasons for the choice of private or public school, national or international schooling, where the school is located, foreign languages studied and other foreign study experiences. Using this information, it was possible to learn how much the interviewees still trust public institutions at the national level, or prefer to find their own educational solutions. This, clearly, is an important indicator of exit strategies, where interviewees can explain their choices, and possibly their exit or non exit options (taking into account local, national and international factors), which might depend on the quality of the national educational system, and the quality of local schools in particular neighbourhoods. Finally, in the fifth section of the questionnaire, we had a series of questions, mainly derived from European surveys, on the representation of society, Europe, globalization, political values and attitudes.

One final methodological point deserves attention. Focusing on networks data impacts the question of interview selection. As we have noted above, all the respondents had to fit some common criteria, and some were deliberately clustered in particular neighbourhoods. However, an important element in the selection was to avoid any snowball effect – selecting respondents who are personally connected with one another – even while not aiming for a representative sample. The emphasis on networks demands that we avoid inevitably interviewing people who know each other and who have similar social practices, friends or values. Different sources were thus used to find respondents, according to the local context examined: we drew upon alumni associations, lists of former students from universities or *grandes écoles*, public lists of engineers, and local occupational associations of managers, as well as basic door-to-door sampling techniques, or visiting schools where respondents might have children.

Mobile but rooted: the upper-middle classes as part of a virtual global society

From our first results, it emerges that most of the upper-middle class subjects we interviewed are in fact very well rooted in their local context. They can neither be considered as 'disembedded' nor 'in retreat' from their urban and national environments. In this chapter we will only discuss three main points concerning the possible partial exit of upper-middle classes from local and national society, as it is not our principal focus (for a fuller discussion of these results, see Andreotti and Le Galès 2008).

Firstly, our interviewees have dense and regular interactions with both families and friends (but not with neighbours) within the cities and sometimes within the neighbourhoods. In contrast to the results of Savage and colleagues in Manchester, our respondents see their friends and families in the city on a regular basis at home or when they go out. They have a dense social life rooted in the city. Secondly, the difference between the groups living in the city centre and those living in the suburbs is not particularly significant. Beyond what we see as exceptions in our survey (one suburban neighbourhood in Madrid, one in Milan), the differences are minimal. These results provide little support for the notion of 'gated communities' or exit from the city, but those relations remains by contrast very homogeneous from a social point of view. Our upper-middle classes are quite part of the urban fabric and they do not seem to exit or to play the secession strategy, but they keep other social groups at a distance in their networks. Thirdly, our interviewees use public and private services (transport, schools, health, social services, libraries and sport facilities) in the city. With some exceptions, there is no pattern of retreat, or abandonment of the public sector. One piece of evidence is the common finding that those services should be much better and should serve their needs better ('voice' rather than 'exit' in our language). In that sense too (and with nuances) our upper-middle classes are not retreating from the city. Most of them are happy to accept some level of interactions with other social groups, but on their terms, when they choose it, when they control the game and if there is a possibility of avoiding the constraints and making some alternative choice when they can (as, for example, with schools).

Given the focus in this volume on questions of Europeanization and globalization, we are rather more concerned with looking at the networks, practices, and values that our respondents might be developing *beyond* the nation-state, and the ways these strategies might be providing what we have called partial exit strategies.

Transnational networks

Most of the upper-class respondents have important transnational connections, though this varies quite a lot in the three cities. In Milan, our interviewees do not mention many international connections; some of them (10 per cent) could not even come up with the name of a friend living in a foreign country. Among those who stated having friends abroad, contacts were not based on a regular interaction, and visits were said to be quite rare – sometimes every three years or even less. However, respondents thought they could, if they wanted, easily mobilize these 'silent' relations, thus somehow abstracting their relationship from time. Similarly, in Madrid or Lyon, belonging to international networks was also relatively limited. Only a small number of managers and engineers (one in four) we interviewed were able to name three friends living abroad.

Foreign friends were usually met at university, or within the firm or organization they work for. The degree of openness to the international arena of these managers and engineers suggests a relatively closed group with few international contacts, except in the case of Paris. Indeed, by contrast, most Parisians mention two or three foreign friends with whom they have regular exchanges, and, in terms of contacts, people living abroad who are completely part of their daily social life. In the Paris case, this element is quite striking. Most interviewees have no difficulty in naming two or three 'good friends' and point to other people with whom they interact on a regular basis. Regular exchange and visits to foreign friends (at least once a year) or to friends living elsewhere is an important part of the Parisian upper-middle class's lifestyle and networks.

It is quite interesting to note – in relation to the discourses on globalization and transnational networks – that the friends mentioned as living abroad tend to be mostly settled in the Western world, and mainly in Western Europe. This regional focus supports this volume's accent on the sociological dimension of European integration. Cities such as London and Paris consistently appear among the first places cited by many Milanese as very close to their lives, although some other cities, such as Barcelona, Madrid or New York, are also mentioned in interviews. In the case of Madrid, the most cited urban areas where friends live were New York, London and Buenos Aires, but Paris and Brussels also appeared in the list. In the Parisian case, the cities mentioned by our respondents are much more widely dispersed, and many Parisians said that they were familiar with many European cities that they visit for weekend trips: first and foremost Italian cities, but also Brussels, Prague, London, and Barcelona. They also named American cities and cities in Asia, South America or more commonly North Africa.

Geographical mobility

In order to analyze the degree of geographical mobility of our managers and engineers, we focused our attention on two aspects: first, experience abroad, the availability to move abroad and their practices related to mobility, and second, their declared knowledge of foreign languages and foreign cities. Both aspects give an idea of the relative internationalization of this group. Knowledge of foreign cities can be an indirect indicator of geographical mobility: the more the respondents know foreign cities, the more they travel.

A significant number of the respondents in the four cities had had professional experience abroad for longer than six months (between 40 and 60 per cent). The city of Paris presents the highest percentage of respondents with this kind of foreign experience. This finding certainly helps to confirm Paris (and its residents) as a more globalized city, with more opportunities to offer to (or sometimes impose on) their employees. Madrid and Milan appear second in the ranking, while the respondents in the city of Lyon appear to lag behind. In part, whether respondents have had experience abroad also seems connected to the size and importance of the company they are working for: the larger the company, the higher the chance of having had this experience. The few women we have in our survey show a lower percentage of experience abroad compared to men. Once again, the city of Paris presents the highest percentage (45.5 per cent), and Madrid the lowest (21.7 per cent).

The second question put to our managers and engineers gives us an idea of their availability to move abroad. Three groups can be distinguished from the analysis which seem to be transversal to the four cities:

- Those who are not available to have this type of experience. The reasons given to explain such decisions are diverse: from the family and the language gap to the fact that they have already reached high positions in the companies they work for and do not need experience abroad. In the latter cases the international reference is used to access more power within the national context, and is not an exit or partial exit strategy.
- Those who are potentially available to move subject to two conditions: that it is a limited period abroad and a desirable country, which usually means West European countries, the United States and, in a few rare cases, China. Africa, South America, Australia and the Middle East are hardly ever mentioned;
- Those who are available to move without any conditions. This kind of respondent is a rarity in all cities.

These group profiles are not explained by the organizational positions and life history of the respondents. There are managers with high levels of responsibility who are not likely to move, and young interviewees not willing to move, particularly in the case of Milan. Yet there are older respondents available for experience abroad. Much depends on the kind of work they do: engineers building infrastructures or working in the energy field, for instance, are more likely to have spent a period abroad and to be available to move, whatever their age. It is quite interesting to note that the ones who have already had experience abroad are more ready to accept another move. Some of the narratives of these people underline the importance of this kind of experience, even though they also point out the difficulties of adapting to new countries and habits, above all when the whole family is involved in the experience. In some cases the interviewees point to this experience having caused a marital break-down. By contrast, those who have not had this kind of experience are less inclined to do it. When we cross the two variables identified – experience abroad and availability to move – two polarized groups emerge: the *immobile*, who have not had any experience abroad and do not intend to, and the *nomads* who have had this experience and are still available to do it again.

To identify interviewees who travel a lot but stay in their native country, we included questions about the frequency of trips abroad for professional and non-professional reasons, as well as the frequency of flying. The sample split into three groups: first, managers and engineers who have not travelled abroad for professional reasons in the last year (50 per cent), second, 25 per cent who have travelled more than four times, and third, another 25 per cent who have travelled between one and three times. Whatever they say, most of the upper-middle class subjects we interviewed in our four cities do not travel much, if at all, for their work. Interestingly, the Milanese in our sample are both more rooted in their city in terms of social and familial networks and more internationally mobile in travel terms for their job (see also Andreotti and Le Galès 2008).

These results are confirmed by the frequency of travel for holidays and leisure. Less than one-third of our interviewees in all four cities has not travelled abroad on holiday in the year before the survey, and almost another third have made more than three trips. In this case no difference between men and women seems to emerge. Those respondents who travelled a lot for professional reasons are also the ones who travel most for non-professional reasons.

Another key indicator that identifies participation in a European and/or global society is the question of language. Our first results suggest that most respondents know at least one foreign language: English. The sample then confirms the existence of two main groups of respondents: those who speak only one foreign language (the minimum required) and those who speak at least two languages (the younger generation). The second foreign language is rather variable, but mainly a European one: French for the Italians and Spanish, German in all four cities, Spanish for the Italians and French, in some cases Russian or Portuguese, in one or two cases Chinese.

Practices

To establish the degree of linkage of our managers and engineers to their national and local environments, and to gain an indication of the internationalization of these groups, we introduced some questions on the use and access of media content in general, and foreign sources of information in particular. We asked three questions: Which newspapers do you read? How often? And which TV channel do you watch (including foreign ones)? Overall, the exposure of these groups to national media is high, indicating in principle a strong interest in national public affairs. In Madrid and Milan, practically all of our interviewees declared they read the national press several times a week, and very often on a daily basis. But what of international viewpoints? While around 12 per cent of the Madrilenian engineers and managers from our sample said they read international newspapers with some regularity, the percentage goes down to virtually zero in the case of Lyon, with only 5 per cent in Milan and 8.5 per cent in Paris. Regarding international TV channels, evidence was somewhat different, with nearly half our Milanese informants saying they watched a foreign channel, and around 30 per cent of Parisian and Madrilenian interviewees saying the same. The case of Lyon appears again as the least exposed to international media content, probably indicating a lower level of involvement of *cadres supérieurs* from this city in world affairs, indeed in the process of internationalization altogether.

Feeling of belonging to Europe

One of the main aspects of the position of managers and engineers in the global sphere is their own self-perception in relation to the different levels in which political and territorial identities are aggregated. In order to account for this element of self-identification, we introduced two specific questions in our questionnaires which asked about perceptions of belonging to different political scales. From the first of these questions, which asked informants to locate their own feelings of belonging along a continuum with the European Union on the one end, and their own nation-state on the other, we aimed at getting a first indication of the perception they have about their own position in the world.

The results showed that Madrilenian managers and engineers had the strongest feeling of national identity when compared with their identification with Europe (with nearly 45 per cent considering themselves only Spanish, or more Spanish than European); French informants were somewhere in the middle (around 39 per cent in both Paris and Lyon selecting these same options). Our Milanese interviewees showed the lowest level of national identification (36.5 per cent considering themselves only Italian, or more Italian than European), a result in line with Eurobarometer figures for Italians.

Those who said they were equally European and members of their own nation-state oscillated between 38 and 46 per cent across the cases, with those declaring themselves to be more European than national varying between the more European Milanese (16 per cent), and the more Eurosceptic Madrilenians – where one of our interviewees admitted to feeling more European than Spanish. However, in Madrid, a record 13.4 per cent of respondents declared a different self-identification to those proposed in the questionnaire, often along the lines of 'citizen of the world'.

These figures tend to confirm the generally received wisdom about the positive relationship of Italians with Europe, but contradict the general conclusions of many surveys conducted among EU citizens in Spain, in which Spaniards tend to identify themselves strongly with Europe and European institutions. Spanish interviewees have indeed a more reluctant attitude towards Europe than the general population of Spain. In general terms, across the four urban settings, women informants also tended to show a higher adherence to national identities that to European levels of identification.

Conclusion

Our results provide some material to respond to the questions we have posed. Firstly, most of the engineers and managers we interviewed do feel part of a virtual global society, but the organization of their life is strongly territorialized within the neighbourhoods of the European cities we studied. Half of them have had some experience of mobility, most travel – although not that much – and they have extensive networks of friends and families close to home. Those who have some long-term experience of living in a foreign country are happy with the experience – yet happy to come back to where they were afterwards. Those who are ready to move tend to favour a limited international posting before coming back, and there are still a good many managers and engineers with no mobility experience at all.

Our results suggest that the idea of partial exit makes some sense. A good many of our respondents spend some time and resources in foreign countries, they keep friends there, and have strong views on the making of a virtual global society – although this applies more to their children than it does to themselves. By contrast, they remain profoundly rooted in their country and their city while feeling strongly European. These results confirm the analysis that Europe still comprises of profoundly territorialized societies.

The internationalization of the groups we studied has a distinctive western-centric bias, mostly European but also directed towards the US. The frequency of interactions within specifically European networks of friends, or mobility between European cities, is rather strong. As is well known, those groups see themselves through strongly European spectacles. However, from the point of view of languages, education and media, their belonging to a European society is limited.

Finally, our analysis, unsurprisingly, shows strong differences between groups in different cities and different countries. National social structures, of course, still matter. But there is a blurring effect of Europe. For example, the engineers and managers we interviewed in Paris display a distinctively more international pattern which is likely to spread to other European cities. Across the cases, elements of a European upper-middle class in the making are appearing, in particular among the younger generation, and especially in the strategies developed regarding their children. Down the road, it may be this aspect of the new strategies of mobility used by upper-middle classes in European cities that will have the deepest impact.

CHAPTER 5

Markets and Firms

Neil Fligstein

> **Key concepts:** economic sociology, markets, firms, trade, efficiency, integrated market economy, Europeanization versus globalization, telecommunications
>
> **Key references:** Polanyi, Granovetter, White, Mattli, Ohmae, Katzenstein, Hall and Soskice, Garrett

Most studies of European integration focus narrowly on political and legal processes in Brussels. This has caused scholars in EU studies to miss how profoundly the European economy has been re-organized by the successive use of European laws and regulations. In this chapter, economic sociology is used to help broaden our understanding of the processes of European integration. I illustrate the degree to which the EU's Single Market and other market opening projects have profoundly affected the European economy by creating new Europe-wide markets and increased trade. The consequence of this re-organization has established a European model of market construction.

The creation of the Single Market across Western Europe lies at the core of European Union. The EU provides a common set of rules that make it difficult for governments to raise barriers to entry to foreign firms, and markets for almost every good or service are now open. Trade today accounts for about 40 per cent of GDP across Europe, and over 70 per cent of the exports from the countries that make up the EU are to other countries in the EU (see Table 5.1, p. 107). Moreover as the EU has expanded, the largest European corporations have made most of their investments in the past twenty years in Europe. These investments have been made by engaging in mostly friendly mergers or joint ventures with companies in other European countries. This means that in many of the largest product markets across Europe, firms with different national identities compete with each other in product markets that instead of being national in orientation are now regional in scope. The interlocking of the economies of Western Europe has become far advanced in two ways. First, there exist common rules and laws to govern most forms of economic exchange which makes it possible for labour and capital to move freely about Europe. Second, firms have taken advantage of these common rules to expand their activities across national borders, thereby making economic integration not just a political project but an economic reality.

In this chapter, I offer an introduction to the characteristic themes and methods of economic sociology. I do this in order to develop a conceptual framework based in the literature that can allow readers to make sense of why the European economy looks the way it does. I then go on to explore what such a theory would suggest in terms of available data which illustrates how the European economy has been 'Europeanized' along these lines. This means that the European market integration project is more accurately viewed as an instance of regionalization, not globalization (Mattli 1999; Katzenstein 2005). I show how large firms have responded strategically to this market integration. I then introduce a case study – the re-organization of the telecommunications industry in Europe – to illustrate how the market project has worked in one sector. Finally, I offer some remarks on whether the market-building process of the EU can be viewed as a good or bad thing for its citizens.

The usual way to understand the changes in the European economy is to view them through the lens of globalization. I argue that this perspective fundamentally misunderstands what is going on in Europe. There has been much convergence across Europe in terms of markets emerging with participants from many societies and firms organizing production in similar ways. But this is not the result of the diffuse process of the global integration of trade. Instead, it is the outcome of the political project of the governments in Europe to create a single market and the use of a single currency. This has created new economic opportunities and European corporations have been quick to expand their operations across Europe. In turn, this has created more competition between European corporations. When Europeans think they experience the threat of globalization, what they are really experiencing is the integration of the European market and the entry into their home markets by other European firms. This stark proposition only makes sense if one understands both theoretically why European economic integration required government action and empirically how this has worked out on the ground.

Economic sociology and the study of integrated market economies

In order to understand what has happened in Europe to create an integrated economy, it is necessary to have some theory about how such economies are constructed. I rely in this chapter on the characteristic tools and conceptions of economic sociology for an explanation of how markets are socially constructed and how governments play a fundamental role in this process. To take one classic definition, that of Karl Polanyi (1957), economic sociology is centrally concerned with all aspects of material production in society, including the organization of both production and consumption. Households, labour markets, firms and product markets are thus all legitimate objects of study for sociologists. The central insight of economic sociology is that all of the processes of material life can be better understood as fundamentally social processes (Granovetter 1985). This means that they are amenable to analysis by the standard tools of sociology such as organizational theory, institutional analysis, political sociology, the sociology of law, and cultural theory.

Economic sociology breaks decisively with the asociological assumptions of neo-classical economics. Neo-classical economics views market processes as fundamentally about supply and demand and the formation of prices. They argue that all market participants are price takers and that market interactions take place between anonymous market actors. For neo-classical economics, governments are mainly viewed as bad for market processes because they come to favour organized political interests, intervening in markets in ways that are seen to undermine efficient market processes. Economic sociology, on the other hand, begins with the view that all forms of market activity are embedded in society and indeed are best understood as social in their character. Modern markets thus cannot exist without governments. Markets are based on institutions, law, rules, and the social interactions that structure the relationships between market participants.

One of the core questions in economic sociology is thus to offer an embedded sociological account of how markets emerge and function. A sociological view of markets argues that markets are social fields that exist for the production and sale of some goods or services. They are characterized by repeated exchanges between buyers and sellers. This idea implies that market exchange relies on rules and social structures to guide and organize exchange. A given market thus becomes a stable field when the producers are able to produce a status hierarchy of firms, whereby some of the largest firms dominate the market and smaller firms find niches in those markets (Fligstein 2001a, ch. 1; Podolny 2005). Once such a structure has emerged, a market can be described as 'self reproducing role structure' where incumbent and challenger firms reproduce their positions on a period to period basis by signalling their activities to one another and reacting in turn (White 1981).

Governments are implicated in the building of market institutions by virtue of their claim to sovereignty in a given territory (Fligstein 2001a, ch. 1). Bureaucracies, courts, police forces and armies are the organizations that represent the ability of a particular state to act. Governments create market rules to govern property rights (who owns what), competitive relationships between firms (what is called competition policy), and the exchange of goods and services. Some governments also own firms and direct investment. Thus, from the point of view of economic sociology, the existence of market rules, the rule of law, and many forms of government intervention in markets promote stable environments for private investment, the growth of jobs and firms, and economic growth.

Economic sociologists do not always think that everything that governments do in markets aids efficiency. They are quite aware that governments often engage in *rent-seeking* behaviour – that is, when they seek to gain benefits from manipulating the economic environment in ways that do not lead to growth – and hence that regulatory apparatuses can be captured by organized political interests. But economic sociologists believe that it is an empirical and historical question as to the degree that the actions of firms, governments and other organized actors in society work to expand economic opportunities or instead, to constrain them. So, for example, in some countries firms have lobbied governments to allow them to control price and production through the legal use of cartels, an agreement among firms to control prices and production, so as to curb open competition. While such cartels stabilize firms and employment to some degree in the short run, they also undermine firm competitiveness in the long run. Empirically, though, this need not necessarily be the case.

A large body of empirical work generated by economic sociology has thus been oriented towards demonstrating that real markets do not work in the way that neo-classical theory suggests. Economic sociologists have demonstrated the importance of government to the behaviour of market actors (for example, see Dobbin and Dowd 2000). They have also demonstrated that the social structuring of particular markets affects supply, demand and pricing (for examples, see Uzzi and Lancaster 2004; Baker *et al.* 1998). These studies use a variety of quantitative, archival, interview and ethnographic methods to demonstrate how real markets are actually constructed.

To begin to make sense of how to think about the EU, it is useful to consider how economic sociologists think about what constitutes an *integrated* market economy. They argue that an integrated market economy will contain firms who can freely trade and invest with each other under a single system of rules. This system typically defines property rights, sanctions legal and illegal forms of competition, and produces rules to govern economic transactions between buyers and sellers. Some scholars might add that a fully integrated market economy also requires a single currency and a single regulatory structure. Most of the historical cases of integrated market economies merged in a single defined geographic territory in reference to a single state – one classic example being the United States of America.

The EU, however, provides an example of an integrated market economy *beyond* the nation-state, which makes it a key new case in the economic sociology of markets. The problem of creating an integrated market economy in Europe is a task that on the surface seems unlikely. Europe before the Treaty of Rome in 1957 – the treaty which founded the European Economic Community, the forerunner to the European Union – was characterized by a group of nation-states, each of whom had their own market rules, their own currencies, and their own legal and political traditions. Moreover, following World War II, Europe was economically decimated. Governments were mostly concerned about protecting their own citizens, jobs, and national firms. European governments had long-standing relationships with their nationally organized economic elites who owned large parts of the economy. In many places in Europe, the government had taken over firms as nationalized industries and managed them as 'national champions'. In the European social democracies, this commitment extended to workers as well. This predisposed governments to not undertake any actions that undermined either jobs or the privileges of national firms. Governments also worked hard to keep regulatory capacity under their control in order to maintain their legitimacy – not to mention the jobs of people who worked for them. In essence each of the European nation-states could be viewed as containing its own national integrated economy.

Given this lack of economic integration across countries, it is remarkable that the EU governments peacefully agreed to create and complete a single market across Europe, in a long process that eventually led to a single currency for much of Europe. To accomplish the creation of the Single Market, the interests of governments, firms, workers, and consumers had to be balanced off. If it had looked as if too many people were going to be potentially hurt by the creation of market rules that would open markets to competitors from other countries, then those rules would never have gained approval by the representatives of the member states in the Council of Ministers. While it was often possible for governments to make trade-offs, it is fair to assume – as would any mainstream political scientist – that they still had to come out of whatever negotiation they entered believing that they were better off with the rules created than they were before.

In 1986, the EU set out to 'complete the Single Market' by removing a whole variety of non-tariff trade barriers (Sandholtz and Zysman 1989; Rodriguez-Pose 2004). The Single Market Program (hereafter SMP) was mainly focused on making it easier for firms who were already exporting to engage in trade across Europe (Fligstein and Mara-Drita 1996). It opened markets in industries that could be logically connected to the completion of the single market: transport, financial services, and professional and business services. There was an effort to create a general European system of property rights, mostly pushed by the British. But, the French and German governments opposed that effort. This preserved the national domination of corporations and made it difficult to engage in hostile takeovers in all of Europe except the UK.

Since 1993, there have been significant changes in many other market institutions. The member state governments have created a common competition policy that has regulated Europe-wide mergers. They have put into place massive state and regional aid to regions that have lagged behind economically. These have particularly helped the newer members of the EU like Ireland, Spain and Portugal. They have collectively invested in upgrading transport infrastructure. They have also produced new market openings in a number of other industries including telecommunications, utilities, airlines and postal services. The logic of market opening in these industries has followed a similar pattern. Essentially, governments have agreed to at least partially privatize their state-owned firms and to stop subsidizing them with state aid. They have also agreed to allow firms from other countries to compete with their national champions. In practice, these market opening projects have worked in a complex way on the ground. The largest corporations have spread out their activities by entering new markets. But they frequently partner local firms either by setting up a joint venture or buying out smaller companies in friendly mergers.

From the perspective of economic sociology, what has happened is that as the governments have cooperated to create new rules regarding trade, labour mobility and investment, they have experienced mostly positive economic benefits. It is these positive benefits that have pushed the governments to make them more likely to engage in further forms of economic cooperation, forms that would have been unthinkable even 20 years earlier. So if, for example, in 1980 an observer had suggested that a single European currency would exist by 2000, no one would have believed it. These new forms of cooperation were sometimes in the form of new market opening projects. But they also worked to create rules to protect consumers and investors by enforcing common health and safety standards and create a common regulatory capacity to govern industries like banking and finance. While this process has had starts and stops, it has consistently ratcheted up increased cooperation in Europe across more market sectors in the past 50 years.

This set of assertions might be startling to readers who are accustomed to understanding increasing market integration in Europe as essentially being driven by globalization: in other words, the general increase in market integration around the world driven by economic free trade. The economic sociology perspective developed here suggests rather that the degree and type of market integration that has occurred across Europe is not only deeper and more organized than it would be if driven by global forms, but generally in fact driven by government actions. Indeed, one of the basic insights from economic sociology is that market integration *cannot* occur without government(s) working to produce that integration. From the point of view of scholars, it is an empirical question as to whether or not this integration has been in response to global forces or government policies designed to integrate specifically European markets. In order to decide whether or not the development of the European economy is mainly being driven by the EU governments or is more just responding to broader global economic forces, it is useful to start considering data that might allow us to understand how things are playing out on the ground in a more systematic way.

I consider a variety of data to support the view that the changing market opportunities brought about by the SMP and the increased cooperation between governments has subsequently created a larger and more economically integrated Europe-wide market. So, for example, if Europe is becoming more of a regional economy, one would expect that trade patterns between European countries and the rest of the world would diverge. I present trade data to illustrate how in the wake of the Single Market, trade specifically within the EU has increased more even as world trade has exploded. I show in the case of the new Eastern European member states that joining the EU also generally works to increase trade for new member states. But even more importantly, it works to also increase their trade integration with the rest of Europe.

Next, I shift to the level of sales and investments by European and non-European multinational corporations. If firms are responding to the opportunities created by the Single Market, they ought to be investing more in Europe than elsewhere. I present data on the activities of the largest European and non-European multinational corporations and demonstrate that since 1987, they have taken advantage of the SMP by investing more in Europe.

Finally, I move from the aggregate level of analysis to a particular case study. The problem of using such aggregate data is that while the data is consistent with the idea that the EU is driving European economic integration, it does not directly show how governments are pushing along the integration process in particular markets. To demonstrate the role of governments more directly into markets, I detail in narrative form how the European governments agreed to transform their telecommunication industries by privatizing national phone companies and allowing foreign firms to engage in competing across national borders in new product markets. This case study shows how the direct intervention of governments created a single market for telecommunications services and equipment in Europe.

Globalization or Europeanization?

To demonstrate the degree to which Europe is a single trade zone, we need to consider relevant data. Table 5.1 shows the ultimate destination of world trade in 1993 and 2005. One can clearly see that exports are divided into three regions: Asia (including Japan), Western Europe, and North America. These regions are often described as the 'triad' (Ohmae 1985). The region that appears the most integrated in trade is Western Europe with 68.9 per cent of trade beginning and ending in Europe in 1993, rising to 73.2 per cent in 2003. 46.5 per cent of Asia's exports end up in Asia in 1993, increasing to 47.2 per cent in 2005. 35.6 per cent of North America's exports end up in North America in 1993, increasing to 55.8 per cent in 2003. Both the EU's Single Market Programme and subsequent market opening projects and the North American Free Trade Area (NAFTA) appear to have worked to increase the concentration of trade in the regions. This supports the view that the world economy is not generally becoming more integrated, but instead, that it is increasingly becoming more regional. In the case of Europe, the policy interventions of the governments through their EU membership mean that the European economy was already more integrated in 1993 and has become increasingly so since then.

Table 5.1 Regional structure of world merchandise trade in exports, 1993 and 2005

	Regional destination							
	North America		Western Europe		Asia		Rest of the world	
Regional origin	1993	2005	1993	2005	1993	2005	1993	2005
North America	35.6	55.8	20.2	16.1	25.0	18.3	19.2	9.8
Western Europe	8.0	9.1	68.9	73.2	8.8	7.6	14.3	10.1
Asia (incl. Japan)	26.4	22.9	17.0	18.9	46.5	47.2	14.2	13.0

Note: Rows sum to 100 within years.
Source: World Trade Organization Annual Report 1996, Table II.1; 2006, Table II.1. Reproduced with kind permission of the publisher.

Table 5.2 Percentage of total manufacturing trade of selected EU countries with others in the European Union

	1970	1980	1990	1997
Austria	53	65	79	78
Belgium	77	86	83	89
Finland	21	35	41	51
France	82	84	86	90
Germany	70	75	79	81
Ireland	27	61	54	42
Italy	70	61	67	70
Netherlands	68	69	77	77
Portugal	28	41	53	64
Spain	43	69	75	81
UK	–	40	56	55

Source: OECD (1998), *OECD Economic Outlook*, Volume 1998 Issue 2, p. 154, www.oecd.org/oecdEconomicOutlook. Reproduced with kind permission of the publisher.

Table 5.2 presents data on the share of manufacturing exports from various EU countries that end up in other EU countries. Between 1970 and 1997, almost every country increased the share of its manufacturing exports ending up in Europe. This is remarkable evidence that European manufacturers really saw Europe as their main market, not the expanding global sphere. The era where these numbers appear to have increased the most was from 1980 until 1990. This was the period when the SMP was announced and implemented. This is evidence that European manufacturers were aided by the changes in EU rules in this period and responded to more trade opportunities by concentrating their sales on Europe.

The countries with the fewest European manufacturing exports include Ireland, Finland and the UK. Finland is a recent entrant into the EU. It also exports many telecommunications products into international markets. Ireland is a platform for many multinationals that use it both as an entry to the EU and also a manufacturing base for their world activities. The UK is the least Europe-focused of the large economies. There is indeed a general British 'exceptionalism' in regional terms. This reflects both the UK's involvement with former colonies and its special connections with the US market. On the one hand, the UK government has allowed hostile mergers to occur in the country and as such, many of the largest British firms have been bought up by their continental competitors. On the other, British firms are the least European in the sense that they distribute their economic activities more widely around the world, and in particular are big players in the US. Of all the European countries they trade the least with Europe and they are not as extensively invested in Europe (a point also shown in the data about the geography of London's global business links gathered by the Loughborough Globalization and World Cities project [GAWC]; see Taylor and Hoyler 2000).

A very different picture emerges for many continental member states, however. The countries with over 80 per cent of their manufacturing exports going to the EU include France, Germany, Belgium, and Spain, while for Austria, Italy, and the Netherlands the figure rises to over 70 per cent. France and Germany have been the traditional leaders of the EU, both because of the relative size of their economies, but also because of their relative economic interdependence. These statistics show in an interesting way why some of the politics of the EU appear to ally France and Germany against the UK. The British depend the least on the EU for their trade, while France and Germany are amongst the largest traders. It is not thus surprising that their governments have been the engine of pushing forward the European integration project, while the British remain more sceptical.

Table 5.2 gives us an opportunity to see how the decision by a country to join the EU affects the orientation of its manufacturing exporters. Ireland joined the EU in 1973. In 1970, only 27 per cent of its manufacturing exports ended up in the EU; by 1980 this figure had increased to 61 per cent. Spain and Portugal joined in 1985 and their exports to the EU jumped during the decade. Finland joined in 1994, and during the 1990s its share of manufacturing exports within the EU climbed sharply.

The story so far concerns the market integration of national economies in Western Europe. But it is also important to explore how joining the EU has affected the Eastern European countries that have recently joined. If joining the EU and accepting European rules, laws and market opening matter, we should observe dramatic changes in the trade patterns of these societies over time. Interestingly, this process begins with the entry negotiations rather than the formal accession that was completed in the EU enlargements of 2004 and 2007. Table 5.3 shows how Eastern European trade changed. The top line of the table shows that overall levels of trade slowly increased during the 1990s and began to accelerate from 1999 onwards as the Eastern European countries prepared to enter the EU. The second line of the table shows that the share of world trade in the region was 3.5 per cent in 1994 and this grew slowly until 1999. Then Eastern Europe increased its share of world trade from 4 to 5.5 per cent, an increase of over one-third.

The most interesting question is the destination of the trade from Eastern Europe. Beginning in 1994, as the Eastern European countries began to apply for EU membership, the share of their trade that went to the EU began at 33.7 per cent and climbed steadily to 47.2 per cent in 1999 and finally 56.8 per cent

Table 5.3 Merchandise trade exports for Eastern Europe (without Russia), 1994–2003

	1994	1995	1996	1997	1998	1999	2000	2001	2002	2003
Total trade (billions of $)	150.1	175.8	173.4	176.7	168.9	169.7	187.6	275.3	302.1	400.1
% of world trade	3.5	3.8	3.9	4	3.8	4	4.3	4.6	4.9	5.5
% of trade within EU	33.7	36.4	38.9	41.2	46.5	47.2	52.6	54.6	56.6	56.8
% of trade with other Eastern European countries	37.4	32.3	30.2	28.4	27.7	28.9	29.2	29.5	26.5	26.5
% Total trade within EU	71.1	68.7	69.1	71.6	75.2	76.1	81.8	84.1	83.1	83.3

Source: WTO, Table III.3, III37, 2004. Website: www.wto.org. Reproduced with kind permission of the publisher.

in 2003. This shows that Eastern European countries began to actively re-direct their trade to the EU. The next line of the table shows how Eastern European trade with the rest of Eastern Europe declined over the period. In 1994, 37.4 per cent of Eastern European trade ended up in Eastern Europe. In 2003, this had dropped to 26.5 per cent. The last line of the table adds up the previous two lines. It shows that over the period, Eastern European trade was 71.1 per cent with the EU and rose to 83.3 per cent in 2003, even as intra-Eastern European trade dropped by a third. The Eastern European economies, which began the 1990s in disarray and were mainly focused on exporting to each other, have now been firmly integrated into the EU trading zone.

Let us now summarize the results of this section. The EU is the most integrated trade block in the world with over 73.2 per cent of EU trade beginning and ending in the EU. The SMP and subsequent market opening projects had the effect of intensifying intra-EU trade, even during an era of rapid economic globalization. Data on the manufacturing sector shows that intra-EU trade in manufactures is high and increasing generally over time. Joining the EU had a big effect on the direction of a country's exports. Every country that joined the EU saw its share of manufacturing exports to the EU increase. Finally, the accession of the ten Eastern European countries to the EU resulted in the revival of the exporting sectors of their economies. Their exports grew dramatically, particularly after 1999. The main shift in trade was from the other Eastern European countries to the EU. These results are powerful evidence that the actions of the EU governments to cooperate to create an integrated European economy have succeeded. In essence, we do not observe a diffuse pattern with increasing integration of the world economy. Instead, we observe a creation of a regionalized Europe-wide economy, led by the creation of a common set of rules governing markets across Europe.

A second question we can answer with available economic data is how large multinational corporations have responded to this market integration project. To get a handle on how large corporations handle their investments, I sought out data from a study of the world's largest multinational corporations in 1987 and 1997 (Stafford and Purkis 1989, 1999). This dataset is unique in that it contains information on the world's largest 450 multinational corporations. It attempts to disaggregate where firms have their main investments and assesses their major markets. The data allow a comparison of how multinationals changed their activities over time. One of the good things about the dataset is that it captures some of the reaction of both European and non-European multinationals to the SMP.

The SMP was announced in 1986, but it was not supposed to come into full effect until 1992. Multinational firms began planning their reaction to the SMP as soon as it was announced, but their redeployment of assets, sales and jobs probably took place over a long period. Thus the 1987 data probably contains the beginnings of the reaction to the opportunities presented by the SMP, while the 1997 data should certainly capture the change in firms' deployment of their resources. The data also allows us to compare the activities of Europe-based multinationals to other firms of similar size and with similar aspirations. One can see the degree to which European firms are like or unlike the multinational firms of other societies.

Table 5.4 presents data on investment of the world's largest multinationals. First, note how EU firms changed their distribution of activities between 1987 and 1997. In 1987, EU-based multinationals had about 64 per cent of their assets in their home country. This decreased to about 57 per cent by 1997. This was a statistically significant reduction in assets. There was an increase in the percentage of assets in Europe but not in the home country from 17 to 25 per cent over the period. There were similar statistically significant decreases in employment in the home country. In 1987, 53 per cent of employees of European multinationals were in the home country and this dropped to 47 per cent. At the same time, the percentage of employees in other European countries increased from 25 to 32 per cent. The shift in assets and employment was mirrored in sales figures. One can conclude that what changed in the decade was that European multinationals spread out their assets, employment and sales across Europe and thereby decreased their dependency on the home country while increasing their presence across Europe. In essence, they redeployed their economic activities to take advantage of the integration of the Single Market.

It is interesting to compare European multinationals with the other large multinationals in the world. In 1987, non-EU multinationals had 71 per cent of their sales in their home country and this decreased to 64 per cent by 1997, a significant reduction. They also decreased their dependence on home assets

Table 5.4 Comparison of the world's largest multinationals, 1987 and 1997

	EU firms			Non-EU firms		
	1987	1997	significance level	1987	1997	significance level
% of assets in home country	0.64 (28)	0.57 (42)	0.05	0.71 (160)	0.64 (176)	0.000
% of assets in Europe, not home country	0.17 (28)	0.25 (42)	0.05	0.2 (91)	0.24 (102)	0.01
% of employees in home country	0.53 (43)	0.47 (50)	0.05			
% of employees in Europe, not home country	0.25 (23)	0.32 (31)	0.05			
% of sales in home country	0.42 (87)	0.35 (87)	0.02	0.7 (186)	0.62 (188)	0.000
% of sales in Europe, not home country	0.3 (69)	0.35 (80)	0.04	0.19 (102)	0.24 (109)	0.01
% of assets in Europe, total	0.81	0.82	n.s.	0.2	0.24	0.01
% of employees in Europe, total	0.78	0.79	n.s.			
% of sales in Europe, total	0.72	0.7	n.s.	0.19	0.24	0.01

Note: Number of cases reported in parentheses; significance level refers to the t-test between the means 1987 and 1997; t-value less than 0.05 is statistically significant; n.s. is t-value greater than 0.05.
Source: Author's own compilation, referring to Stafford and Purkis (1989, 1997).

from 70 to 62 per cent. Thus non-EU multinationals became more 'global' from 1987 to 1997. One interesting question is how much of this redeployment in Europe was in response to the SMP. The last two rows of the table show that non-EU multinationals increased their sales in Europe from 19 to 24 per cent and increased their assets from 20 to 24 per cent (both statistically significant). This shows that Europe was a huge focus of non-EU multinationals. Half of their shift in assets (4 per cent of 8 per cent) was towards the EU market during the decade 1987–1997. Even more impressive is that 71 per cent (5 per cent of 7 per cent) of their shift in sales out of their home countries was accounted for by Europe. Non-EU multinationals may have been 'globalizing', but a majority of their globalizing in this period was in fact accounted for by their move into Europe.

Markets and Firms 113

What can be concluded from these results? Large European multinationals responded to the opportunities created by market opening projects by expanding into other European countries. They were not globalizing, but Europeanizing. Multinationals from other parts of the world also perceived the new opportunities in Europe. They expanded across Europe as well. The largest European corporations, as others elsewhere, made most of their investments by engaging in mostly friendly mergers or joint ventures with companies in other countries.

One caveat needs to be added. Despite the clear evidence of Europeanization, most of the largest corporations remain national in their ownership. Only a few of the large mergers have produced truly cross-European ownership of firms. One rare example is EADS, the company that makes Airbus. The largest firms in the European economy remain resolutely British, German, French, Swedish or Italian in ownership and investment. The main reason for this persistence is that European governments have, while enabling trade in other ways, resisted creating a single market for property rights. As a result, it is difficult or impossible to engage in hostile takeovers of continental European firms – except in Britain, an exception again in the European market. So when firms do decide to merge cross-border, it is generally a friendly alliance that leaves national management in place.

A case study: the telecommunications industry

So far, I have presented aggregate evidence of how the whole European economy has changed over time in response to the Single Market Programme. Aggregate data is useful for capturing these broad trends. In the wake of the Single Market Programme and the continued attempts to open markets across Europe, trade has expanded, European firms have invested more across Europe, and sales and employment have increased as a result. This kind of data, though, does not tell us much about the actual role of governments in the reorganization of particular markets. The EU and the member state governments did not just agree to provide new rules to open markets. Frequently, governments were deeply involved with many of their largest firms either because of their national regulation of the market or their ownership of the firm. This meant that as EU rules came into force, governments had to change their relationships to their national firms. This meant not only changing the way they related to those firms, but asking those firms to make different kinds of new investments. It is here that a case study of a particular industry can help us understand the role of governments in integration processes much more clearly.

I have chosen to examine the telecommunications industry. My strategy here is to reference secondary studies as well as use some original data collection to create a narrative that shows how the European telecommunications industry was dramatically reconstructed over a 20 year period through the conscious acts of government officials across the governments of Europe. Historically, the largest telecommunications firms were government-owned bureaucracies. But beginning in the 1980s, the member state governments, with prodding from large supplier firms and the EU, began to liberalize the industry. The EU governments agreed to extensive privatization and deregulation of the telecommunications industry. As the telecommunications industry became revolutionized by new products during the 1980s and 1990s, the governments sold off large shares of their national firms and opened their markets to competition – the first steps toward Europeanization. In 1990, the telecommunications industry in Europe, with the exception of the UK, was owned and controlled by national governments. Almost all of the business was in landlines that were used for telephones. Subsequently, though, the industry exploded in many ways. The sector saw the emergence of new firms, the privatization of existing national champions, as well as innovation brought by new products such as the internet, the use of cable for text and data, the creation of wireless telephones, and then the use of wireless phones for text and data.

But here again, it is possible to see the continued influence of governments. Even today, the German and French governments continue to own large (if minority) shares of their telecoms companies. Other governments have not wanted their national phone companies to fall into the hands of foreigners. It has only been a few of the small national phone companies which have been sold to larger firms. Instead, there has been the development of extensive alliances across countries, whereby firms jointly own ventures, particular for cellphones. As Europeanization has proceeded, most of the smaller national firms have not disappeared, but instead entered into ownership alliances with the larger firms, particularly in the cellphone field. So while the telecommunications sector has been reorganized at the European level, governments still sit closely by to ensure that citizens have access to phones that are provided by a nationally-owned firm.

It is easy now to look back and see that this process seemed obvious. But in the late 1980s, both the governments in the EU and their national phone companies were trying to resist any changes. The telecommunications companies resisted new products and were concerned about losing their national monopolies, while governments worried about the jobs of the large workforces employed by telecommunications companies. Why did governments eventually decide to open these markets up, and in the controlled way they eventually chose? There were four key elements to making these changes: the Single Market initiative being negotiated in Brussels; the general perception amongst EU governments that their high technology industries were in danger of being shut out of world markets by virtue of their being behind in product innovation; the support and lobbying of large technology industries who wanted new and growing markets and found themselves in conflict with the government owned phone companies; and the actions of the European Commission which was able to begin the process of market deregulation in telecommunications and, as this took effect, get governments to agree to privatize their telephone companies (Sandholtz 1993, 1998).

Beginning in the late 1970s, there was a great deal of technological change in the industry (Couhey 1990; Hart 1988; Hills 1986). The microelectronics revolution made possible a new range of telecommunications equipment. As computers became hooked up to the telecommunications network and new forms of transmission media evolved, such as microwave, satellite, or fibre optics, the possibilities grew for new services such as data communications, data processing, database sharing and storage, electronic mail, teleconferencing, and of course, mobile wireless phones.

In Europe, producers and providers of these telecommunications technologies found themselves increasingly at the mercy of national phone companies. Producers of new technology found that national telephone companies used their proprietary technologies to make it difficult to connect to the existing phone system. And even if one could connect, national phone companies made equipment makers conform to national standards. This was made even more difficult for firms trying to work across national borders.

American firms thus leapt ahead during the 1980s in a more open environment. Even where European phone companies tried to incorporate new markets and products, customers still had to face the problems of connectivity across countries. Different standards for sending voice and data across countries made costs high and the process difficult. Governments across Europe began to recognize that if such services were to be created and offered, national telephone companies would need to adjust. During the 1980s, the Thatcher government in the UK began the privatization of what became British Telecom. The government set up the firm in 1981 and sold a majority of the shares in 1984. It still protected the main business of local landline phone service but gradually opened up the other telecommunications markets. Vodaphone and Cable and Wireless pioneered the wireless phone industry in the UK. In 1989, the French government allowed firms other than France Telecom to participate in all markets except for landline telephones, although it still made it somewhat difficult for them to do so. In 1989, Deutsche Telekom was separated from the postal service but maintained its monopoly over landlines (Sandholtz 1993). Italy, the Netherlands, Denmark, and Belgium followed suit to varying degrees.

In 1983, Etienne Davignon, the EC Commissioner, gathered a group of business and government leaders together to form a group called the Senior Officials

Group for Telecommunications (SOGT). The basic rationale was that Europe was falling behind high technology industries in the US and Japan. The group agreed to a set of proposals that eventually became the official programme of the EU. These proposals called for an open EU telecommunications market where there would be common standards for connectivity and the opening of public procurement (European Commission 1983). They also agreed to introduce new networks and services and collaborate in producing new technologies.

In 1987, the Commission published a Green Paper outlining its ideas for creating a standards-setting organization to ensure compatibility across Europe (European Commission 1987). Several directives were passed to encourage more cooperation between the telephone companies and equipment producers to set new standards for products across Europe. The 1987 Green Paper also called for market liberalization. The European Commission called for an end to public procurement policies that favoured national champions and an end to phone company monopoly over services.

In order to push this along, the European Commission took unusual action. They invoked Article 90 of the Treaty of Rome to end the telephone company monopolies. They were able to put into effect directives that immediately opened up the modem, telex terminal, PABX, fax machine, mobile phone and satellite markets to any firm. The French government tried to have the authority of the European Commission overturned and took them to the European Court of Justice. In 1991, the Court sided with the Commission. The governments agreed in 1991 to a directive that opened up all markets except for local land-based telephone markets. As part of the Single Market Programme, the Commission was able to push through a directive that opened up equipment sales to competitive bidding in 1992.

The first wave of reform was partially welcomed and partially met with resistance. The British government felt that their firms would do well in an open market and did not oppose the liberalization that the Commission was pushing. The German government generally sided with the British as their large telecommunications producers stood to gain in a deregulated market. They were concerned to preserve the national monopoly over line-based phone lines but were willing to open other markets. The French, Spanish and Italian governments resisted liberalization the most, trying to preserve as much of the privilege of their local phone companies as possible.

By the 1990s, many of the technological breakthroughs began to create huge new market opportunities. It was ultimately the realization that these new markets were too big to ignore that brought the governments round to the position that the telecommunications market across Europe needed to be more integrated. The governments realized that continued support of their national telecommunications companies was a rearguard effort defending the past.

During the mid-1990s, they agreed to an even more ambitious market opening project. They agreed to privatize their national champions. They also agreed to allow firms to enter into joint ventures and alliances in order to exploit the new technologies. These changes were embedded in a series of directives that were to take effect on 1 January 1998.

Table 5.5 shows how the privatizations were carried out. Many of the firms remain at least partially owned by their governments, suggesting the governments still retain an interest in their success. This has meant that they are unlikely takeover targets unless government officials agree to sell their share. There has only been one merger of any consequence that combined former national champions – that between the Swedish and Finnish companies. The Italian government decided not to sell Telecom Italia to Deutsche Telekom, and instead to keep it nationally owned by selling it to Olivetti. There have been attempts to sell off some of the other companies in the smaller states, like Austria (which sold a share of its state-owned company to Telecom Italia), Portugal, Spain and the Netherlands, but so far governments have baulked at giving up their control over these firms.

While much of the structure of the national champions has been preserved, there has been a huge growth in the number of companies and players in the market for wireless phones and other services. Many of these new entrants are spin-offs or partially owned subsidiaries of the former national champions. Table 5.6 shows some of the main subsidiaries of the largest firms. It can be seen that many of the subsidiaries are jointly held by more than one firm. British Telecom, Deutsche Telecom, Telia (Sweden) and France Telecom have been the most successful of the former national champions suggesting that their national governments were correct in supporting deregulation. But the new market entrants from America and around Europe have been able to form alliances with the smaller firms in the other member states as well.

Firm entry into other European markets means either setting up a subsidiary in each country or else partnering with local firms. There are three layers of these developments that are worth describing. The new subsidiaries are mainly organized on the national market level. First, new entrants have emerged in the wireless, internet, and cable business. In Europe, firms like Cable and Wireless, Vodaphone and Viag have prospered. Second, many of the phone companies have opened up subsidiaries in other countries that they wholly own. So, for example, Telia (the Swedish company) owned ventures in Denmark, Finland and Eastern Europe. More frequently, there has been a proliferation of joint ventures between existing national phone companies and foreign companies, particularly in producing wireless companies. For example, Wind in Italy was owned by Deutsche Telekom and France Telecom. Third, these ventures often include firms from outside the telecommunications industry, like banks or

Table 5.5 Privatization of European telecommunications companies

EU Country	Date of effective liberalization	National operator (former PTT)	Date and method of privatization of national operator
Austria	1998	Post & Telekom Austria	75% state-owned, 25% owned by Telecom Italia
Belgium	1998	Belgacom	1995: Sale of strategic stake
Denmark	1996/97	Tele Danmark	1994: International offering; state retains 51%
Ireland	1998 (December)	Telecom Eireann	1996: Sale of strategic stake
Finland	1994	Telecom Finland	Government sold 80% in 1990s. 2003: sold to Telia
France	1998	France Télécom	1997: International offering; state retains 80%. 2003: state share 55%
Germany	1998	Deutsche Telekom	1996: Public offering: state retains 74%, 2003. 2004: state share 46%
Greece	2001	OTE	1996 & 1997: 20% of equity sold on Athens Stock Exchange over two offers
Italy	1998	Telecom Italia	1997: Privatization completed through second offering; sold to Olivetti, 2001
Luxembourg	1998 (July)	P&T Luxembourg	100% state-owned
Netherlands	1998	KPN	1994 &1995: Public offerings
Portugal	2000	Telecom Portugal	1995, 1996 & 1997: Public offerings. State retains 25%
Spain	1998 (December)	Telefonica	Privately owned. State's remaining 20% equity sold in 1997
Sweden	1991	Telia	71% state-owned in 2004
UK	1991	BT	1984–93: fully privatized over three international public offerings

Source: Standard & Poor's (1999) *Standard Corporation Descriptions*, New York: Standard & Poor's. Reprinted with permission of Standard & Poor's Financial Services LLC, a wholly owned subsidiary of the McGraw-Hill Companies. All rights reserved.

Table 5.6 Shareholdings of main European telecommunications companies, circa 2003

Firm	Holdings in
Deutsche Telecom (Germany: land, wireless, internet)	TMobil (wireless, US, France, UK, Germany) Maxnmobil (wireless, Austria) Enel (wireless, Italy) Wind (wireless, Italy) Federa (wireless, Netherlands) Eurobell (cable, UK)
France Telecom (France: land, wireless, internet)	Orange (wireless, Belgium, UK, US, Switzerland, Germany, Netherlands, France) Mobistar (wireless, Belgium) Panafon (wireless, Greece) Wind (wireless, Italy) Airtel (land, wireless, Spain) Sonofon (land, Denmark) TeleDenmark (land, Denmark)
British Telecom (UK: land, wireless, internet)	9 Com (wireless, France) Viag (wireless, Germany) Albacom (wireless, Italy) Telfort (wireless, Netherlands) Telenordia (wireless, Norway, Sweden) Europolitan (fixed lines: Sweden) Airtel (land, wireless, Spain)
Vodafone (UK: wireless, internet)	Verizon (wireless, US) Belgacom (wireless, Belgium) Mannesman (wireless, Germany) 9 Com (wireless, Italy) Libertel (wireless, Netherlands) Panafon (wireless, Greece) E-plus (land, wireless, Germany) Omnitel (wireless, Italy) Sonofon (land, Denmark)
Telia (Sweden: land, wireless, internet)	Sonofon (wireless, Denmark) Telia Denmark (wireless, Denmark) Telia (wireless, Norway) Sonera (land, wireless, Finland) Telecom Eireann (land, Ireland)
Telecom Italia (Italy: land, wireless, internet)	Telekom Austria (land, wireless, Austria) Telestet (wireless, Greece) Retevision (land, wireless, Spain)
KPN (Netherlands: land, wireless, internet)	EPlus (wireless, Germany) Base (wireless, Belgium) Hutchison3G (wireless, UK)

Source: Standard & Poor's (1999) *Standard Corporation Descriptions*, New York: Standard & Poor's. Reprinted with permission of Standard & Poor's Financial Services LLC, a wholly owned subsidiary of the McGraw-Hill Companies. All rights reserved.

manufacturers. An example is the Italian company Albacom which was owned by British Telecom and two local partners, BNL (a bank) and ENI (a government-owned manufacturing conglomerate). This has created a plethora of new companies that produce services within and across national boundaries.

In 2004, the EU passed a set of directives (European Commission 2004a) that tried to provide a combined set of rules to govern telecommunications markets, mergers, market entry and standardization of equipment. These directives are now the framework for the working out of industry alliances. It now appears as if the wireless market has matured in Europe, where 87 per cent of possible consumers have purchased phones. It remains to be seen if this complex structure of firms will survive a slowing market. As long as national governments hold shares in their telephone companies, any consolidation is unlikely to involve the biggest players. More likely is the consolidation of subsidiaries or firms that are privately owned.

The evolution of the telecommunications market is a case where industry moved from being highly regulated with nationally owned and closed national markets to open markets that allowed participation of firms from other countries. The result has been to shift the players around, create larger firms, and complicate industry structure by producing a plethora of joint ventures and subsidiaries that operate across borders. While there has been some privatization of the industry, several of the largest players, France Telecom and Deustche Telecom, remain partially government-owned. National firms still exist and governments have been reluctant, with a few exceptions, to letting their national telecommunications companies be merged into larger competitors. Still, European telecommunications has been reorganized on a European basis. In the fastest growing market, wireless telephones, European firms have partnered to produce a Europe-wide industry.

Costs and benefits of Europeanization

Who benefits from Europeanization? Corporations have successfully pursued new strategies as part of European market integration. Has this been a good or bad thing for average Europeans? A sociological approach to the European market ought to also say something about this fundamental question.

Contemporary political rhetoric across Europe suggests voting publics are most fearful of globalization, neo-liberalism, and immigration. All of these fears are tied up with European perceptions that national economies are being buffeted by new sources of competitive pressures that will not be mediated by government action. Globalization is thought of mostly as the increasing competitive pressure being brought by developing countries which have lower wage structures. Those who view these competitive forces as determinative argue that if firms from one society figure out the most efficient way to produce a set of products, then firms from all other societies will have to emulate those firms or fail (Strange 1996; Castells 1999).

Neo-liberalism is the idea that the only thing governments can do in the face of the onslaught of a competitive world is to remove all forms of social protection, on trade, finance, and working conditions. Governments that persist in producing trade barriers, protecting workers, and engaging in too much taxation of firms, will over time lose firms and jobs to societies where firms have friendlier arrangements. This allegedly forces governments to dismantle worker protections, free up capital markets, and deregulate other markets (Crouch and Streeck 1997; Boyer and Drache 1996; Garrett 1998). This is thought to translate into a race to the bottom that will force the social welfare states of Europe into decline.

As I have argued both theoretically and empirically in this chapter, this perspective is wrong. The market integration project in Europe has been entirely the work of freely elected European governments who have democratically decided to cooperate on a large number of issues in order to produce economic growth and jobs across Europe. The evidence presented in this chapter shows quite clearly the power of those governments both to agree to make changes and to have those changes create an integrated European market.

Earlier, I argued that the main reason that governments have cooperated and expanded their cooperation was their perception that the integration of the European economy had basically positive results. It is useful to consider the evidence. A recent report by the EU (European Commission 2004b) argues that between 1993 and 2003, the Single Market Programme directly created 2.5 million jobs across Europe. It was responsible for 877 billion euros of additional economic activity in Europe a year, about 5700 euros per household in Europe. These calculations are conservative in that they are the direct benefits of more trade. They do not include the lower prices for many things people in Europe consume all the time, from phone calls (prices have dropped 50 per cent) to plane tickets (prices have dropped 41 per cent). Nor do they include the stimulation of European creativity towards the production of new and novel technologies – such as the advances in wireless communication, many of which were invented in Europe.

Governments and firms have profoundly changed the way the economy works in Europe. The Europeanization of business has brought about more competition in Europe, but it has also increased economic opportunities and lowered prices for many of the goods and services Europeans consume. European citizens who see globalization and neo-liberalism as the cause of their anxieties miss the real transformations brought about by governments and corporations that have increased their standards of living substantially. This positive story is not widely known outside scholarly circles. It is ironic that the governments which have signed on to these policies rarely explain what has happened to their publics.

Thus the problem with the apparently plausible arguments about the dangers of globalization in Europe is that there is little evidence that globalization or neo-liberalism are having these effects here. This has been a point made by a number of authors linked to the 'varieties of capitalism' school of political economy, such as Hall and Soskice (2004; see also Fligstein and Choo 2005; Pauly and Reich 1997; Wade 1996; Rodrik 1997, 2003; Garrett 1997). The evidence that they put forward about Europe's distinctive form of 'economy and society' – in the Weberian sense – particularly its distinct stance on balancing welfare protection and growth, regulation and legal oversight, supports the view proposed here. The world economy contains three large, distinct trade zones: the EU, North America, and the Asian area. These zones have become more and not less economically integrated, as the regional analysis of Mattli (1999) and Katzenstein (2005) has also argued. Studies typically show that governments continue to sponsor a great number of policy interventions in capital and labour markets. There is little evidence that there has been a race to the bottom to undermine the protection of workers in advanced industrial societies. Indeed, what evidence exists suggests exactly the opposite: countries whose economies are more open to trade offer more, not less social protection to workers (Rodrik 2001).

So if it is not globalization and neo-liberalism that are driving the transformation of the European welfare state driven economy, what is going on? I have demonstrated that the member state governments of the European Union have been engaged in a fifty-year-long market opening project that has allowed firms and corporations to create new markets, implement new technologies, and expand on a Europe-wide basis. European industries are increasingly becoming more organized at a European level. As a result of the Single Market and subsequent market opening initiatives, firms have shifted their attention from controlling national markets to becoming increasingly focused on their competitors from other European countries.

European governments have proved quite willing to push their former national champions to transform themselves into larger players who would try and sell products across Europe, given shifts in technology and opportunities for new business. While there was some resistance on the part of governments at different points in the process, the French, British and German governments generally saw mostly advantages to 'Europeanizing' their economies. Creating Europe-wide markets has mostly meant the preservation of the identities of national firms. While there were extensive mergers and the creation of joint ventures across national borders, national firm identities were preserved. So in the case discussed here, the three largest telecommunications companies before deregulation became European players by starting new companies as joint ventures and entering into partnerships across Europe with smaller phone companies. One can still recognize British Telecom, France Telecom, and Deutsche Telecom – indeed, the latter two remained partially state-owned.

The EU has played a fundamental part in all of these market changes. The European Court of Justice and the European Commission play an important role in adjudicating and acting to solve market governance problems. By and large, the member state governments have been the main agents who have pushed this agenda to produce Europe-wide markets. The dynamics by which national firms became more oriented towards a Europe-wide market occurred as opportunities emerged, governments changed policy, and the EU intervened to create new collective governance. One way to sum this up is that as a result of the actions of European governments through their cooperation in the European Union, the European economy has not become globalized, but Europeanized.

Conclusion: economic sociology and EU studies

It might be useful to end this chapter with a brief recapitulation of what economic sociology can bring to the study of the EU. Economic sociology offers two sorts of insights into market integration processes.

First, it makes such processes more concrete by providing the idea that governments, firms, and other actors in society are responsible for the shape of market rules and practices. It forces us to consider these processes, not as out of our control or being directed by some unobserved entity (like 'the market' or 'global capitalism'), but instead as the outcome of political, legal and economic decisions made by organized actors like firms, political parties and governments. An economic sociological analysis of any market begins with an understanding of the legal and social underpinnings of the market. Markets have histories and the leading firms in the market have created a social structure that benefits them. The stability of that structure depends on their common perception of what other actors are doing. Markets are reproducible to the extent that in a given period, the main actors preserve their positions in the market. Markets also contain a cultural understanding of what the market is about so that firms can interpret each other's actions. Economic sociology's analysis of changes in rules and laws for markets begins by situating market and government actors in a historical, social and political relationship with each other. These relationships explain what is going on and what it means. In most economic sociological analyses of such arrangements, it is important to get into the details of market rules. This is because these rules will reflect local understandings of the market.

Second, economic sociology invites us to ask whether or not market changes that are occurring have had good or bad consequences for the societies that have undertaken them. As I argued earlier, some market changes might narrowly benefit one group over another in society if these groups manage to capture the market integration process. While there are always winners and losers from economic changes, it is important to understand how the gains and losses are allocated. So, for example, in Europe, social democratic states have generally worked to mitigate the negative effects of trade on jobs for those workers who have proved to be vulnerable. It is also clear that in the aggregate, citizens both as workers and consumers have benefited from European economic integration. I would argue that the tools of economic sociology suggest that in this case, there is a win–win situation here for citizens. I note that this outcome is not predetermined by market logic, neo-liberalism, or some more general principle: it is the practical politics of the situation that produced the character of the market openings. The EU did in fact create level playing fields for firms who wanted to enter markets in other countries, and this has worked to the benefit of citizens both as workers but also as consumers. An economic sociological analysis of this situation allows us to de-mystify what has occurred and understand it more concretely. In this case, the benefits have been mostly positive.

PART II:
Politics and Policies

As well as the study of the social foundations and social consequences of European Union, sociology can also be used to study some of the more traditional questions of politics and policies in the EU. The second half of the volume thus homes in on how sociological tools might be operationalized to study more explicitly *political* integration. They suggest how sociologists might still offer something new in this crowded arena, by focusing on the emergence of trans-European or EU 'fields' – a key term picked up from the sociology of Pierre Bourdieu – in approaches to political mobilization, the media, EU politics and EU policy-making. They thus offer startlingly new conceptualizations of otherwise familiar processes and institutional venues in the EU, new methodological tools, as well as fresh empirical insights.

Much has been written during the last decade about the need to develop a European 'public sphere.' Such normative debates would greatly benefit from a better empirical understanding of the extent to which political mobilization and the claims it articulates has been Europeanized, and whether or not it has been publicly represented in the media in these terms. **Virginie Guiraudon** was involved in one such comparative empirical study (Koopmans and Statham 2010) which used quantitative discourse analysis of claims-making and frame analysis of the press, as well as interviews to study the potential development of a European 'public sphere'. Here, linking up with this work, and focusing on the policy areas of immigration, race and gender, she takes stock of the broader import of the social movements literature into EU studies for the understanding of the EU political sphere and the reconfiguring of cleavages and alliances across EU member states. She reconceptualizes Europeanization in terms of the political mobilization of various non-state actors in European politics. Also drawing upon her qualitative research on NGOs and public interest lobbies in Brussels and transnational advocacy coalitions (Guiraudon 2001, 2004), she asks who gets access to European channels, how they use them, and what it tells us about the specificity of the EU 'composite polity' (Tarrow 2001). The EU is often proposed as an elite-driven pluralist model of democracy. Guiraudon's work suggests how empirically we might assess how much the EU in fact enables mould-breaking politics beyond the nation-state, and hence the redefinition of balances of power in various policy domains.

Niilo Kauppi's chapter on EU politics also examines the specific resources of political actors engaging in EU political careers, linking up with the essential questions of power and democracy in the EU. As with several of the authors in this volume, Kauppi uses the notion of 'fields' as a key heuristic concept in his approach to the EU. In his book *Democracy, Social Resources and Political Power in the European Union* (2005) he helped pioneer the use of Pierre Bourdieu as the source of a new approach to studying the EU (see also Kauppi 1996b, 2003). His chapter is also an exemplar of the research conducted in the Strasbourg research centre on the EU (currently known as GSPE PRISME). Kauppi conceptualizes the EU as a distinctive power structure and form of social organization. In order to understand how it works, he argues that before studying the effects of its policies, one must focus on the human dimension of EU politics, on the individuals and groups who make up the EU, where they come from, what kinds of resources and networks they have access to, how they perceive their roles, the institutions in which they work and, more broadly, their conception of the social world around them. He draws upon his work on the European Parliament, particularly the careers and profiles of MEPs and the processes of socialization and professionalization that they reveal. In this way, Kauppi illustrates how useful the import of the concept of 'fields' might be, and pinpoints its distinctiveness to existing political science approaches.

Frédéric Mérand's chapter on EU policies further complements the political sociology of European Union presented in the previous chapters. When conceptualizing EU policies, sociologists focus on the social construction of policy problems by asking questions such as: who defines policy problems, do they fit pre-existing solutions, and why are some solutions never even contemplated? Mérand borrows from the classical concepts and methods of sociologists such as Goffman and anthropologists such as Lévi-Strauss to answer these deceptively simple questions. More specifically, Mérand analyzes EU policies as a set of practices embedded in social fields and informed by social representations. He observes that EU policy-making looks like *bricolage*, whereby policy actors experiment and strategize on the basis of their practical knowledge. He thus takes ethnographic methods into the heart of a policy field normally taken up only by international relations scholars and diplomatic historians – European military and defence cooperation (Mérand 2008). His interview-based research offers extraordinary insights into the minds of senior military officers of several major member states who have been going through their own process of Europeanization. The chapter also alerts us to some of the methodological precautions that political sociologists must take when conducting field work to study EU policies: key reflexive notions long identified in the sociology of Bourdieu, such as going beyond common sense, constructing the research object, taking practices seriously, and keeping a critical perspective.

Finally, **Hans-Jörg Trenz** links up the empirical focus of our volume with contemporary social theory and the role that it can play in rethinking EU studies. In doing so, he revisits the main theoretical approaches in contemporary sociology to identify the kind of research agenda that they inspire, while linking up to a core concern of all political and legal EU studies – the question of integration. The chapter also recapitulates the main questions that are examined in the book, bringing us full circle to some of the broad guidelines of the sociological tradition introduced by Díez Medrano. Building on Durkheimian and Weberian traditions, Trenz explores the concept of integration in discussions of European integration, only re-read through the concerns of classical and contemporary social theory. The chapter shows the added value of this approach, distinguishing between macro-, micro- and meso-levels of reflection. Trenz highlights the relevance of Europeanization from below, in the form of transnational and intercultural relations and contentious politics, not simply the result of purposeful top down policy processes (a view also developed in Trenz and Eder 2004). He underlines that social theory predicts that Europeanization will also bring further differentiation within societies, as well as integration. In his view, this will help us comprehend European society as the emergence of a new social entity, a genuine reconfiguration of the European social, political, economic and cultural space.

CHAPTER 6

Mobilization, Social Movements and the Media

Virginie Guiraudon

> **Key concepts:** social movements, mobilization, transnational collective action, operationalization, pluralism, interest groups, non-governmental organizations (NGOs), lobbying, protest, public sphere, media, political communication, Europeanization, fields, frames, networks, immigration, race, gender, mixed methods.
>
> **Key references:** Tarrow, Keck and Sikkink, Tilly, Dahl, Olson, Haas, Lindberg, Moravcsic, Marks and McAdam, Habermas, Bourdieu

Scholars of social movements only belatedly showed interest in transnational collective action within the context of the European Union. In one of the first volumes taking stock of the Europeanization of collective action published in 2001, Doug Imig and Sidney Tarrow could still write: 'We know much more about participation in consultative committees in the five square kilometres of Euroland in Brussels than we do about contention over the effects of their decisions among the 375 million people who have to live with their consequences' (2001: 7).

Three empirical developments in the 1990s prompted social movement studies to shift their attention to the European Union. First, the excitement around Europe 1992 and the completion of the Single Market and the debate on the significance of several revisions of the Treaty of Rome led to a heightened awareness among Europeanists that the EU had become a source of authority and decision-making. As Simon Hix (1994) aptly put it, the European Community was a 'challenge to comparative politics' and difficult to ignore even for social movement scholars.

Second, in the wake of debates on the EU's democratic deficit and scandals on the lack of transparency of the European Commission, the latter funded a number of projects to address these concerns: these often focused on the question of a possible 'European public sphere' – a transnational communicative space where the EU would be debated by its citizens – or on the notion of 'organized civil society' – a deliberately vague term often used in the European Commission's White Papers on Governance and on Communication to point towards potential democratic foundations for the European project (Commission 2001, 2006). Quite a few comparative quantitative databases on social movements and the 'claims-making' of different forms of mobilization in the mass media have thus seen the light, often with EU money (see below, and also Trenz, Chapter 9 in this volume, on Habermasian studies of European civil society).

Third, the 1990s also witnessed the emergence of the global justice movement, and other forms of transnational collective action, starting by way of the 1994 international solidarity movement with the Chiapas rebellion and culminating in the 1999 anti-WTO protest in Seattle (see della Porta and Tarrow 2004). With this new 'cycle of protest' in motion (Tarrow 1998), scholars wondered about the targets of cross-border mobilization and the role of international institutions as friends or foes of such movements. They were also inspired by international relations research such as Keck and Sikkink's *Activists Beyond Borders* (1998), which posits a 'boomerang effect', through which weak domestic actors can use alliances with external allies, mediated through other states and international institutions, to advance their claims against their own governments (see also Risse *et al.* 1999). The dense web of European-level institutions thus became an interesting case study for those interested in the transnational politics of contention. Whether the EU or the Council of Europe have provided resources for transnational organizations or served as a target for common mobilizations, they could be seen as a kind of 'coral reef' (Tarrow 2005: 27) around which a number of different claims and movements have clustered. There are thus some similarities between the findings of EU scholars and those working on global institutions. For instance, they all point to the importance of non-governmental organizations (NGOs) in setting the agenda, especially prior to important intergovernmental conferences. They also underline insider/outsider collaboration.

There have thus been two premises to the study of European mobilization. On the one hand, there has been a tendency to identify the European Union with a new type of polity and consider that interest groups and movements would shift the scale of their actions to adjust to the new locus of power just as they had in state-building and later nation-building eras. On the other, an analogy has been drawn between the EU and other international institutions. In this view, European movements are mere localized versions of wider global trends. For instance, the European Social Forum that first took place in Florence in

2002 was a regional chapter of the World Social Forum that had first taken place in 2001 in Porto Alegre. A first key research question could thus be phrased as follows: Is the 'Europeanization' of mobilization part of a process whereby activism has become globalized, or are mobilized groups migrating from the national to the European level to follow the shift in policy competence to the EU? Of course, the Europeanization of collective action could be a symptom of both and empirical research would also seek to determine how the two dynamics interact.

In fact, this first research question subsumes another one. When collective actors target European institutions or policies, frame issues as supranational ones, or organize across borders, is the dynamic top down or from below? Linked to this, is the repertoire of action privileging protest from the outside or insider lobbying? The questions are historically important, because social movement scholars such as Charles Tilly (1978) consider contentious politics as a dynamic element of nation building. In this perspective, mobilization by those affected by European developments would be the motor for a process of Europeanization from below. Imig and Tarrow have argued that the current situation in Europe is analogous to state-building times in early modern Europe, when there was a jumble of overlapping jurisdictions, unstable political alignments between local rulers and centralizing elites, and thus a range of potential coalitions and entry points for 'ordinary people' (Tarrow 2001). Tarrow posits that today's Europe provides opportunities for ordinary people that can play national governments against European institutions or vice versa. Linking European integration with polity building thus allows for 'Europeanization from below'. Non-elite publics and social groups that were previously mobilizing at the national level could now shift the scale of their action to the European level (see also della Porta and Caiani 2007). However, other accounts, stemming from theorists of European integration, suggest that, with the exceptions of farmers' groups, the Europeanization of collective action is a top down phenomenon driven by EU institutions that favours lobbying by interest groups and international NGOs rather than social movements using protest as a repertoire of action. This diagnosis is largely shared by sociologists (Marks and McAdam 1996) and political scientists (Greenwood 2007; Balme *et al.* 2002; for a cross-disciplinary study see Favell and Geddes 2000).

For these scholars, a specific system of interest intermediation has emerged as part of European integration, whereby the EU has opened up opportunities for all sorts of interest groups (Mazey and Richardson 1993). This is a pluralist version of the EU. Pluralism is a group-based approach to politics that had its heyday in the 1950s and 1960s when the behaviouralist paradigm dominated social science. According to pluralists, society is composed of various interests that coalesce into groups and vie for influence over policy outcomes. The state is subject to the competitive demands of various groups, and, depending on the variant of pluralism, policy either aggregates these interests or reflects those of the most powerful social groups (Dahl 1961).

Interestingly enough, theorists of European integration known as 'neo-functionalists' were very much influenced by the pluralist approach when they wrote in the 1950s and 1960s (Rosamond 1999). For Ernst Haas (1961) and Leon Lindberg (1963), European integration would alter the strategies of groups trying to influence policy outcomes: they would shift their activity towards the new loci of power, organize transnationally and change their tactics, provided of course these groups had direct access to the new supranational institutions and could bypass national governments. Some neo-functionalists, however, believed that a number of societal actors and organized interests would have a hard time adapting and would continue to act collectively at the sub-national or national level, in particular labour, farmers, and resource-poor actors. As Philippe Schmitter provocatively put it, paraphrasing Karl Marx's famous definition (1844) of the modern state apparatus as a committee for managing the affairs of the bourgeoisie, 'the Euro-Bourgeoisie has at long last found in the EC the 'Executive Committee' for managing its common affairs' (Schmitter 2003).

Scholars with a rational choice perspective, meanwhile, pick up from Mancur Olson's famous foundational work on collective action, which focused on the incentives for mobilization that groups must provide to individuals who otherwise can get a 'free ride' on the efforts of others, and on the costs and rewards of mobilization, providing a taxonomy of groups according to their capacity to mobilize (Olson 1971). Scholars in this line have also been sceptical about the apparent 'pluralism' of the EU: Richard Balme and Didier Chabanet believe that adding a new institutional layer raises the costs of collective action and may also be an unfavourable venue for groups creating situations of 'cumulative exclusion' (2008: 39). Others, based on field work, think that not all economic interest groups are able to integrate the EU in their lobbying strategies (Grossman 2004). The debate continues as other scholars maintain that the EU is more open to a variety of interests than national systems, where entrenched interest organizations dominate. They argue therefore that there is a distinct European system of conflict resolution or interest intermediation that could be labelled 'Euro-pluralist' (Claeys *et al.* 1998; Coen and Richardson 2009).

The first section of this chapter examines the existing literature on European integration and collective action and its shortcomings. The second section devises ways of answering the questions raised in the literature by turning them into testable hypotheses, a process called operationalization that we have emphasized throughout this volume, which involves circumscribing a research object, elaborating a research design, and choosing appropriate methods. The following section then illustrates how to go about studying EU-related mobilization and the emerging 'European public sphere' based on quantitative and qualitative research I have conducted in individual and group projects on both race and gender equality and immigration policies. I conclude by underlining not only the need for comparative and multi-method research designs but also for projects that combine different levels of analysis in a field where the 'meso' level (go-between organizations such as NGOs) dominates.

European mobilizations: symptom or cause of European integration?

From the founding fathers of European integration theory such as Karl Deutsch and Ernst Haas to contemporary social movement scholars focusing on Europe (Imig and Tarrow 2001), many scholars have believed that the single market project and other shifts of policy regulation to the European level would lead contentious politics to increasingly occur with or against European institutions rather than at lower levels of government. Ernst Haas called this process 'political integration' and defined it as 'the process whereby political actors in several distinct national settings are persuaded to shift their loyalties, expectations and political activities towards a new political centre' (1961: 196). Since then, some have dismissed this statement as outdated idealism (Schmitter 2000). Yet a number of integration theory schools, including new institutionalism, neo-functionalism and multilevel governance, still believe that over time, as the locus of power shifts to the EU, domestic actors will indeed adapt to this new playing field (Rosamond 1999).

For instance, the institutionalist school of integration theory has stressed an interactive dynamic between the strategies of political actors and the development of EC/EU treaties and rules: 'The new rules create legal rights and open new arenas for politics; in this fashion they structure political processes thereafter. Actors – including governments, private entities and EC bodies – adapt to the new rules and arenas ... adapt their preferences, strategies and behaviours to the new rules' (Sandholtz and Stone Sweet 1998: 18–19). This implies that the level of Europeanization of mobilization correlates with the extent to which competence has been transferred to the European level in each policy domain. The expectation is that there should be more contention directed at EU institutions in supranational domains than in the more intergovernmental policy areas where the role of EU institutions is circumscribed or in sectors where the EU still plays a marginal role. The main hypothesis is that Europeanization varies across policy sectors rather than across cases.

Andrew Moravcsik, whose work is known as 'liberal intergovernmentalism', would propose a different hypothesis (1998). In his view, national policy preferences drive European integration. There are intense domestic debates over integration between interest groups which national governments 'aggregate' yet they vary 'by both issue and country' (1998: 28). Think of agriculture, an old common EU policy; not all member states have the same stakes in this sector so there is cross-national variation. It is crucial in French politics, yet in that same country, other issues may be of lesser importance. The determinant is not that the sector has been supranationalized but rather the preferences of member states. Here, Europeanization varies by country in a given sector. A salient issue in national politics is likely to generate both the Europeanization of this policy area and contentious activity against the EU.

Where do social movement scholars stand in this debate? Those that focus on protest expect that movements will slowly shift their attention to the European level. For instance, Gary Marks and Doug McAdam have stated that to 'the extent that European integration results in the replacement, or more likely, the decline in the importance of the nation-state as the exclusive seat of formal institutional power, we can expect attendant changes in the forms and dynamics of social movement activity', although they have also pointed out that not all social actors could adapt, in particular trade unions (1996: 273–6). Thus scholars have expected a small rise in the overall number of transnational mobilization as the pace of European integration picked up in the mid-1990s, and this trend was in fact validated by the first rough quantitative estimates (Imig and Tarrow 2001; della Porta *et al.* 1999). Imig and Tarrow (2001) also thought that 'domesticated contentious action against the EU', whereby national actors are targeted for action over EU integration would first dominate before any cross-border coordinated action against EU institutions. Thus the forms of action might evolve over time: first, as predicted by 'intergovernmentalists', domestic actors would mobilize against mobilization at the infra-European level, and only later, as institutionalists and neo-functionalists would expect, organize to directly address European institutions.

Notwithstanding, contention would vary across types of mobilized actors (for example, trade unions versus business associations) depending on whether they could unite across borders or adapt to new forms of collective action. As Carlo Ruzza (2004) has shown, one must take into account both *ex ante* national regimes of collective action and the specificities of the EU political system. In his view, while there is cross-national and cross-sectoral variation in mobilization 'cultures', there are specific moments or opportunities in the EU policy process for non-governmental actors to voice their demands. This implies possible cross-national and cross-sector variation regarding the Europeanization of contention depending on the characteristics of challengers (their resources, identity, repertoire of action and history), the degree of cross-national divergence hindering coordinated action, and the seizing of opportune moments for agenda-setting. One could even surmise that, even in areas such as the environment, where the global arena and the EU have been obvious targets and frames, there is some form of backlash against the shift of scale to a higher level: there is rather more attention paid to the local and more radical forms of protest emerging alongside the institutionalization of environmental interest groups (see Rootes 2003). In brief, Europeanization can also vary across time, in other words, ebb and flow.

There is another tradition under the broad 'civil society' umbrella: the 'public sphere' school, which stands squarely in the lineage of the German social theorist, Jürgen Habermas (1969). As Hans-Jörg Trenz argues in this volume (Chapter 9), they believe that polity building at the EU level drives the Europeanization of civil society. In fact, they also posit that there *should* be a transnational communicative space where the European political order could be debated and contested in a fairly unrestrained way (Eriksen 2005a). Public sphere scholars are deeply aware of the importance of the locus where debate takes place and thus of the media. In spite of global market trends that encourage uniformity, one can still speak of twenty-seven media fields in Europe. Public sphere scholars thus remain sceptical in empirical terms about a European arena of debate (Fossum and Schlesinger 2007, Díez Medrano 2009, Vetters *et al.* 2009), in spite of the 'post-national' enthusiasm of their Habermasian intellectual source (Habermas 2001).

After this brief review of the various perspectives on contention in the European Union, one can see that they generate contrasting testable hypotheses regarding Europeanization. Notwithstanding this, what should be a dynamic process remains in all these positions a fairly static view of interest groups and political institutions. Groups seem to pre-date European integration and must adapt so that they can 'influence' EU institutions whose features are also taken for granted. To get beyond this, let us zoom in a little bit on the meso-level: the actors in organizational structures inside and outside the EU. It is unclear who is knocking on whose door and who is influencing whom.

I am not referring here simply to the archetypal career trajectories whereby NGO staff members move within the EU Commission or Parliament secretariat, or when retired insiders become private consultants, although these instances are numerous. More generally, those lobbying the Commission are also shaped by the Commission. The Commission outsources *expertise* and seeks to *legitimate* its policy proposals by referring to the demands of organized civil society. This often means creating and financing associations, umbrella organizations or platforms. Non-governmental actors must be able to play along and deliver relevant proposals. In this respect, they must possess certain *resources*, adopt certain *structures*, and use certain *repertoires of action* and *framing* strategies to play their part properly. Moreover, it is not clear who is creating opportunities for whom: EU actors or non-governmental actors. So let us zoom in further, to the micro-level, where the individuals in NGO structures are political entrepreneurs creating their own opportunities for action. They have not just been sitting at home, in their national capitals, waiting for the EU to acquire competence in the policy area that they wish to shape. They have not just been waiting for Commission policy proposals to be put on the negotiating table so that they can migrate to the EU decision centre, Brussels. In fact, a big part of their job is precisely to carve out a European space for action and thus actively take part in this shifting of competence. Given that there are regular and frequent revisions of European treaties, or open fora such as the one set up to draft the Charter of Fundamental Rights (Michel 2009), non-governmental actors can seize these moments to set the agenda and argue for the European relevance of their issue. There are key individuals in these processes; 'mediators' between national and European levels that are crucial for alliance building and transnational networking (Ruzza and Bozzini 2008).

To reiterate the main point here, functionalist and institutionalist approaches do not allow us to think enough about the role of agency and the capacity of political entrepreneurs to create their own opportunities rather than just seize existing ones. At the same time, this does not mean that actors are independent from European institutions. On the contrary, they rather live in a symbiotic relationship with them, which needs to be investigated.

From theory to research design: studying EU-related contention

Now that I have reviewed the literature and extracted from it some general propositions that could be empirically tested, step one in the operationalization is to define precisely what it is that I am studying: that is, delineate clearly what is the *object* of my research before identifying indicators of the phenomenon that I want to observe. As a rule of thumb, in the construction of the research object one should first avoid being trapped in common sense conceptions (from the media or everyday talk), but also avoid the reproduction of the idiosyncratic conceptions of the academic sub-discipline, in this case social movements or mobilization studies.

Common sense would suggest that interest groups pressure political institutions to defend their interests and influence decisions. In fact, interest groups and social movement organizations spend quite a significant amount of their time and resources doing more: defining what their 'interest' is, building a common identity, raising funds, and many other things that have nothing to do with directly pressuring the powers that be. Moreover, at the national level, according to elitist or neo-Marxist theories, powerful economic actors often do not need to make demands since politicians need business confidence to ensure public trust and, more prosaically, their own re-election (Poulantzas 1968). In Brussels, large multinational corporations have their own lobbyists, use consultants and participate in a range of organizations, yet this costs them almost nothing, given their resources, and compared to the benefits that might follow from securing a single comma in an EC regulation, or a 'could' instead of a 'shall' in an EU directive. At the same time, one should also be wary of taking for granted the terminology used by policy actors themselves, that is, native categories, as opposed to constructing analytical concepts, aimed at understanding what is actually going on. 'Organized civil society' might be an attractive concept for a researcher, but it is a good example of European Commission jargon that sounds like social science – indeed, has been borrowed from social science – yet is as elusive to define and as rhetorically malleable as the European 'public opinion' or European 'identity' that Eurobarometer reports assert that they measure.

As I have just stated, 'influence' is not a very useful concept and masks the fact that public policies are, after all, one way of ordering society and regulating the relations between different social groups. If influence is reciprocal, one ends up with a form of circular thinking or an analytically flat statement about the co-production of public policy. Other reciprocal effects (and concepts) may be more relevant to our understanding of the relationship between organized interests and EU policy makers: co-legitimation of institutions and policy frames, cross-pollination of expertise, circulation of personnel, or exchange of resources (material versus non-material resources). In any case, the idea is to have an open mind about what it is that interest groups (can) do, not assume that it is just about measuring their influence.

A further problem is that the mainstream academic next door may be as biased as the wo/man on the street when it comes to thinking about EU mobilization. Your colleague is interested in 'social movements' and may in fact have been involved in a couple. S/he has read and taught all the classics with their book covers showing pictures of colourful banners and picket fences, or paintings from nineteenth-century revolutionary demonstrations. For them, European contention will therefore primarily be about mass protest and the search for an elusive 'transnational social movement' (Tarrow 2005). It is so much more fun to interview chatty activists who may be socially proximate to you, than to sit in on a EU affairs training school, interview savvy heads of communications in a Brussels consultancy, or listen to the excruciating details of European Court of Justice decisions told in perfect legalese by an enthusiastic EU 'native'. Comforted by groundbreaking scholars who focused on national or cross-national protest event count analysis, mobilization scholars have thus tended to look for the obvious, for example, dramatic cross-border demonstrations. These turn out to be rare and are often 'over determined', such as the much studied French-Belgian-Spanish 'Eurodemo' when the former French industrial champion Renault closed a car factory in Vilvoorde (Belgium) in the middle of a French presidential campaign, and in a district where the Belgian Prime minister was elected, only a few miles away from the seat of the EU in Brussels (Lagneau and Lefébure 2000). But do such obvious cases of mobilization, in which people literally march on the streets, give us the whole picture? In social science terms, how biased or representative is this sample? When one sees that protest event analysis in fact shows little Europeanization of protest in the environmental field (Rucht 2002), isn't it time we actually tried walking the corridors of Brussels institutions, where even Greenpeace, an NGO known for its spectacular repertoire of spectacular protest, is also known for smoothly presenting its serious and informed reports?

As we will see below, social movement scholars have advanced on these points, and now seem to go beyond protest, to include all modes of 'claims-making', that is, publicly articulated political positions that might be registered in the media or other forms of discourse. Still, there is always a need to look beyond the obvious. Legal mobilization, for example, is a normal mode of politics and rule-making in the EU. Yet the sociology of law is not always valued in EU social movements work. Most scholars focusing on strategic litigation and other forms of judicial contention come, unsurprisingly, from 'the nation of lawyers', the US, and rarely work in sociology departments. This in effect means that there has not been enough attention paid to the use of courts and more generally to the predominance of law and lawyers as resources for mobilization.

Let us go back to protest and activists. What is a 'European' protest? How does one delineate what is or is not one? There is a need to look below the surface and go inside an event that might be of interest to social movements scholars. An example is the European Social Forum, a recurring conference held by members of the Global Justice Movement. Is this about the EU? Perhaps not. 'Another Europe'? Probably. There may still be an added value to the study of certain types of transnational mobilization that do not target the EU, yet are laboratories to study the possibility of a multilingual communicative space. Recent studies using ethnographic methods have come up with interesting findings on the scope provided by European Social Forums, which are dominated by old timers, for new types of voices and activists (Dörr 2007).

Here is another example. European Parliament elections are second order, according to national political heavyweights; European careers are considered second-best by national elites. But this means the results favour non-professionals, women and small parties (see Kauppi, Chapter 7 in this volume). It may be the same therefore with activists: there might be a space in these multinational settings for those ignored in other contexts (women, migrants, Eastern Europeans). Yet this does not prevent us from being aware that the label 'European' may be overstated for strategic reasons. Was the 1999 'Battle of Seattle' a truly global protest? Most of the participants in the demonstrations against the World Trade Organization were in fact local residents or at any rate, North American activists, including Canadian citizens living just across the border. Similarly, 'European networks' are often binational or only include a few individuals. The rule of thumb again, then, is to keep a distance between the actors' self-definition and one's own indicators in order to define a phenomenon.

I will take one last example to illustrate my point about the construction of the research object. A failed or incomplete attempt or non-attempt at Europeanization is as interesting as one that apparently has succeeded. This is a question of research design. Statisticians call 'selecting on the dependent variable' a strategy where you only focus on one kind of outcome, for example visibly successful movements. Qualitative studies that resort to the case study method and thus focus on one object of research must also be careful to anticipate some of the biases in their case selection. If scholars only focus on the few transnational protest events that have taken place – such as the unlikely 'march of the unemployed' (Chabanet 2008) – and ignore the rest, they miss the opportunity to understand the obstacles to Europeanization, and the reluctance or lack of resources that may be behind some decisions not to initiate a multilevel strategy.

This completes step one of the operationalization. Next, I need to define the 'Europeanization' of contention and decide how to study it. I will address this in the sections that follow. I present here a research design to test existing hypotheses about the macro trends in EU-related mobilization, while also pursuing new methods at the meso and micro-level that help reveal the dynamics whereby EU policy fields are created with an important role for non-governmental actors. The research design that I present is both comparative and historical and includes both quantitative statistics using a database of claims coded in daily newspapers and on the Internet, and ethnographic research on movements and actors within European institutions (see Favell and Recchi, Chapter 3 in this volume, for a comparable multi-method approach).

A mixed method approach to studying mobilization: the politics of immigration, race and gender in a comparative perspective

Operationalization 1: a quantitative analysis of claims-making

Between 2001 and 2004, I participated in a project involving research teams in seven member states, led by Ruud Koopmans in Berlin, called 'The Transformation of Political Mobilisation and Communication in European Public Spheres [EUROPUB]' (see Koopmans and Statham 2010). As the French partner in the project, my main purpose was to test some of the hypotheses that I have outlined in the first part of this chapter. Does mobilization follow treaty competence or not? Are certain types of actors more able to Europeanize their claims than others? Starting with an operational definition of what the Europeanization of the public sphere could mean, our central research agenda was to document empirically the forms and degree of Europeanization of collective action, public debates and the media (including the internet) in seven countries, across six policy fields and over time.

The project outline comprised five possible forms of Europeanization of the public sphere, collective action and public debates: (1) supranationalization; (2) increased national focusing on Europe; (3) vertical convergence from above; (4) horizontal convergence through cross-national diffusion; and finally (5) Europe as a new conflict dimension in public spheres (Koopmans and Statham 2002). *Supranationalization* would imply the development of well established European media, such as exist for political and economic elites (for example, the *Financial Times*), or the development of the internet as a means of transnational political communication. *Increased national focusing on Europe* instead would mean that movements and media remain national yet increasingly mention European policy developments. For instance they might address their claims to EU institutions or frame their demands with reference to Europe. *Vertical Europeanization* refers not only to the presence of European institutions and actors in national debates but more to the fact that EU guidelines and laws would be adopted at the national level and thus the same ideas would be found in policy debates across cases. *Horizontal Europeanization* entails the diffusion of collective action campaigns and public debates from one national public sphere to another and exchanges between national media such as editorials published simultaneously in daily newspapers in different languages and EU member states. *Europe as a new conflict dimension* would suggest that there are tensions between the winners and losers of European integration and EU market liberalization and that these are expressed in the public sphere through parties or social movements that criticize EU institutions or propose 'another Europe'.

This conflict dimension could also be expressed across borders through the denigration of European neighbours in public debates. Beyond these five forms of Europeanization, other forms of de-nationalization (globalization and decentralization) were also considered and included in the research design.

To investigate political claims-making, the research team used data drawn from content analyses – that is, the quantitative analysis of arguments and references made in everyday political life – of daily newspapers in seven countries including Switzerland, a non-EU member state. There was also a special dataset based on claims made in EU news sources. We focused on the news coverage of mobilization, public statements and other forms of claims-making by non-media actors and thus the units of analysis are not articles, but individual instances of claims-making (Koopmans and Statham 1999). The dataset includes the whole spectrum of claims-making acts related to six selected policy fields (monetary politics, agriculture, immigration, troop deployment, retirement and pensions, and education) and the general field of European integration, irrespective of the actors involved. This includes civil society groups such as employers and trade unions, NGOs, and European campaign organizations, but also political parties and state actors, including the courts, legislatures, local and national governments and supranational institutions. Instances of claims-making are included irrespective of their form, and range from protest actions and public demonstrations to legal action and public statements. EUROPUB took two policy fields where EU competences had extended furthest (monetary, agriculture), two intermediate ones (immigration, troop deployment), and two where nation-states retain autonomous control (retirement and pensions, education). Acts were included in the data if they involved demands, criticisms, or proposals related to the regulation or evaluation of events in the six selected policy fields and in the general field of European integration.

The dataset provides important information on the collective actors who make public statements through their reports, interviews, and press conferences, by litigating, and by protesting in conventional and unconventional forms. There are biases in a dataset on political claims-making collected from newspapers, of course, since many instances of political communication and mobilization are not publicly visible. Still, it affirms that executive leaders dominate media coverage when it comes to EU affairs, and make the most claims (Koopmans 2007). The relationship between opportunities and claims-making would look curvilinear if plotted on a graph: there is very little claims-making from those collective actors who have insufficient material and non-material resources, nor from those that do not mobilize 'because their position is considered the legitimate orthodoxy' (Guiraudon and Statham 2002).

The results of this kind of survey are mainly descriptive. In my principal field of interest – immigration – there has been a Europeanization of claims-making over time, mainly through a European framing of the issue either on instrumental or normative grounds by national actors. Cross-border debates have also been fed by issues such as the Sangatte camp near Calais, which created tensions between France and the United Kingdom, or the deaths of Chinese migrants in a truck in Dover, which forced national leaders to respond during an EU summit.

A number of large comparative research projects on the European public sphere, most of which involve media content analysis, have been conducted or are under way (pioneers include Holli *et al.* 2000 and de Vrees 2001). This is the case with the project that studied the Europeanization of newspapers in Bremen (Wessler *et al.* 2008) and 'Transnational public sphere and the structuration of political communication in Europe' at the Humboldt University, Berlin (Trenz 2004). Others are still ongoing, such as the RECON project (Reconstituting Democracy in the European Union), coordinated by ARENA, the Centre for European Studies at the University of Oslo.

Large-scale studies such as these identify key trends that qualitative studies on, for example, EU journalism, can then explore further. For example, Baisnée's (2007a, 2007b) ethnographic study of Brussels correspondents and unsuccessful attempts at European media ventures such as Euronews (Baisnée and Marchetti 2000) explains why a 'European public sphere' does not exist (if it ever did at the national level), in spite of generous EU Commission funding to make it happen. His research highlights the historical development of the role of EU correspondents from the early days when Brussels attracted many 'federalists', to today's situation where journalists are socially embedded in Brussels' 'Euroelite' circles and dependent on EU institutional sources and insider old timers. In this way, he shows why EU coverage remains a hard sell in national newspapers, regardless of the importance of EU policy decisions: Brussels correspondents are cut off from national journalistic circles and connections. Of course, this does not preclude attempts at developing transnational or horizontal 'public spheres', but it does suggest why it has been so problematic. In this work and other media studies, there are also stories that explain why quite a number of European newspapers have almost made it to the news stand, but failed, or only survived for a few issues (see, for instance, Neveu 2004). As this shows, the trials and tribulations of journalists with a European project tell us a lot about media production and reception in general and about how 'Europe' is perceived by the broader industry. The EUROPUB studies show that there is increasing contention directed at the EU, but also underline that the national media rarely cover Europe. In short, it just does not sell. And even the highbrow newspapers rarely engage with debates in other countries (Vetters *et al.* 2009; see also Favell and Zimmermann 2010 for a thorough discussion of the literature, as well as Trenz, Chapter 9 in this volume).

While comparative datasets of claims-making are useful to validate or falsify general hypotheses about the direction, extent and forms of the Europeanization of contention, it does not tell us much about causal mechanisms and the dynamics at work within the Europeanization process. This is why it is important to complement such data analysis with a qualitative research strategy, where one might observe actors *in situ*, putting a human face on the process. Enough of the 'bird's-eye view' of the EU (Guiraudon 2006), then; it is time to be a fly on the wall!

Operationalization 2: a qualitative study of EU immigration and race politics

As in the chapters on EU politics and policies by Niilo Kauppi and Frédéric Mérand that follow in this volume, I here now borrow Pierre Bourdieu's concept of 'field' (Bourdieu 1981). This notion is particularly useful in a heuristic sense in order to explain the emergence of transnational political spaces (see Bigo 1994 and Mérand 2010 for concurring views). I use the concept as Neil Fligstein has done, as a general theoretical tool to describe a meso-level social order (Fligstein 2008, and in this volume). It helps me understand the emergence and functioning of relatively autonomous settings of social relations as well as the positions of the agents therein. As Fligstein put it in a recent interview: 'With field theory, you come back to what do human beings do and how they make collective action happen' (Denier 2010: 61).

So is there a European field of immigration? When and how did it emerge? Who are the players and what are the rules of the game? Who? When? What? How? And why? Just in reading the research question, it is clear that the approach is historical in nature: it involves going back to a period prior to Europeanization, at the genesis of the process, to identify failed and successful attempts at scale shifting (moving from the national to European level) and to determine whether there were already activists or pro-migrant interest groups before the EU had competence in this area. Second, it is also an actor-centred approach. It looks for those who are creating the organizational structures and the arguments and co-writing the rules of the game – in Bourdieu's terms, those that have 'a feel for the game', and those who fall by the wayside (Bourdieu and Wacquant 1992: 223). The field is embedded in an overarching structure of power relations but is in some way autonomous. How it becomes relatively stable and relatively closed is an important question. Political scientists would speak of 'process tracing' to study 'institutionalization'. Whatever the conceptual language, the key idea is to study dynamics over time. The last crucial element is that the approach must be comparative and multi-sited, not only to compare various fields but to situate actors to see whether they are multi-positioned;

moreover, this is a cross-national political space (Europe) and a cross-sectoral issue field (immigration). The contours of the policy area at the European level are not likely to match those pre-existing at the national level. It is precisely in this agenda-setting or defining moment that interest groups and even a handful of non-governmental actors can have an important role: they frame policy in the literal and not so literal sense of the word. By stating what the immigration issue is about, they delimit what is in and what is out, just like the frame of a painting. That is, they determine who is legitimate to take part in the debate, to voice demands, in an expert or 'pro-migrant' capacity. This will have repercussions on the types of countries and structures that collective actors come from, as not all will somehow fit the frame.

The existing literature on the politics of immigration in Europe gives us further clues. In 1994, sociologist Yasemin Soysal argued in *Limits of Citizenship* that international organizations and transnational actors diffuse 'postnational norms', that is, new understandings of 'belonging', of participation in the polity and rights that are de-linking citizenship and nationality. Her thought-provoking argument launched many further studies, and although it has been challenged by later sociological studies that failed to find any evidence of post-national frames in national claims-making (Koopmans and Statham 2003), her work spurred interest in the capacity of supranational institutions such as the EU, as well as, in a more limited way, the Council of Europe and the European Court of Human Rights in Strasbourg.

In this line of work, I and a number of other connected researchers started investigating what was in fact happening in Brussels. At one point, we joked that there were more researchers than either collective actors or even informants in Brussels! In the same building there could be several NGOs listed but in fact the same person answered all the bells. The fact that the organizations were small was not necessarily a sign of weakness; the fact that they are still few showed there was a monopolistic logic in Brussels, where NGOs can act as gatekeepers for national collective actors and where the Commission likes to have a single interlocutor. The fieldwork undertaken by these researchers consisted first of all in interviewing collective actors and informants in Brussels, and later extended to institutional and collective actors at the national level (see for example Monteforte 2008). As I found out, over time 'observation' increasingly became 'participant observation', as I would also be invited as an 'expert' in the field among 'practitioners', which in turn was useful to understand the relations between different institutions and organizations. Of course, I also analyzed the material provided in the campaigns of the NGOs to determine the type of framing strategies that they adopted. I also studied them over a rather long period of time, which gave me the opportunity to see if there were any entries and exits in the field, and also to see how actors adapted to the evolving institutional context, comparing the strategies adopted before each important constitutional moment (such as treaty revisions) and observing successes and failure in such agenda-setting.

In the immigration field, Favell (1998) argued that to mobilize in the EU context required the knowledge of local Brussels norms and practices, known as *habitus* in Bourdieu's theory, which only certain actors had. This was the case for NGO activists who could mobilize expert networks and make alliances with Commission insiders. Concomitant research (Geddes 2000; Guiraudon 2001) also emphasized the success of initiatives by lobby-like structures whose EU know-how included interpersonal relations with the members of relevant Directorates General such as Employment and Social Affairs, the knowledge of emerging agendas that they could exploit to carve out a space for new policy issues, and more generally a knowledge of EU law and institutional dynamics.

This was particularly the case with the Migration Policy Group, which mobilized a handful of Anglo-Dutch lawyer–activists who combined a strong commitment to anti-discrimination legislation with a high level of EU-related technical know-how. They coordinated the Starting Line Group, founded in 1992, which asked for the inclusion of an anti-discrimination article in the Treaty, a successful campaign which saw the final Article 13 greatly resembling their original proposal, with the EU institutions rallying in favour and not just their 300 key signatories. Their success is explained not only by their organizational structure but also by the fact that they drew from EC legal resources surrounding market integration, which provided the principles of non-discrimination and equal treatment and called for provisions located in the EU's core first pillar (the single market principles). They argued that the absence of anti-discrimination provisions impeded the operation of the single market by, for instance, acting as a barrier to movement by people of immigrant and ethnic minority origin who feared racial discrimination when exercising EU rights. They also linked their proposal to the 'social exclusion' policy frame that was developing in the early 1990s (Geddes 2000). This particular frame was more successful than the 'citizenship' frame that more bottom-up migrant organizations, brought together as the EU Migrants' Forum, were using. This meant that policy in fact could not be elaborated by the beneficiaries of the policy – the migrant communities themselves – because they did not have the resources of the better placed elite actors in Brussels, and their base organizations remained state-centred and not tailored to the EU institutional field (Guiraudon 2001).

Even when successful, Brussels 'think and do tanks' organizations have no real social or organizational base that they can activate at the national level when seeking to socialize actors into a new and imported policy model. Their success at the Euro-level thus does not imply an easy implementation of the EU law based on Article 13. Shifting competence to the EU and seizing upon EU legal opportunities involves different actors who have never before come into contact with other key players at the national level. For example, in France, SOS Racisme, a large NGO that has launched testing strategies in the area of race/ethnicity, and is involved in anti-discrimination case law, never attended Brussels meetings of the Starting Line Group. They considered it irrelevant, given their media-friendly repertoire of action (Geddes and Guiraudon 2003). After plotting the policy process in Brussels, the research agenda thus calls now for a wider focus on whether NGOs and trade unions are in fact mobilizing EU norms at the domestic level. This calls for a next step in the research design. In the next section, then, we discuss an interesting precedent that will serve as a comparison to validate our findings: gender equality.

Operationalization 3: bringing in gender politics as a comparative control case

Given what I have learnt from my research on the Europeanization or lack thereof of mobilization on immigration and race, can I gain further confidence in my results by extending the study to a related field such as gender equality? This calls for a comparative strategy, a close 'most similar case' that might shed light on the first case studied. Gender equality differs, though, in that it is an area where scholars have more hindsight than in the case of immigration and race: it can tell us a lot more about the ways that movements have or have not mobilized EU gender equality laws at the national level, or have sought to change them with the example of 'mainstreaming'. The gender equality field, with its power battles, cleavages and struggles over the meaning of gender and equality itself makes it particularly interesting. How do national feminist groups position themselves in relation to EU policy? Who are the key players or mediators in Brussels? What types of resources – in particular non-material ones such as expertise – are mobilized at the EU level?

Quite a few studies on gender equality in the EU have focused on EU legal norms and litigation. EC Article 119 (now Article 141) on equal pay for equal work has been in force since the Treaty of Rome; the relevant directives on gender date back to the 1970s. Yet soft norms and non-binding mechanisms such as the Open Method of Coordination may also have an impact. In fact, legal routes had been exhausted by the 1980s and EU gender equality policy was thus reframed in the 1990s, partly following global trends, with non-binding instruments put into place: what is called 'mainstreaming' and the inclusion of gender equality in the European Employment Strategy national action plans (Jacquot 2010). There are now fewer possibilities for strategic litigation after the reference to subsidiarity in the Amsterdam Treaty of 2007. There was also the legal case in 1995 (*Kalanke* v. *Freie Hansestadt Bremen* ECR [1995] I-3051) against a positive action scheme for the employment of women in a German *Land*. There have clearly been developments, though. Throughout these evolutions, the role of feminist insiders (known by scholars of state feminism as 'femocrats'), the women's movement, and Brussels-based lobbies have been scrutinized (Hoskyns 1996). Scholars have identified what Alison Woodward (2004) has called a 'velvet triangle': informal relationships between policy makers, social movement organizations and academics in the field of equal opportunities. This is an example of the importance of expertise and insider contacts in EU lobbying, just as in the immigration case. The informal network exists alongside a more unwieldy social movement organization, the European Women's Lobby, founded in 1990. The latter now federates over 2,000 national women's platforms and NGOs. Although it can be efficient at certain times, such as intergovernmental conferences prior to treaty revisions during which 'multilevel action coordination' is needed (Helferrich and Kolb 2001), it has been slow at other critical moments, such as EU eastern enlargement. It is interesting to compare this organization with the failed EU Migrants' Forum, which no longer exists, and the newer European Network against Racism.

While EU equality norms were written into the original Treaty to protect French economic interests (the relatively decent wages of women in the now defunct French textile industry), some women's groups have used these norms strategically. EU norms can be construed as way of overcoming challenges at home in a way reminiscent of the 'boomerang' metaphor in Keck and Sikkink's (1998) book on transnational contention, which documents the way resource-poor groups use international organizations against their own government. To be successful, though, this requires a tradition of strategic litigation, which is not widespread in Europe. Most academic articles have focused on an emblematic case where change occurred: the United Kingdom (Alter and Vargas 2000). The main puzzle, though, seems to be to explain resistance to change or inertia in most member states. The staying power of shared understandings and their filtering role in the face of exogenous change from the outside should not be underestimated. EU legislation always goes through national cognitive filters. Notably, Ostner and Lewis (1995) have argued that gender equality does not have the same meaning in different national settings, ranging from equality as sameness to equality of difference. Similarly, the idea of the family and the organization of work differ. Gender relations may even be so internalized that people unintentionally use certain gendered concepts like equality (Giddens 1984).

Notwithstanding, for gender studies scholars who focus on the EU, a key aspect of feminist struggles has been continuous debates over the actual meaning of gender equality, a meaning which varies, as political actors 'strategically' stretch, shrink or bend it to fit the particular institutional setting, policy frame or political mood (Lombardo *et al.* 2009). For instance, when the proposal for a treaty article on discrimination was discussed among NGOs, women's groups including the European Women's Lobby were keen to state that they were not a minority or a group but in fact more than half of the population. They did not want to have their cause diluted. Framing strategies generally serve to navigate institutional constraints. This question thus brings us to classical works in sociology on 'framing' as a way of understanding the world and rationalizing experience (Goffmann 1974); it is a crucial aspect of mobilization (Snow and Bedford 1988; Bedford and Snow 2000). In fact, ongoing research projects using frame analysis examine how EU policies are appropriated or 'domesticated' by civil society actors. They compare member states where the history of the women's movements and their relationship with the state differ (for example, the QUING project headed by Mieke Verloo in Madrid on Quality in Gender+Equality Policies).

To recap the comparative point briefly. There is an added value here in studying gender in the same way that immigration and race were studied: coupling comparative studies that document claims-making over a sufficient period of time with interviews and observation that reconstitute and analyze the characteristics of the European gender equality field, in particular the trajectories of key individual actors, relations with insiders within EU institutions, and informal networks. All this is easier to grasp with a qualitative methodology. Gender also brings its own perspective. There is a strong emphasis on the role of discourse analysis, and it is a particular policy case, given the already important presence of strategic litigation in the field. The final stage of the project would be not just to compare mobilization on immigration and race and mobilization on gender but to see how the fields overlap and networks interact if at all. 'Intersectionality' between race (or ethnicity) and gender was at best a pious vow but never a priority for European gender equality NGO actors. Changes in the context now make alliances between pro-migrant groups and women's groups more necessary, but still not necessarily easy (Woodward 2007). The situation constitutes an occasion to study cross-sectoral coalitions and the reframing that it entails. In brief, as always, there is still work to do.

Conclusion

The European Union – and more broadly European supranational organizations, which includes the Council of Europe and its Court of Human Rights – constitute a unique regional setting in which to test the literature on global protest, transnational social movements, and lobbying that targets international organizations. The thick web of institutions built in Europe in the post-war era allows us to observe and analyze the development of various forms of mobilization, from small NGOs to advocacy umbrella organizations and trades unions, and repertoires of action, from strategic litigation to lobbying and violent protest. This can be done in a variety of policy sectors and countries.

Scholars can thus compare how organized public or private interests at the national or local level incorporate this new level of regulation in their strategies, and test various hypotheses regarding the resources necessary to even think about 'going European', whether the unit of analysis is an individual or an organization. Given that European countries have different traditions of mobilization, languages, configurations of state–society relations, the EU is like a small-scale version of transnational collective action.

It is thus a pity that sociologists, along with some political scientists, are often caught in national cognitive maps (and research funding schemes) that were late to shift to studying the EU. There is thus still much to explore with regard to the dynamics of multilevel contention in Europe and the challenges that actors must face: building cross-border networks, allocating resources across levels of government, adjusting issue definition and frames both horizontally and vertically to fit the same goal.

In this chapter, I have highlighted some research questions, and shown how in two sectors, immigration/race and gender, the Europeanization of mobilization could be studied. There are some features in the research design adopted that could be useful for further research. First, Europeanization cannot be studied in isolation. The research question and design must take into account other processes, such as globalization, and distinguish their respective effects. Second, turning this around, there is a need to explore 'effects of Europe' at different levels from the global to the national and local. For a global INGO such as Amnesty International, the EU is a possible partner in promoting human rights using its trade power, or a target to criticize; either way it requires a special Brussels bureau. For a local NGO, the EU may be a source of funding and legitimacy. For a national movement, it may just be a nuisance because new EU competence requires an investment in expertise and personnel, a change in action repertoires, costs that are inevitable yet with uncertain benefits.

Lastly, I would make a simple point about research design and methods. I have shown it is important to zoom in on the 'microcosm' that is Brussels and study with a microscope the members of transnational advocacy networks that in the end play a key role in shifting the scale of contention. Yet one also needs a hovering satellite: ethnographers also need a GPS in this complex multilevel political space, just as activists keep in touch through Indymedia or other websites. Big surveys are thus also necessary to grasp the full picture and compare what is happening cross-time, cross-policy domain and cross-country. In brief, the use of mixed methods and a comparative approach seem necessary to capture the complexity of phenomena that happen in various countries and policy sectors yet often hinge on the trajectories and personal networks of a few individuals.

CHAPTER 7

EU Politics

Niilo Kauppi

> **Key concepts:** fields, power, structural constructivism, domination, institutionalization, specialization, power, roles, resources, social capital, embedded agency, embodied institutions, homology, methodological nationalism, autonomization, turf wars, framing, practices, social representations, democratic deficit
>
> **Key references:** Weber, Bourdieu, Powell and Di Maggio, March and Olsen, Berger and Luckmann, Abbott, Mann, Putnam, Goffman

A block of over 500 million inhabitants, the largest single economic player in the world with 20 per cent of global imports and exports, and the most complex political system ever realized, the EU also comprises a bureaucracy of around 30,000 civil servants, a massive corpus of European law, a currency (the euro), numerous policy sectors and a complicated structure of inter-relations with historically grounded national political systems. But our understanding of EU politics – as it is conventionally described above – is mostly limited to the picture created by political scientists, economists, and legal scholars. In this picture, the EU is either a depersonalized, self-sustaining institutional complex, or – in a manner that evokes Thomas Carlyle's 'great man' theory – a battle-ground of super-individuals, such as Nicolas Sarkozy and Angela Merkel, manipulating everything from on high. What is missing from our understanding of the EU is a human dimension. A sociological account makes clear what should be self-evident: the EU does not do anything by itself; it is people as everyday political agents who make the EU happen. To understand the EU as a distinctive form of social organization and power structure, its influence and the effects of its policies, one has get inside the politics to know who the individuals and groups making up the EU are, where they come from, what kinds of resources and networks they have access to, how they perceive their roles, the institutions in which they work and, more broadly, the social world around them. This is what a sociological approach to EU politics is all about.

In this chapter, I will therefore discuss some of the intellectual tools that sociology can mobilize in the analysis of European Union (EU) politics, and then follow with a presentation of empirical sociological work that has pursued these issues. To illustrate this approach to EU politics, I concentrate on the European Parliament, the most democratic European institution, composed of 785 members directly elected from the current 27 EU member states. I will contrast what a sociological approach to this institution can tell us with other more familiar approaches in EU studies, so as to show its added value.

Fields and power

As this volume amply illustrates, the process of European Union provides a variety of new objects of analysis for sociologists working on political issues as well as for political scientists with a sociological bent. A sociological approach to EU politics should be interested in the specifically *social* factors that influence and shape these politics. This can be studied at the level of the individual and the social group, and in terms of what I will refer to as *fields* of action. A *field* is the social space which structures and orientates the individual actions and interpersonal struggles that make up society. *Fields* are thus, like maps, analytically specifiable *constructed* spaces consisting of familiar objects such as institutions and social groups, social practices and cultural conventions, rather than roads and towns or oceans and mountains. I take a slightly different approach to the most famous version of the concept – that is Pierre Bourdieu's conception of the field, with its roots in the theory of the structural linguist Ferdinand de Saussure. In this conception, the value of a field's elements is dependent solely on its internal structures (see also Martin 2003 and Sallaz 2006 for discussion). In contrast, the interpretation developed here comes closer in some respects to Max Weber's (1922) action-oriented idea of value spheres (see Kauppi 2000 and 2005 for a fuller discussion).

EU politics is thus conceived as social action that takes place in relation to historically evolving fields of *power* that include symbolic and material elements such as EU institutions, various groups and individuals, social representations and public policies. In the sociological approach developed here, the link between individual and politics is never direct. Individuals are always members of various groups and enact various social roles, both inside and outside politics. Furthermore, individual action is conditioned and channelled by various institutions such as elections, political parties, parliaments, and so on – a point also made in the well known sociological institutionalist approaches of March and Olsen (1984) and DiMaggio (1988). Agents can be individuals, groups or even organizations and institutions (Mayntz and Scharpf 2001). All fields of action that encompasses individuals, groups, organizations and institutions involve political aspects. The political field proper is formed of all the individuals, institutions and procedures that regulate politics in the traditional sense of the term.

Engaged in action in the world, individuals and groups mobilize available resources in their struggle for power. Following a classical definition by Max Weber, power is the ability of an agent to realize his or her will even against the will of others. This can be done through a variety of means: physical force, charisma, persuasion, blackmail, guilty conscience and so on. Power limits and empowers (on this, see Elias 1982, Foucault 1990 and Lukes 2005), not just individually but also collectively. Agents' scope of action is always constrained by a variety of social, economical, technological and other factors. Through empowerment individuals and groups, and even weaker ones in some circumstances, can influence and even transform reality. A sociological approach helps highlight the central role of power structures that keep the EU together by analyzing individual and group action. Some groups wield more power than others and rely on a variety of social resources and institutionalized processes – such as, for example, professionalization – to protect their status and increase their power. The macro-level process of European integration is conditioned by a myriad of field level struggles for power and influence.

Instead of a theory in the traditional sense of the term, the sociological approach developed here serves as a heuristic device or thinking tool by which the scholar can mentally construct a simplified object of research. Here it follows a method characteristic of structuralist or (more precisely) *structural constructivist* approaches (Lévi-Strauss 1963; Bourdieu 1989). As a tool of reflection, this device enables the scholar to analyze in a structured manner the phenomenon under scrutiny, in this case EU politics (see Kauppi 2005 for a more thorough analysis). To illustrate this, and drawing on my own studies of the European Parliament, we might divide the *space* of EU politics under scrutiny along two salient dimensions: executive power/legislative power and supranational/national. This would give the simplified 2 x 2 representation of the field shown in Figure 7.1.

The 2 x 2 representation of a field is a classic device in structural constructivist approaches. In it, both axes can be interpreted as representing characteristics of individuals, groups or institutions as well as power strategies and resources. In the case of the evolving European political field they represent different types of political resources at agents' disposal: these lie along the executive-legislative axis (axis A) and/or the European-national axis (axis B).

EU Politics

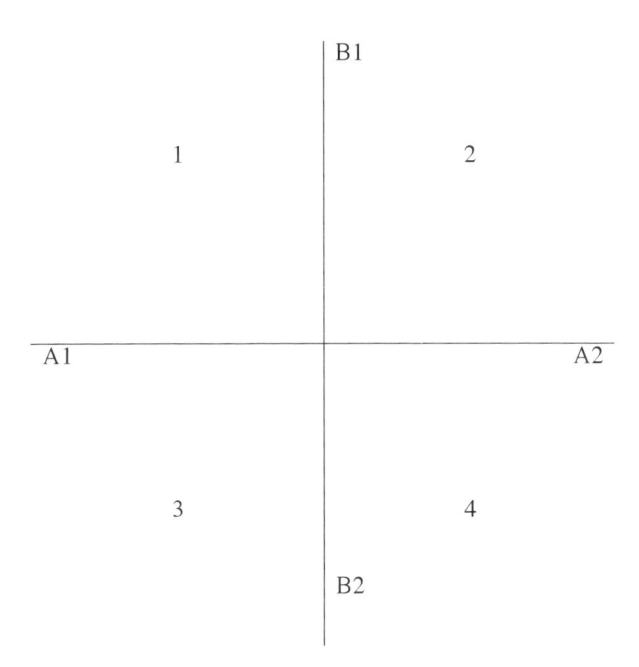

```
                    │ B1
                    │
         1          │        2
                    │
                    │
                    │
─────────────────────────────────────────
A1                  │                  A2
                    │
                    │
         3          │        4
                    │
                    │ B2
                    │
```

Figure 7.1 Political space as field

Groups and individuals situated close to A1 would have at their disposal executive resources while those closer to A2 would have at their disposal legislative resources. Similarly, those closer to B1 would have at their disposal European sources of power whereas those closer to B2 would have national resources. Cross-referencing these positions, group 1 (upper left box) would be composed of individuals with a lot of European executive resources, group 2 of those with European legislative resources, group 3 with national executive resources and group 4 with national legislative resources. These group features can then be correlated with other characteristics that might determine where political agents lie within the typology, such as nationality, gender, education, political activities and so on. For instance, those with considerable European executive resources are empirically more likely to be men than women, at least in most political fields. This same formal heuristic device (dimensions A1–A2 and B1–B2) can in fact be applied to any research topic in sociology (see for instance Kauppi 1994 and 1996a for analysis of French political and intellectual radicalism in the 1950s and 1960s). Analysis of correlations and correspondence between various social variables provide the statistical extension of this heuristic device (see Bourdieu 1984 for a sophisticated application, and Le Roux and Rouanec 2004 for further elaborations).

The European Union constitutes a kind of 'superfield' that is composed of a variety of smaller-scale, relatively autonomous fields of action such as national political fields (the French political field, the Finnish political field, and so on), institutional fields such as the European Commission and the European Parliament, and specialized sectors of public policies (for instance defence, transport or social policy). For instance, still largely nationalized policy sectors such as social policy will be located in sectors 3 and 4 while highly Europeanized policy sectors such as competition policy would be situated in sector 1. Policy sectors also correlate with decision-making modalities (the Communitarian method, the Open Method of Coordination, etc.). Each field of political action is comprised of individuals, groups, institutions, procedures, local knowledge and policies. In Bourdieusian terms, some elements are dominant while others are dominated. That is, certain institutions, policies or assets will have more value and carry more power than others. This complex architecture evolves and is variably structured: some fields such as competition policy or institutional locations such as certain Directorates General are more structured, others less so. Perhaps the key characteristic of the EU as a social organization is its permanent transformation. Because of its numerous phases of deepening and expansion, it is in fact a good social laboratory for the analysis of institutional change. In the following, institutions such as the European Parliament are thus analyzed as fields of action in which politicians are integrated.

Roles and resources

One of the key aspects of a sociological approach to EU politics is that it seeks to link politics to broader social and cultural factors and processes – at the level of the individual, the group and the various fields of action. The object of a sociology of the EU is thus not the EU or its political institutions as such, but rather the individuals as part of collectivities and social groups who make up the EU and the interaction between agents and, more broadly, the local worlds in which they live. Certain sociological concepts link all these levels (individual–group–organization–institution–field) to one another, forming a prism through which EU politics can be analyzed. In this, *institutionalization* (Berger and Luckmann 1966) and *specialization* (or professionalization: see Abbott 1988) are key terms.

Institutionalization refers to the establishment of customs, practices and patterns of social interaction. Specialization refers to the fact that society is becoming more complex and requires that individuals specialize in certain tasks through the creation of new professions such as those of Member of the European Parliament (MEP) or European Commissioner. Institutional *role* is another key concept. A role refers to the identity an individual has to acquire to be a competent agent (Gerth and Mills 1954). For instance, a French politician who is nominated to the post of European Commissioner in Brussels has to learn a new role that carries with it certain obligations and rights such as those of representing the EU and not France (for a recent analysis, see Egeberg 2006). In this case, the institution in question imposes certain values on the individual.

To simplify a great deal, it is not the person that creates the institution, but the institution that creates the person. However, if the institutional role in question is a new one, for instance a newly created Commissioner's post in charge of a new policy area, the individual creating the post (its first occupant) might have significant influence on the definition of the role in question. In that case, the social characteristics of the individual can also have effects on the form the institutional role takes. If, on the contrary, the institutional role is already strongly codified (institutionally regulated), individual influence is more modest. Seen this way, the formation of institutional roles is a key element in the broader process of socialization of individuals, of learning to act in a competent manner, and more broadly of the institutionalization of policy sectors. Certain institutional roles will be included in the policy sector and others excluded. Institutionalization involves the construction of roles and of organizational structures (for a general presentation, see Powell and DiMaggio 1991) and procedures that regulate action and distribute power and knowledge.

A further key sociological concept is that of social resource; through this concept we can link individual action to broader social structures. Political power can thus be analyzed through the social resources agents have access to. By social resources I mean any kind of socially valued symbolic entities that can legitimately be used to influence outcomes in a specific field of action. Economic resources of this kind include money and other financial means; physical resources include qualities such as strength and beauty (or their lack as in the case of a handicap); cultural resources, education and knowledge; political resources, political recognition, legitimacy and other means of influencing political outcomes (such as running for political office, voting, donating money, or writing letters to decision makers). Central questions in the analysis of social resources (see, for example, Bourdieu and Wacquant 1992; Imig and Tarrow 2001; Mann 1986) concern their accumulation (how does one get more resources?), their conversion (how does one use economic resources to get political resources?), and usage (how does one use economic resources in politics?).

Social resources vary as to their level of tangibility and generality. Material or tangible resources can be stocked and reused as such or converted into other resources. Material resources can include, for instance, financial resources such as money and stocks, or educational resources such as diplomas. Although their value fluctuates to some extent according to context, these objectified resources (that is, they are externalized and separated from individuals) are relatively stable. They can be transported from one context to another without them losing their value, in the same way that a euro is a euro in Europe or in the US. At the other end of the spectrum of resources, symbolic resources such as political resources are, more than material social resources, based on social recognition. They are intangible and thus more unstable, requiring from their users action that sustains their value. The often discussed notion of *social capital* – that is the social resources enabled by relations of trust and durable interpersonal connections and recognition – require constant upkeep and usage. They are also more bound to certain social configurations. A German politician might have a lot of social capital in Berlin but this social capital might have little value in Brussels. Unlike physical objects and their usage (usage equals depreciation in value), symbolic objects require usage and recognition (usage equals increase in value). More recognition equals more symbolic credit, which equals more potential for action for the individual having access to the resource in question. Political elections, for instance, are a way to acquire political resources. But the winning candidate has to use the symbolic credit that has been attributed to him or her, otherwise its value will depreciate.

Individual usage of resources is not enough by itself because action never takes place in a social vacuum but rather in socially structured fields of action. This might be referred to as *embedded agency*. Reproducing resources horizontally (across various fields where the individual occupies positions) and vertically (for instance, transmitting resources to one's offspring) requires collective action and work. For instance, money as a form of resource that is relatively easily transported, transmitted and reused might owe its high value as a type of resource to the fact that it is universally recognized and taken by all competent individuals as a legitimate form of power. Because it is the 'bond of all bonds' (Marx 2000) it can be used as such in more specialized fields of action like politics, transmitted to other individuals or converted into other resources (such as time, contacts, services). But this form of resource is, of course, exceptional in its convertibility.

Apart from their degree of materiality, social resources can also be distinguished from one another in terms of their generality. More generic resources such as social capital are necessary in any social configuration. Without social relationships between individuals, society would not exist. Robert Putnam (2000), for instance, distinguishes between binding and bridging types of social capital: the former resemble close group or family ties, while the latter are the 'weak ties' enabled by associations or other public networks. Unlike monetary capital, though, these forms of capital might not be very transportable out of certain contexts.

More specialized types of resources are even more particularly linked, such as European political resources linked to European political fields and their institutions: for example, the European Commission, the European Parliament, the European Court of Justice, and so on. Resources here can be collective or individual. Collective resources include those that an organization like the European Parliament offers to its members. These can be office space or facilities, but also the right to speak in its name or to mobilize others and collective resources around a project connected to it. Individual resources might have to do with physical attributes or 'gifts' for instance.

A variety of conventions control the conversion of collective resources into individual ones. For instance, educational diplomas can reinforce perceptions about individual qualities. Certain political institutions such as those represented by one individual – the European Ombudsman for instance – are prone to a mixing of collective and individual resources. In fact, the European Ombudsman is expected to use collective resources of various kinds such as representing and speaking in the name of the EU, and using taxpayers' money to travel all over the EU to promote the office of the Ombudsman, and so on. The types of social resources that interest us in this chapter are, then, relatively symbolic and intangible (they require constant action) and relatively specific (they are restricted to European fields). These relatively specialized resources are linked in multiple ways to other, specialized and generic resources.

All kinds of social groups are involved in EU-related political activities. When we study politics, we are of course primarily interested in the specialized field of action in which the politicians act politically as such. As highly sophisticated symbolic constructions, political institutions are both instruments of political power and objects of a wide range of political struggles that aim at determining the scope and nature of their policies. Because of their intangible character, they exist simultaneously in the heads of individuals and in objectified reality. But in order to access the subjective level, the sociologist needs to combine objective data (via quantitative studies of biographies, for example) and qualitative techniques, such as interviews and observation. Otherwise, the institutions will be detached from the individuals working in them, and the concrete ways institutions function will be distorted and misrepresented.

Advantages of the sociological approach

The sociological point of view developed here has several advantages compared to mainstream institutional or organizational approaches analyses of EU politics. Firstly, ethnographic fieldwork, involving interviews and participant observation of political events and rallies, can be combined with statistical analysis, while also engaging in a more general investigation of cleavage structures and structures of symbolic domination. In this way, the micro-level can be analyzed from a macro perspective and the meanings individuals give to their actions taken into account (a good example is Gaxie and Hubé 2007). For instance, individuals involved in the activities of the European Parliament apply specific symbolic structures in their social practices that, in turn, perpetuate specific power relations. Individuals operating in the same local world frame their actions in similar ways. The way people occupying positions in a field frame issues can find resonance in the way other individuals in similar positions in other fields frame other issues: something that can, after Bourdieu, be referred to as the principle of *homology*.

This principle suggests that individuals in dominant positions in different fields might find out they share certain interests with individuals in other fields because of their parallel dominant positions, a situation that would resemble an elite consensus. Another example is how, by recurring displays of open contempt toward the European Parliament and its elections, national ministers reinforce the public perception that the political influence of the European Parliament is weak. From this example, we see how certain types of political action indirectly delegitimize – that is, downplay the significance of – certain resources, in this case legislative political resources, and reinforce the elector's view of the EU as simply a battlefield of top leaders from large member states. This delegitimation then actually plays into the hands of some politicians, and allows these very same politicians with significant executive political resources to have 'common sense' and public opinion on their side. This type of common sense is confirmed every day in the European media and is even reinforced by some academic theories like intergovernmentalism (Moravcsik 1998). One side effect of these field spillovers – that is the spilling of discourses, values, instruments and practices from one field of action to another – is that, in this process, competing academic visions and political alternatives (such as those discussed by Manners 2007 and Rosamond 2000) are pushed to the background and delegitimized. Going beyond political science perspectives and the official normative rhetoric about the EU, the current sociological approach thus highlights the new career trajectories and possibilities that the changing European political field offers national political, administrative and economic elites.

A second advantage is that, in contrast to the dominant practice of political science or international relations, sociological terminology can free itself from the traditional nomenclature used in describing the European nation-state. This deals directly with the issue of *methodological nationalism* (Glick-Schiller and Wimmer 2002; Beck 2006). New insights may be enabled. The terms used here – field and resource, for instance – are analytical tools that can be applied within any area of research and any national context. This enables sociologists to develop a less state-centred approach.

Following from this, sociology takes into account not only institutional and legal structures but also, and perhaps most significantly, systems of meaning and cultural/symbolic structures (on this, see also Beauvallet 2007and Díez Medrano 2003). In this way it provides analytical tools for entering into perhaps the most difficult aspect of EU politics: the analysis of European nation-states in relation to the cultural/symbolic role of the European Union. Frequently missing in political science work that centres primarily on institutions, work that analyzes meaning structures requires qualitative analysis and a great deal of familiarity with the culture in question. The sociological approach developed thus has the advantage of combining social structural *and* cultural/symbolic structures in one analysis. The transformations induced by European integration are not only quantitative but – indeed, most importantly – qualitative. This is precisely what makes them difficult to grasp.

From this perspective, scholars have examined European institutions such as the Commission and Parliament through analysis of resources and their usage, including conversion into other resources. Here, political groups, such as Commissioners and MEPs (Members of the European Parliament), political careers, European parliamentary elections and their campaigns, and civil society (the media, intellectuals ...) are the primary objects of scrutiny. These studies have shed light, for instance, on the transformative effects of European Parliament elections in national political fields. These studies show that the value of a political investment in the European Parliament is extremely variable from one national political field to another, and from party to party.

In France, for example, small parties such as the Communist party and the extreme-right Front National have found in the European Parliament a strategy of political survival. Had the European Parliament not developed in the way it has, these parties might not exist today. Gaining a seat in the European Parliament is not only a way to secure political resources, however. For some, like political novices, a seat in the European Parliament provides a 'back door' opportunity to access national politics. In the Finnish European Parliament elections of 1999, it was seen how political novices were provided with an opportunity to convert cultural resources (such as media fame) or economic resources (especially private wealth) into political resources by buying airtime or by being prominently displayed on television. In the Finnish context, these novices linked political representation and group interests in a new, creative way. Labelling these elections as of second or third order – as is often the reflex of traditional political science (Reif and Schmitt 1980) – does not in the least clarify their political status and uses. On the contrary, it devalues and underestimates their social and political functions. Instead of disqualification, what is required is a 'phenomenological' study of European Parliament elections in different national political fields that would demonstrate the varying meanings attached to and the political usages, whether populist or elitist, made of the institution. Using the same approach in other contexts, such as the analysis of the European Commission, similar insights can be achieved.

A third advantage of the sociology argued for here is its sensitivity to the links between (to put it simply) state and society, as well as the institutional arrangements which structure power and produce forms of domination. The analysis of resources links political action to society in the broad sense of the term. In the French case, the role of social movements such as the 'Hunters' movement (Chasse-Pêche-Nature-Tradition, CNPT) for instance, and the political strategies of the French Communist Party, as they try to reinvent themselves through EU politics in a dramatically transformed political landscape, both illustrate specific uses of the European Parliament. The conceptualization of the meaning of the European Parliament and the attempts to frame this conception in the public space are determined by such strategies relying on resources. Through the analysis of European Parliament party campaigns, one sees that the links between 'Europe' as it is conceived and 'Europe' as a new political system help explain party strategies. An analysis of political praxis enables us to link micro and macro levels of analysis and to focus on political power and resources.

The Strasbourg school

Although it is not well known in the English language oriented mainstream of EU studies, a large body of work, mostly published in French, has already put into practice many of the characteristic methods and conceptualizations discussed above (for introductions, see Guiraudon 2000, Kauppi 1996b, Favell 2006). I will outline here some of the main contributions for what has become known as the Strasbourg school, as many have been produced by scholars working at or collaborating with the Center for European Political Sociology (CEPS) in Strasbourg, France. For a comprehensive survey see Georgakakis (2008).

In its endeavour to study the human dimension of EU politics, the Strasbourg school has defined new objects of study and new research questions in EU studies and mobilized a variety of quantitative and qualitative research techniques. Again, one central concern has been the statistical analysis of the characteristics of the groups involved in European politics, such as Members of the European Parliament, European civil servants and judges of the European Court of Justice. Scholars have painstakingly collected this statistical material from a variety of sources such as administrative directories and official EU almanacs (see Beauvallet 2007; Beauvallet and Michon 2009; Georgakakis and de Lassalle 2008b; Kauppi 2005). They have thus examined the influence of education, gender and political experience on political careers and group formation, in what are called prosopographic studies that reveal the structural cleavages of institutional fields. These works have shown that certain social qualifications such as degrees from elite schools like the National School of Administration (ENA) in France or ministerial political experience are necessary to make it to the top in European politics. In the Commission, moreover, structural tensions have developed between individuals with permanent positions and those with temporary ones, between those involved in highly integrated policy sectors and those in less supranational sectors, and so on. Qualitative studies based on in-depth interviews of individuals, ethnographic fieldwork and discursive analysis of historical documents have complemented quantitative analysis. They focus on the perceptions and interpretations that individuals attach to their actions and to the institutions in which they operate. They thus enrich the more numerical analysis provided by statistical analysis.

The Strasbourg school now encompasses a wide range of distinctive empirical EU studies informed by the sociological principles presented here (key examples include Beauvallet and Michon 2009; Dakowska 2009; Madsen 2006; Mangenot 2009). Beauvallet and Michon (2009) study the evolution in the social characteristics of French MEPs and especially the growing place of female MEPs in the French contingent to the European Parliament. This increasing role of women in the European Parliament is contrasted with the relative absence of women in other sectors of the French political field. Dakowska (2009) scrutinizes the role of German political foundations in the construction of European political foundations. Political entrepreneurs close to German political parties have been central in the shaping of European transnational political formations. In his study on legal integration, meanwhile, Mikael Rask Madsen (2006) shows how transnational group strategies are linked to national fields and to the positions individuals hold in these fields. Mangenot (2009) examines the institutional configurations and political strategies that led to a significant innovation in the European legal field, the creation of the European Union's Judicial Cooperation Unit, Eurojust.

The leading research question of many of these works has been the sociological analysis of the processes of *autonomization* of a space for political power that has been constructed around the EU, its institutions and public policies. Scholars examine this general process of transformation of ties of dependency *vis-à-vis* the European nation-state at different levels by mobilizing a sociological conflict model. Following this model, social fields are the sites of incessant power struggles and alliances between various social groups. The policies and political goals groups promote are best understood in relation to these ongoing struggles. More specifically, in many of these studies individual biographies are related to broader professional *turf wars* between different social groups such as representatives of national governments, lawyers, national experts or full-time civil servants in the Commission. In this process, certain types of social resources and professional definitions have succeeded in imposing themselves.

One of the most representative edited volumes of the Strasbourg school is a work on the professionalization of European groups (Georgakakis 2002). It looks at the professionalization of European Commissioners and civil servants in different policy sectors (Buchet de Neuilly, Georgakakis, Smith), as well as a variety of national or even regional agents such as representatives of regions (Costa, Lavignotte), journalists (Bastin, Lefébure and Lagneau), business managers (Davoine) and social networks revolving around educational institutions such as the College of Europe in Bruges (Schnabel). Constructed from the points of views of the individuals and groups involved, these studies show the complexity of EU integration, which is neither linear (from less integration to more integration), nor self-evident for the individuals involved. For instance, in his chapter on European Commissioners, Andy Smith relates the difficulties of becoming a Commissioner, of learning the social and institutional role. There is a relative lack of models to follow, which has considerable political consequences for the Commission as a political institution. The Commission is situated between the extremes of technical agency and political institution. While institutional structures define institutional positions in the Commission's organizational structure, social positions are embedded in the numerous social networks in which individuals participate. More idiosyncratic factors relative to the individual in question can give cues on how the role will be acted out. In other, more recent works the shift has moved from analysis of professional groups to the analysis of the characteristics of the (relatively) autonomous space itself, the structural tensions that constitute this space and shape group strategies.

In another volume edited by Hélène Michel (2006), sociologists present a sophisticated picture of lobbying and lobbyists in the EU through an analysis of the field of EU lobbying. Contrary to a widespread representation of lobbyists as a group sharing a common identity, sociologists find that their social identity remains heterogeneous and differentiated. The field of EU lobbyists is composed of two poles around which repertoires of action and practices have developed. The professional pole of the field is composed of those lobbyists with considerable economic clout and media visibility. At the opposite pole, the activists of non-governmental organizations constitute a newer group of lobbyists that has become more powerful as a result of the organization of interests opposing industrial lobbying. The field of EU lobbying is thus differentiated, with competing profiles and social roles. Another interesting finding of this sociological research is the proximity, in terms of recruitment and social attributes (in other words, in terms of education, social and cultural dispositions) of the representatives of European institutions. These people are the 'Europeans', as they are called by the locals in Brussels, and the representatives of civil society. The same individuals in fact circulate in both universes. Future research is needed to elucidate the political effects of this sociological proximity. It might constitute one of the social conditions for the detachment of the field of EU lobbying from other fields of action such as the European and national administrative fields.

Two further recent edited volumes concentrate more on European public policies. A volume on the construction of public problems deepens our understanding of the links between knowledge (that is, cognition, frames, and so on) and public policy in a fragmented European institutional field (Campana *et al.* 2007). Here, empirical studies scrutinize the processes by which public problems are constructed and transformed from instruments of objectification to social dispositions of political and administrative action. This transfer, or better, translation, is dependent on the structures of the fields in which political and administrative agendas are set. Meanwhile, the studies contained in another edited volume on the notion of governance in the EU (Georgakakis and de Lassalle 2008a) discuss the evolution of this concept through the prism of the *White Paper on European Governance* published by the European Commission in July 2001. The studies are grouped into analysis of the genesis of the European Commission's White Paper on European governance and the political uses of European governance. The uses made by various agents of the concept of governance reveal a fundamental sociological process, the structural differentiation of fields of public action, fields in which the uses of and meanings attached to 'good governance' vary a great deal. For instance in the field of development aid the European Commission makes intensive use of 'good governance' as part of a broader strategy of global governance.

Social practices in the European Parliament

I will now here present a more in-depth discussion of one specific case study, using a sociological approach, that I developed in my own work on the EU and the European Parliament (see, for instance, Kauppi 1996b, 2000, 2005, 2007, 2009) My research started in the mid-1990s from an empirical puzzle. Despite the limited political value of the European Parliament in French and (later) Finnish politics and its limited legitimacy in the European political field as a whole (Abélès 1990; Katz and Wessels 1999), it can be shown that the European Parliament has played a significant role in the transformation of the French and Finnish political fields. It has enabled dominated groups such as female politicians, regional politicians and political novices to build political careers for themselves and legitimize issues that would otherwise have been left off the political agenda. Moreover, since the first direct elections to the European Parliament in 1979, the political status of the institution has evolved from a weak institution to one that has more and more political power.

Instead of concentrating on institutional structures as most EU-related research does, I directed my empirical enquiries towards social practices, in other words, focusing more on processes than objects, on what people actually do. This approach is grounded in several considerations. Firstly, the European Union is an emerging field in which institutional structures are commonly not as strongly codified as at the level of the nation-state, even considering the partial reorganization of the latter. The analysis of individuals within the changing field thus reveals key features of the European Union (see, for instance, Ross 1994). Secondly, the analysis of social practices gives a clearer picture of the forces that keep the Union together. One can scrutinize the practical factors that explain political decisions, for instance, and more broadly, study the social mechanisms that maintain relations of power between individuals and groups. The comparison of political career patterns in the same political field over time is a case in point. By assessing different social groups' political investment in the European Parliament at the beginning of the 1980s and again at the end of the 1990s, the changing (and often implicit) value judgments that condition political action and shape the various European political institutions are revealed.

This sociological perspective focuses on framing and classification struggles, drawing on the famous work of Erving Goffman. Framing refers to the use individuals make of basic cognitive structures to represent reality. This amounts to an analysis of the 'metapolitical' level that conditions traditional political action and policy-making in the EU. A third argument for an analysis of practices is that it leads us to an understanding of how individuals – politicians, civil activists, intellectuals and bureaucrats – have negotiated the transformations the EU has brought about. At this level of analysis, the macro-level convergence of national political fields is necessarily a local phenomenon, embedded in specific national cultures, meaning structures, and institutional positions (see, for instance, Kull 2008). The opportunities and constraints created by this macro-level process directly challenge the political habits and social skills of these individuals (Fligstein 2001). Despite the fact that the European Union has become more structured as a result of nearly fifty years of integration and imposes social practices and habits on those working within its institutions, individuals still behave in manners characteristic of their national political culture and in relation to their positions in domestic political fields.

For example, politicians are faced with contradictions that they have to solve on a practical level. There are the tensions European Parliamentarians must negotiate between the imperatives of representing constituencies within the nation-state, the national interest as a whole, and the interests of the European *acquis*. More broadly speaking, the contradiction-rich circumstances generated by the EU lead to a variety of political innovations. These become only fully visible once we abandon standard institutional and normative approaches to EU politics. A fourth advantage of the processual approach is that one can analyze not just quantitative transformations, such as the evolution of the distribution of seats in the European Parliament from 1979 onward (Reif and Schmitt 1980), but more importantly, the qualitative transformations the EU has brought about. These include new institutions like the European Ombudsman, institutional roles like the High Representative for the Common Foreign and Security Policy and new social identities, for example 'European', 'federalist', and so on.

In order to reveal this underlying aspect of EU politics, studying institutional structures is not enough. We have to analyze the categories or frames that enable individuals to interpret this reality consistently. As institutions are always embodied, an analysis of social representations and perceptions can deepen our understanding of how European institutions work as part of a broader social environment that encompasses European societies (a point also made by Rumford 2002).

The general process of European political field-formation – the regional formation of a transnational and national space of power and action – induces individuals to take into account the institutional context at the European level and, through different political strategies, to adapt themselves and their immediate habitat as they move from one practical regime to another. On the one hand, individuals make use of European political resources; on the other, they take part through, for instance, the introduction of European directives, guidelines and the creation of new administrative positions, in the differentiated adaptation of EU institutions and practices to domestic political fields. For instance, for national civil servants and politicians, European careers are integrated into domestic career trajectories. European bureaucrats are not just an elite: they are an elite of national elites. In this sense, European institutions are extensions of national political and administrative fields (contrast, for example, a purely national analysis such as Suleiman and Mendras 2000).

To simplify a great deal, attainment of the post of Commissioner or MEP represents two different modes of career integration and political legitimation: the first as an avenue toward executive legitimacy, and the second as a means of legislative legitimacy (see also Mény 1996). These two types of political resources have been of increasingly uneven value in the European Union ever since the first elections to the European Parliament in 1979. While French European Commissioners have become ministerial-level politicians, French MEPs are situated at a relatively low level, between regional politicians and national deputies. From this it can be clearly deduced that experience in the European Parliament is, for the moment, a minor appendix to a politician's curriculum vitae. However, there are signs indicating that this is changing. For instance, the current Finnish foreign minister, Alexander Stubb, is a former MEP with no domestic political experience. Experience as a Commissioner, in this case, is increasingly seen as a necessary stepping-stone for an ambitious politician, enabling him or her to be classified as a 'European statesman' and integrated into supranational and global executive multilateral networks (see also Garth and Dezalay 1998; Sklair 2001; Zürn 2004).

In the French political field, for instance, political groups in executive positions utilize European posts as an extension of the domestic ministerial cabinet system, whereas other political groups use these posts as a means to enter national electoral politics through the back door provided by the European Parliament. Sociological research reveals that certain types of social resources and characteristics are necessary to make it to the top in the field of EU politics. These include social and educational resources in the form of inclusion in powerful networks such as those of the College of Europe or the National School of Administration; political resources in the form of membership of large political parties such as the Socialist party; and political experience in national governments, which can be national resources (for instance being the German candidate for a position 'reserved' for German nationals) or gender resources (although a handicap for many top positions, being a woman can be an asset in certain conditions and contexts). As in any social field, an individual is more likely to reach a position if s/he has access to certain social resources. But exceptions exist, and resources can also lose their value and lead to changes in social groups' strategies of power.

One of the difficulties with the EU is that fields change with successive waves of expansion and deepening. This is clear also in the case of the European Parliament. Since the first direct elections to the European Parliament in 1979, the Parliament has gained more power and resources. This transformation is due to both endogenous and exogenous developments. Political work inside the Parliament has become more professionalized, although unevenly so. The French representatives in the European Parliament have, in contrast to their British and German counterparts, for instance, have acquired the reputation of 'bad' Europeans for not taking their work seriously. Yet sociological research shows that professionalization has touched even the French contingent. From amateurs of European legislative representation, numerous French members of the European Parliament have become real professionals of Europe (see Beauvallet 2007). For many of them, it is not only a full-time job instead of a secondary occupation but it is also a more and more specialized job. Some MEPs specialize in environmental issues, others in issues relating to economic

Table 7.1 European Parliament, national and international (including ministerial experience and experience in other EU institutions) experience of MEPs, 1979–1994 (%)

	MEP experience	National parliamentary experience	International political experience
1979 N=81	12.3	45.7	38.3
1982 N=81	11.1	41.2	29.6
1989 N=81	31.8	27.3	53.3
1994 N=87	35.6	46.1	60.0

Source: For elaboration, see Kauppi 2005: 93.

development or transport. In this sense, career development in the European Parliament has become increasingly dependent on the specific competence MEPs can acquire in the European Parliament itself and not just on previous political experience in the French political field. Indeed, many of them do not have previous political experience. In other words, specialization and professionalization have become dependent on factors endogenous to the European Parliament as a political institution (for similar analysis of the European Commission, see Smith 2004). Table 7.1 illustrates these developments with an increase in MEPs re-elected and having political experience in EU institutions.

A European legislative elite has thus developed, an elite that is set to further the development of a transnational democracy of a new kind. This process has been simultaneous with important transformations in the European Union as an expansive political field, and more specifically in the evolving relationships between its key institutions, the European Commission, Parliament and Council. European integration deepened with the Single European Act, the treaty on the European Union and the Amsterdam Treaty. The European Union has also expanded considerably to become a polity with twenty-seven member states. The position of Parliament has strengthened. This process of empowerment has given backing to the specialization process inside the European Parliament. However, this institutionalization of the European Parliament has also been dependent on national developments in the member states of the European Union.

To illustrate this point, the European Parliament elections of 1999 played a crucial role in French political history, introducing several innovations. Despite France's foundational role in the European Communities in the 1950s, it was the first time that French political parties had to elaborate their own interpretations of issues such as a European defence policy and European taxation. Lists and parties imagined their own vision of Europe and of France's place in it. 'Europe' became an important element in the legitimation of political action. French intellectuals also got involved in this process of symbolic construction of Europe. By criticizing the Socialists and the Communists, extreme-left Trotskyist movements represented by Arlette Laguiller and Alain Krivine won seats in the European Parliament. In general, the elections empowered small political parties and voiceless anti-establishment movements to present their own versions of France's role in the European project. Some lists, such as that organized by the Communist Party, included members from outside their own organizations. The French Communist Party (PCF) included non-Party social activists of colour, for example. By elaborating the idea of double parity – single parity being the equal representation of women – the Communists moved to bring voiceless groups such as France's immigrant-origin minorities and the unemployed into the political process.

It was found that throughout these changes, while individuals perpetuate domestic structures and their inbuilt power relations, there are also innovations. Because European Parliament elections are considered less important and thus more accessible to alternative political entrepreneurs, certain French politicians, civil activists and intellectuals have used them to challenge the dominant political values of their national political field. Political parties and lists constructed their own image of what Europe should be, and in the process questioned the official, executive-level vision of the EU. Unlike the latter mainstream discourses that concentrated on a unified, republican France, several left-oriented candidates who stood in the elections constructed a vision of an alternative, more democratic Europe, where non-Christians, the unemployed, women and regional representatives would also have a public voice.

Another example can be see in the Finnish political field, where in the course of the political campaigns to the European parliament in 1999, a new type of political representative was invented. Elected diplomats are Finnish MEPs who act in the interest of the country as a whole rather than the interest of any specific political group. The cultural condition for the invention of this type of political representation is the collective sense of exteriority to Europe felt in Finland. To this can be added the political condition, which is the withdrawal (as part of a delegitimation strategy) of the top political leaders from the European Parliament election campaigns. The elected diplomat is thus chosen more on the basis of his/her cultural resources than of the traditional collective political resources a politician normally has access to.

More generally, the sociological perspective developed here enables us to give new light to the notorious issue of democratic deficit in the EU: the claim that the EU is not a democratic polity. An analysis of the democratic deficit requires close scrutiny of the concrete social representations and practices that produce it. Two factors seem to contribute to the current perception of the democratic deficit of the European Union. First, supranational executive networks have become more autonomous, reinforcing the dominance of the social resources they control in the heuristic matrix composed of the dimensions 'European–national' and 'executive–legislative'. As we have seen, these two axes socially structure EU politics and can be seen as cleavage structures conditioning individual trajectories. The problem summed up in the term 'democratic deficit' is that major political decisions are made in executive networks relatively detached from democratic control. Some of the mechanisms of this detachment have been described above. The second reason for a perception of a lack of democracy is that while the evolution of the European political field has induced convergence of institutions, practices and norms, the numerous historically more established national political fields continue to constrain this development. The European Parliament is still a (relatively) weakly valued institution. This is because, for the individuals and groups involved in EU politics, domestic political culture is still a Weberian 'iron cage' that conditions the status of European political resources and the desirability of posts in various European institutions, especially the European Commission and Parliament. Through their everyday political activities and choices in their local social orders, individuals reinforce these more general symbolic relationships of power – often without realizing it.

Conclusion

The sociological approach outlined in this chapter advances a new social theory that provides a more comprehensive description of the EU politics. We have focused on the characteristics of individuals, on institutional roles, and on the historical development of EU institutions through concepts such as institutionalization (institution building) and specialization (the development of the social division of labour). We have used the concept of *fields* – more or less structured spaces for action – in which individuals and groups struggle for power and valued resources. Through a variety of social resources such as nationality, education, political experience and gender, individuals and groups maintain and reinforce specific subjective and objective forms of political domination. In this process, certain individuals and institutions like the European Commission have accrued more power while others such as national parliaments have lost it. The sociological approach developed in this chapter presents four advantages compared to more traditional approaches. First, it links politics to the development of European societies and their national political fields through the use of historical analysis. Second, it takes individual perceptions seriously, concentrating on the embedded agency of individuals and groups, their collective identities as key elements of the EU. The objective qualities scholars attribute to political institutions are dependent on the social representations that the individuals in the field have of these same institutions. These representations shape their actions and aspirations. Third, sociology analyzes political action as strategic action in a more or less stable context. Fourth, in contrast to traditional institutional approaches, the sociological approach presented here introduces critical thinking tools that transcend European national specificities, narrow political agendas and the ideology of the European Union (Kauppi and Madsen 2007). Conflict lines go beyond official EU divisions that traditional political science has studied and legitimized.

Scholars have laid the foundation of a sociological field theory of European integration. Others are encouraged to use these insights to further develop the field dynamics of the EU that would help articulate a more complex and extended view of EU integration. A sociological agenda for research on EU politics needs to continue exploring both the subjective and objective dimensions of EU politics through deepening of broad sociological processes of institutionalization and specialization. This way a more comprehensive and sophisticated account of EU integration can be developed.

Future avenues for sociological research include the following. First, more systematic research is needed in analysis of the social attributes of European elites and the fields in which they operate. Deepening our understanding of embedded agency and what might thus be thought of as embodied institutions will shed light on the complex links between social structures and policy-making. In what conditions and how do social attributes of elites influence policy framing and decision-making? What are the links between institutional location and social networks, or between social attributes such as professional formation or dispositions and political strategies? The broader, crucial issue is the ways in which individuals, elites and ordinary European citizens contribute to the shaping of the social fields in which they operate. Second, qualitative comparative analysis is needed on group dynamics and professional structures. How have specialized groups like European Parliamentarians historically differentiated in national political fields, and how has the broader institutional field of the EU (and the relationships between the main institutions) influenced this social genesis? What forms has specialization taken in different national administrative fields where distinctive models of the professional have developed – such as the generalist in the UK, the jurist in Germany, the alumnus of the ENA in France, and so on? Third, what are the links between European policy-making and global processes? How could the relative autonomy of the EU as a field of action be sociologically assessed? Fourth, structural analysis has to be complemented with analysis of the contingent aspects of

European integration. How do unforeseen, extra-institutional events such as the fall of the Berlin wall or the current financial crisis or broader transformations such as the rise of human rights or technological innovation influence the power relationships between institutions and social groups? What kinds of groups are able to take advantage of these exogenous transformations? Last but not least, sociological research is urgently needed to untangle the complex ties between the social scientific study of EU integration and the political agendas of EU integration. In what ways has the development of research been dependent on the political agendas of national and supranational decision makers? How have broader conditions shaped sociological research on the EU and the division of labour between sociology and competing disciplines such as political science, law and economics? A sociological approach to EU politics is equipped to begin answering these questions.

Chapter 8
EU Policies

Frédéric Mérand

> **Key concepts**: constructivism, bricolage, EU policies, European defence, field, habitus, social representations, socialization, frames, practices, translation, routines, isomorphism, interpretation, reification
>
> **Key references**: March and Olson, Lévi-Strauss, Bourdieu, Mauss, Goffmann

The European Union produces a lot of public policies. Approximately a hundred EU laws (that have been called 'directives' and 'regulations') are adopted every year, to which we should add a host of other policy instruments, including strategy and framework documents, benchmarking procedures, spending programmes and joint actions. Scholars usually pay attention either to the characteristics of the process that leads to policy decisions or to their impact. It is tempting indeed to believe that EU policies are created just to solve collective EU problems. But while they may end up doing that, a sociological approach begins by asking tricky questions, such as: Who gets to define what a problem is? Aren't problems sometimes invented to fit pre-existing solutions? What, other than the ubiquitous existence of problems, leads some solutions to be sought while others are never even contemplated? Do only officials get to influence the policy process? Can we really assume that policy outcomes reflect far-sighted intentions? To answer these questions, this chapter borrows from the classical concepts and methods of sociology. More specifically, I analyze EU policies as a set of *practices* embedded in *social fields* and informed by *social representations*. It extends the efforts by Guiraudon and Kauppi in this volume to develop a distinctively sociological approach to the study of EU politics.

The chapter is organized as follows. After reviewing political science approaches to EU policies, I elaborate on a few sociological concepts, especially social fields, social representations and practices. My analysis focuses on the practice of *bricolage* as a useful way of understanding EU policy-making. I will illustrate the usefulness of these concepts with a case study based on my own research on the European security and defence policy (ESDP). It should become clear that the focus on social fields, social representations and practices also has important methodological implications for the study of EU policies and politics more generally.

Political science approaches to EU policies

An EU policy is any action led by an EU authority, alone or in cooperation with other public and private actors, which is justified in terms of solving a collective problem. This action can take the form of lawmaking, regulation, public spending, creating a new organizational body, making personnel available to provide a service to the people, or simply engaging in a speech act on behalf of the EU. A typology of EU policies is given in Figure 8.1.

Giandomenico Majone (1996) has called the EU a *regulatory state*. By that he means that Brussels shapes the lives of Europeans more through rules, norms and legal decisions than through budgetary or fiscal means. In other words, the relatively cheap environmental or visa policies affect more people than the EU's big budget items, such as the Common Agricultural Policy (CAP) or regional policy. Indeed, the EU decides on many policies it does not pay for. The CAP notwithstanding, the European Commission has access to a relatively small budget of approximately 120 billion Euros, which is a bit over 1 per cent of the EU's Gross Domestic Product (GDP). By contrast, European states typically spend between 30 and 50 per cent of their country's GDP, mostly on welfare policy. EU personnel amount to 25,000 people – fewer than the number of municipal employees in a big city like Paris. The EU does not employ what Lipsky (1980) calls *street level bureaucrats*: most EU policies are 'transposed' in national legislation and implemented by national governments. So, rather than provide social services or spend money which it does not have, Brussels produces rules which member states are then forced (or encouraged) to implement. Some of these rules regulate behaviour, such as when they set the timeframe for the hunting season. Other rules have a distributional impact: for example, monetary policy affects the purchasing power of Europeans since it determines, by setting the Euro's interest rate, how they will finance a mortgage, what they will pay for imported goods, or the likelihood that their employer will increase their salary.

Policy analysis, mostly developed in a US context, has been widely applied to the EU in recent years, with a view to understanding how social problems

Figure 8.1 A typology of EU policies

The production of EU policies is complex because the EU, as a system of multilevel governance, is complex. Numerous actors are involved, from regional governments to transnational interest groups, from national parliamentarians to Brussels-based civil servants, who all come from different policy-making traditions. In contrast to a nation-state like France or Britain, no policy actor can claim to control the political agenda; there are several entry points depending on the nature of the problem and the availability of institutional solutions. This has led Héritier (1996) to characterize the EU's policy process as a *patchwork*. But in this patchwork we can probably distinguish three types of policy field, each with its own logic of practice.

Supranational policies where the EU has been granted a great deal of executive authority, such as monetary policy, competition, the functioning of the internal market, agriculture, or fisheries. The Commission (or the European Central Bank for monetary policy) is the main actor in these policy fields. It creates binding rules (called directives, regulations, etc.) for all of the EU. These laws, which must be approved by a majority of member states through the Council and a majority of the citizens through the European Parliament, can usually be enforced by the European Court of Justice. This is also called the 'Community method'. Here, the EU almost functions like a traditional state.

Multilevel policies where the EU has specific resources that it can bring to the table in order to influence other public actors, such as in the areas of regional policy, industrial policy, education, or research and development. These resources usually consist of funding but they may also include the Commission's expertise or executive power. As the holder of a substantial purse, the Commission can be a key partner for member state governments, regional authorities, or private actors. This 'distributional mode' corresponds well to the image of multilevel governance, where many different actors are involved in the production of public policies.

Intergovernmental policies where, using the EU as a virtual meeting place, national governments try to coordinate or even harmonize their domestic policies, such as employment, criminal justice, defence, or fiscality. In these policy domains, the Commission or the Parliament are only two of many policy actors and the European Court of Justice (ECJ) plays a very minor role. The rules that are produced are said to belong to soft law, that is, there is no constraining mechanism to enforce them. But their increasing popularity attests to the growth of transgovernmentalism, whereby domestic governments interact constantly with each other with a view to developing common policy solutions for the EU as a whole.

become specifically EU problems (Peters 1994). Some authors study under what conditions the Commission can play an important role in bringing social problems to the fore (Pollack 1997). Others argue that the European Parliament has a 'conditional agenda setting power' (Tsebelis 1994). Domestic and EU civil servants may also help shape the agenda through their involvement in one of Brussels' 900-odd working groups, through which policy ideas percolate to the top (Christiansen and Kirchner, 2000). In fact, the literature shows that all kinds of policy entrepreneurs can seize on windows of opportunity to highlight 'their' problem or promote 'their' solution at the EU level. In that regard, the role of interest groups (Greenwood 2007), experts (Radaelli 1999), policy networks (Falkner 2000) and advocacy coalitions (Sabatier 1998), all of whom are configurations of like-minded entrepreneurs, has been well studied.

Policy analysts usually start with an idea about a problem (such as 'we need to tackle climate change' or 'we should liberalize the energy sector') that eventually made it onto the EU agenda. The presence of an item on the EU agenda can be attested through media coverage, EU summit conclusions and so on. This transition from simple idea to EU policy is traced back by looking at how specific entrepreneurs promoted the notion that 'something has to be done' in various political fora, selecting strategically the one venue where their demands are likely to have the greatest impact. If the EU appears more accommodating than national governments in this *venue shopping*, then policy entrepreneurs will converge around Brussels and push it to action (Baumgartner and Jones 1993; Guiraudon 2000). Whether the EU succeeds in producing policies, however, depends on several factors, such as the absence of *veto players* who would block any EU initiative; the ability of the Commission to forge an effective policy discourse and craft coalitions with the Parliament, national governments and private actors; and, of course, the institutional constraints set by EU treaties about whether the EU is competent or not in a particular policy domain (Tsebelis and Yataganas 2002).

When it comes to public policy, most scholars believe that radical change is more the exception than the norm. There are strong institutional constraints on the agency of policy makers. In general, the policy process is characterized by inertia. As Baumgartner and Jones (1993) argued for the US case, policy dynamics are characterized by long periods of stability ('punctuated equilibria') followed by brief critical junctures where external pressures shift the boundaries of policy-making. This seems congruent with what we observe in the EU, where inertia is strengthened by what Fritz Scharpf (1999) calls the *joint-decision trap*: there are, Scharpf argues, several veto points in the EU's complex institutional architecture, that is, several key decision makers who can easily grind the policy process to a halt.

But change is not impossible. Recently, by looking at the EU's anti-smoking and bioterrorism policies, Princen and Rhinard (2006) adapted Baumgartner and Jones's framework to understand agenda-setting dynamics in the EU. They argue that agenda-setting is shaped simultaneously by political institutions (from above) and through policy experts in working groups (from below). Some policies are more likely to be determined at the political level, for example through intergovernmental conferences, while others percolate through the mundane activities of working groups, which bring together member state officials. We can say that there is a critical juncture when the two meet on some level, often because current arrangements are perceived to have failed.

Since the 1970s, however, scholars have begun to argue that policies are not a rational response to collective problems. In fact, we should distinguish three partly autonomous streams in the decision-making process: the *problem stream*, where problems are set on the agenda; the *political stream*, where actors compete with each other over alternative ways forward; and the *policy stream*, where solutions are devised by experts on a continuous basis (Kingdon 1984). The puzzle is that these streams do not necessarily follow a logical sequence: policy makers may look for problems upon which to impose pre-existing solutions, politics may interfere with the design of a policy, and so forth. We refer to this continuous state of organizational anarchy, in which actors have a very limited understanding of the policy process, as the *garbage-can model*. For Cohen, March and Olsen (1972: 1), who coined the term, decision-making is based on 'simple trial-and-error procedures, the residue of learning from the incident of past experience, and pragmatic invention of necessity'.

The garbage can model dovetails nicely with what is known as constructivism, which argues that policy makers do not follow a logic of consequences but a logic of appropriateness (Guiraudon 2003). That is, people follow social norms and ideas more often than they calculate the consequences of their acts rationally. Not surprisingly, constructivism is the approach that has done the most to introduce sociological concepts in EU studies, importing concepts such as *framing* or *socialization*, which help explain how people promote ideas or incorporate norms (Christiansen *et al*. 2001). But constructivism has also put aside other equally important sociological notions, especially those that pertain to power structures. In what follows, I try to develop a sociological perspective on EU policies that, while remaining close to constructivism in spirit, proposes a more exhaustive framework and a more rigorous methodology. This perspective borrows from the classical sociology of Max Weber, Emile Durkheim and Marcel Mauss, but also on the more contemporary work of Claude Lévi-Strauss, Pierre Bourdieu and US based sociological institutionalists. The general idea I put forward is that sociology's distinctiveness lies in its focus on social fields, social representations and practices.

EU policy-making: a sociological approach

Social fields

In recent decades, French sociologist Pierre Bourdieu and American sociological institutionalists have argued that social action takes place in a world of social *relations*. The 'relational sociology' that they propose is based on the concept of social *field*, which is a hierarchical space of social relations centred on a specific stake, such as politics (for example, winning the election), business (dominating one's competitors), or culture (being in vogue). Every social field has rules of the game, some of which are formal, others informal (Martin 2003). In most fields, relations between social groups are scripted; the rules of social interaction are informal but it is tacitly understood that deviating from them is costly. While some relations connect people of relatively equal standing, many social relations are actually hierarchical. Race relations in a segregated society or capitalist labour markets are good examples of hierarchical fields. Social relations are also often contentious, as actors struggle to obtain valued goods (prestige, money, power, influence, etc.).

Social fields go a long way towards explaining how policy makers relate to one another. In the policy context, a social field is the pattern of social relations wherein different actors struggle for influence over the policy process. Policy analysts usually focus solely on official organizations like the Commission, national governments, and interest groups, which are bound together by formal links – the EU's organizational chart, so to speak. Although this is important, we are missing out on a lot of what is going on in the daily lives of policy actors, on their informal ties, and on the social traits that characterize them. Take the role of the ECJ. The Luxembourg court has had a tremendous impact on EU policy-making through its 'preliminary rulings', such as the famous *Van Gend en Loos*, *Costa* and *Cassis de Dijon* judgments, all of which forced member states to make their legislation compatible with EU treaties. A preliminary ruling means that a national court referred the case to the ECJ for advice before making a final judgment. But we don't really know why national courts decided to do so or why member states agreed to implement the ECJ's rulings; EU treaties would have made it relatively easy to avoid these 'obligations' (Alter 2001). From a sociological perspective, the key is to understand why European judges appeared *legitimate* to their national counterparts. To explore what legitimacy means, it is useful to know how different categories of judges are positioned *vis-à-vis* each other in the judicial field; what kind of social networks or organizational resources they can muster; what sort of symbolic authority they may derive from their experience or national origin; what is the role of law in modern societies, and so on (Vauchez 2008). This is the kind of crucial information that can we only get by studying social fields.

One important characteristic of social fields is that they generate power relations. Social fields determine the resources that policy actors have access to, be they cultural (for example, credentials, manners), social (connections), economic (budget) or political (administrative position). Sociologists, for example, have shown that in the Commission, certain educational trajectories, such as having studied in prestigious US law schools or the College of Europe in Bruges, provide one with social connections and ways of behaving that constitute a professional asset when trying to reach the top positions (Georgakakis 2008a). Similarly, the fact that a British Permanent Representative on the EU Council is the personal embodiment of the strongest military power in Europe, that he speaks 'Oxford English', and that he can rely on a competent group of Foreign Office diplomats, explains his influence in the policy process as well as the Council's rules of procedure (Mangenot 2003). Because the EU bestows authority, it is also a *field of power* in which various actors compete for political influence and prestige.

The concept of field thus forces us to be attentive to political, social and symbolic struggles. Although one may derive power from the possession of economic, social, political or cultural resources, power struggles are always a way of interpreting and engaging with the symbolic world. For example, when the Agriculture Commissioner and the Trade Commissioner bicker over agricultural subsidies in Berlaymont, the seat of the Commission, it is not just a matter of finding a rational policy proposal. The struggle is also between two profoundly different bureaucracies (Directorates General of Agriculture and of Trade), with distinctive histories, entrenched collective memories and client networks (the farmers' unions for the former and business firms for the latter), both of which are trying to defend their standing in the European field of power (Smith 2004b).

Indeed, the notion of field is much broader than this image of a Commission meeting implies. Beyond the bureaucratic politics of Brussels, we can observe all kinds of political conflicts which pit organized groups against each other in the policy process. For example, the 2006 Bolkestein directive, which the Commission proposed to liberalize the services sector in the EU, led a loose coalition of trade unions, environmental groups and left- as well as right-wing political parties to mount a large social movement, with the complicity of the media, against the Commission, business groups, and the national governments that supported the directive. All of this took place during harsh referendum campaigns on the constitutional treaty in France and the Netherlands. In this complex political clash, Western trade unions turned against Eastern unions and governing political parties campaigned against their own government (Nicolaïdis 2007). Such a conflict, which was Europe-wide but was played out differently in each country and at the EU level, did not fit the traditional cleavages of national politics. It attested to the emergence of a European field of contention around specific policies.

While political scientists define European integration as the centralization of government power in Brussels, sociologists see it as the constitution of new social fields at the European level, be they political, economic, social, or cultural. These European fields are usually not as strongly institutionalized as national ones, but they can strengthen or undermine them (Fligstein 2008; Adler-Nissen 2008). For example, some actors will use their involvement in the European field of power to bolster their position in the national field of power. This is allegedly the case with national judges, who have used the potentialities of Europe's quasi-constitutional order to strengthen their position *vis-à-vis* their own government (Cohen and Vauchez 2007). Conversely, the creation of a European field can be detrimental to some of the actors that held a privileged position in the national field but cannot make Europe work to their advantage. An illustration is provided by trade unions, which have been so far incapable of organizing themselves effectively on a European level, even though their influence on national governments is threatened by single market rules (Martin and Ross 1999). By redirecting our attention from formal decision-making rules to the social fields that surround them, we can get a better understanding of the dynamics of policy-making. Looking beyond Brussels thus improves our leverage on what goes on inside the corridors of EU institutions.

Social representations

We now know that policy makers are embedded in social fields that are much larger than the organization they work for and constrain or enable them to do certain things and not others. But what do these people *want*? Most of the research on EU policy rests on a sharp and mutually exclusive distinction between interests and ideas, which more or less corresponds to the debate between rationalists and constructivists. Policy makers either pursue their (economic) interests, it is surmised, or they follow certain ideas. Sociologists for their part doubt the meaningfulness of the interest/idea dichotomy. Is it not sufficient to assume that actors are genuinely invested and therefore *interested* in the social games they play? Ideas and interests are then two facets of the same practical attitude, or what Pierre Bourdieu (1990) calls the 'logic of practice'. Policy actors have motives, they want to 'fulfill their preferences', but the content of these preferences is determined by the rules of the game, which people internalize. Doing otherwise, for a sociologist, is like trying to explain the strategy of an ice hockey player on the rink by reference to his income or ideology.

Rather than impose abstract motives on actors (X pursues his interest while Y cares only about ideology), we may prefer to talk in terms of *social representations*, or ways in which individuals make sense of the concrete world they live in. Social representations are intimately connected to the social field, to which they give meaning. In the political field, for example, they may include the role ascribed to the state, acceptable ways of intervening in the economy, the perception of dominant political cleavages and one's position *vis-à-vis* them, etc. These worldviews are not the same in, say, the French and the British political fields. The emphasis on social representations makes sociology a natural ally of constructivism. Like constructivists, sociologists believe that symbols, ideas and norms matter. But these social representations are not free floating: as Emile Durkheim argued, they make sense only in a particular social context. Paying attention to context means that, when a Member of the European Parliament asks for fiscal harmonization, we have to try and understand where s/he is coming from: what sounds like a progressive policy for a French Green may smack of reaction and xenophobia for a former Eastern dissident, even though both formally sit on the left (Kauppi 2005).

In addition to helping understand motives, social representations provide schemes of perception and action with which actors interpret and shape their social environment. This is what Bourdieu (1990) calls *habitus*. Erving Goffman (1974) uses the term *framing* to understand how social representations in turn structure our perception of political issues, but also how one can label a political issue according to a pre-existing narrative, which then makes selling this issue as a 'problem' to the public easier (Daviter 2007). Frames can be cognitive, that is, used to interpret problems or model solutions. Calling a policy initiative 'European' does not carry the same meaning in Spain, where for historical reasons it is associated with modernity and democracy, as it does in the UK, where it is linked to undermining parliamentary sovereignty (Díez Medrano 2003). Frames can also be used strategically to justify a certain type of intervention. For instance, framing the working time directive (which limits the working week to 48 hours in the EU) as a health and safety issue allows the Commission, which has broad legitimacy in this policy domain, to intervene much more forcefully than if it were framed as a labour issue, where the Commission's authority is contested.

As Durkheim and his followers showed, social representations come from one's *socialization*. Like other individuals, policy makers have internalized 'principles of vision and division' in their childhood years, in formative experiences such as schooling, and during their career. Socialization is an ongoing process. An official's worldview, for example, may be informed by his past trajectory (for example, as a former trade unionist in Portugal) but also by his current position (as an incumbent *chef de cabinet* for the Transport Commissioner in Brussels). Some constructivist literature in EU policy studies argues that, in addition to individuals, *states* can also be socialized. So, for example, France and Germany would have 'internalized' EU norms and identities to different degrees as a result of belonging to the EU and through the process of conforming to EU directives (Risse 2001). For a sociologist, however, states are corporate entities. In contrast to human beings, they cannot act and cannot think. Thus, unlike individuals who may be socialized by the school system into specific ways of perceiving the world, it is *a priori* inconceivable that states would be socialized into anything.

In the EU context, an interesting sociological question is to examine whether Brussels-based civil servants adhere to national or to European social representations. The question is not only whether they feel more European or, say, Spanish, but whether they have adopted social representations that are peculiar to the EU political field or, on the contrary, whether they stick to views that make sense only in the Spanish context (Beyers and Trondal 2004). This can help us understand their motives and behaviour. For example, have they incorporated a transversal left/right cleavage that transcends nationality or do they frame issues through an opposition between 'new (Eastern) Europe' and 'old (Western) Europe'? Through interviews and ethnography, the sociology of EU professionals finds that, although some cleavages are emerging that are unique to the EU level, for example between liberalism and corporatism, or between the Nordic and Mediterranean political traditions, EU officials remain more national than European in their worldviews and ways of behaving (Hooghe 2002; Georgakakis 2008a; Egeberg 1999). Spanish officials working in Brussels view the world more like Spanish civil servants than like other EU officials. In other words, national social fields, in which these Brussels-based civil servants are no longer fully implicated, still have a lasting impact on the majority of them.

This is an interesting result, for it questions the possibility that European officials will ever become the equivalent of the political elite that we find in most European nations. 'Eurocrats' would not have the same cohesion, the same *esprit de corps*, the same unity of purpose that we have come to expect of government elites in nation-states (Bourdieu 1996; Shore 2000). Perhaps it should not be surprising, since these individuals come from a very wide variety of family, ethnic and class backgrounds, have attended different schools, speak different languages, are involved in separate social networks, and possess different kinds of cultural capital. But it means that, for the moment, it is probably premature to speak of a dominant European elite. Because they remain fragmented, the European political field and European social structures in general have not produced European social representations. In Bourdieu's (1990) terms, there is no European *habitus*, no common social representations and no common ways of behaving that would be unique to European officials (see also Kauppi, Chapter 7 in this volume).

Bricolage as practice

The weight of social fields and social representations explains why it is so difficult to launch new policies or modify existing ones. A social problem may exist, but whether it is perceived and acted upon depends on a variety of structural and representational hurdles. Will powerful actors notice? If a Polish-born Commission Director-General was brought up in the worldview that state intervention is bad because it smacks of Communism, it is unlikely that he will see the lack of a Europe-wide minimum wage as a problem, even though many French unionists may ask for it. A policy proposal has to 'resonate' with officials' social representations (Mérand 2006). But even supposing the DG is favourable to such regulation, will he do something about it? It is indeed likely that interest groups such as Business Europe, which are very powerful in the economic field, would do their utmost to block it, by way of lobbying, for example. Institutionally, Business Europe does not have a vote at the Economic and Financial Council; but politically and symbolically, it can do a lot of damage to a policy proposal. Paying attention to social structures and social representations allows us to avoid the voluntarist fallacy, or the mistake of believing that, barring institutional veto points, all you need is a policy entrepreneur and an opportune situation to transform an idea into a policy.

Yet despite the weight of social structures and social representations, new policies are launched every week in Brussels. So sometimes there is change. Rationalists argue that this is because smart people have figured out a way to promote their interest; constructivists believe that policy makers are more likely driven by what they think is 'right'. Sociologists, for their part, prefer to look at practices before giving an informed opinion. A practice is not what someone says s/he thinks or says s/he wants; it is what someone *does*. If we observe practices carefully enough, we see patterns emerging that tell us a great deal more than official documents, organizational rules, or self-justifications.

As Vincent Pouliot (2008) writes, 'practices are the result of inarticulate know-how that makes what is to be done self-evident or commonsensical'. The life of a policy actor, whether a minister, bureaucrat, or a lobbyist is quite routinized. Policy actors meet with stakeholders, circulate memos, draft work plans, and try to spend their budget by the end of the fiscal year. Ethnographic studies have shown that, in EU countries, government officials are developing bureaucratic practices that are increasingly alike, from Spain to Sweden (Ekengren 2002). Through doing the same things over and over again, policy makers accumulate a great deal of practical knowledge; that is, they develop a repertoire of social networks, behavioural attitudes, standard operating procedures, rules of thumb, tactics and strategies that help them cope with the practical problems they face every day.

One such regular pattern is that, while individuals tend to repeat more or less the same routines every day, they also show some creativity by virtue of accumulating a stock of practical knowledge. This practical creativity is what anthropologist Claude Lévi-Strauss (1968) calls *bricolage*. It plays an important part in the art of crafting policies. In *The Savage Mind*, Lévi-Strauss describes handymen who solve technical problems by picking up whatever resources are available around them. To build something, they try materials that work and discard other materials that don't work, following their practical sense to change the object incrementally. *Bricolage* is a sort of making do. Each step is caused by the desire to solve a local problem (such as fixing two pieces of wood together). New problems arise in the process which are also addressed by whatever comes to hand. In a process that is similar to Charles Lindblom's (1959) 'science of muddling through', these individuals eventually end up with something completely different from the rough 'problem solver' they initially had in mind, even if they had something in mind at all. *Bricolage* is the art of invention (*ars inveniendi*) within the 'reasonable' limits set by practical knowledge.

Many sociologists believe that modern individuals, including policy makers, continue to act in the 'way of the savage'. We strategize all the time, we effect change, but not with a clear design in mind. The reality described by *bricolage* is one in which policy makers respond to local organizational problems, often in haste, by drawing from a background of practical knowledge. This know-how is made up of the social representations that they have internalized over the course of their careers and before, and the feeling for what is possible in the current social structure. Getting a feel for the game, knowing the right people, seizing contingent opportunities as they arise, and having the sense of one's place are thus key to shaping policy (Bourdieu 1990). Strategic policy makers instinctively know what is feasible and what is not, that is, what will be deemed acceptable by influential social actors in the social field.

This means that the policy process does not follow a well-designed path towards a clearly identified goal. While constructivists probably give too much importance to norms, as if we couldn't get around them when we really want to, the mistake made by rationalists is to proceed backwards, to deduct a series of rational moves from the observed outcome as if each past decision was necessarily and evidently leading to this outcome. This neglects the fact that practices are often *pre-reflexive*: not clearly thought and often almost instinctive. One way of grasping this is to think of these responses as bodily dispositions: actors responding to situations as players do in a game. Also neglected is the importance of *time*: policy makers adapt their practices constantly in the policy process, reacting to new events, trying out ideas, discarding others – in other words, *bricolaging* their way through. Finally, policy actors show an incredible creativity in subverting or altering the goals of a policy instrument in the process of implementing it; policy-making involves a practice of *translation*, of giving new meaning to policies that may appear set in the stone of the Official Journal of the European Union (Jacquot and Woll 2003). This multilevel *bricolage*, however, takes place in a rigid world of social fields and social representations, which constrains what is feasible and what is not.

To illustrate this point, it is a documented fact that EU member states are adopting education, health, welfare, or intellectual property policies that are increasingly alike (Cowles *et al.* 2001). Some of these developments have to do with formal Europeanization, through the transposition of directives. But there is a great deal of policy convergence in the EU that does not involve Brussels at all; this is what Bastien Irondelle (2003) calls 'Europeanization without the European Union'. For example, universities are switching to similar curricula, armed forces are developing similar force structures, and governments are adopting similar labour market legislation with virtually no input from EU institutions. How are we to account for this? The notion of *bricolage* suggests that, faced with local organizational problems such as student mobility or labour market rigidities, policy makers tend to look around for tools, such as policies implemented in other countries that appear successful, which they try to plug into their own institutional framework. In this process, which sociological institutionalists have described as 'isomorphism' or the reproduction of organizational forms, practical strategies yield policies that are converging even though they remain different and patchy. Thus there is a great deal of policy innovation that comes from policy makers emulating each other, without a grand design, inadvertently producing Europeanization. But these strategies are refracted through domestic social structures and social representations; they are *bricolaged*, using different combinations that are layered onto each other, subverted or reoriented, which explains why Europeanization is not uniform.

To summarize this section, we can say that using a sociological lens to focus on fields, social representations and practices such as *bricolage* helps illuminate elements of the EU policy process that remain obscure to other political science approaches. It suggests that a supranational policy field does not function in the same way as an intergovernmental or a multilevel policy field, but not only because the formal rules and competences of the Commission, the Parliament and the Council differ. To be sure, the actors will not be the same: EU officials have more authority in supranational policy than in intergovernmental policy, where they have fewer political resources; non-governmental organizations may be able to deploy their social networks more efficiently in a multilevel policy field than in a supranational one. But social representations will also differ: in competition policy, neo-liberalism is the frame used by dominant actors, while when it comes to the CAP, *dirigisme* (as opposed to market forces) is a commonly

EU Policies

accepted principle of vision and division. Finally, the variety of practices must be taken into account. While the so-called Community method and the search for common interest dominate supranational policy debates, intergovernmental policies are characterized by the search for consensus and the importance attached to domestic considerations.

The case of European defence policy

With these few concepts in mind, we can now turn to the European security and defence policy (ESDP). The dream of a European military structure is as old as the EU itself. Fiercely debated but rejected in the early 1950s when it was called the European Defence Community (EDC), the project resurfaced in 1998, when Jacques Chirac and Tony Blair launched the European Defence Initiative at the Franco-British Summit of Saint-Malo. Enshrined in the 2000 Treaty of Nice, ESDP is now a decision-making structure, based in Brussels, which enables the EU to launch crisis management operations and pursue its foreign policy objectives with an array of military and civilian instruments. Europe's military ambitions have grown since 2000, culminating in EU-led military operations in Macedonia, the Congo, Bosnia, and Chad. As of the summer of 2008, there were a little under 8,000 peacekeepers deployed under EU command across the globe (see Figure 8.2). Although ESDP does not yet herald a European Army, it constitutes the most ambitious project of military integration in peacetime.

Figure 8.2   The European Security and Defence Policy

ESDP is an intergovernmental policy. The decision-making structure is located in the EU Council. Under the authority of the Council of Foreign Ministers (aka General Affairs), which functions by unanimity, a host of political-military bodies have been created: the Political and Security Committee, the Military Committee, the Military Staff, and the European Defence Agency. This structure allows the EU to deploy civilian and military crisis management operations throughout the world. In cooperation with the Commission's DG External Relations and DG Internal Market, ESDP is also meant to help the EU develop better crisis management capabilities and rationalize defence procurement. But military capabilities and the right to use them remain for the most part in the hands of national governments; the role of the Commission and the Parliament is limited and that of the Court of Justice is non-existent.

In this section, I argue that sociology provides a useful perspective on this policy. Rationalists have treated ESDP as a rational response on the part of national governments to the evolution of the security environment, while constructivists have portrayed it as resulting from the convergence of European norms on the use of force (see Howorth 2007; Mérand 2008). To show the difference a sociological approach can make, I will focus on four methodological principles that I tried to uphold in my research; they will serve to illustrate the use of concepts such as social structure, social representations, practice and *bricolage*.

Going beyond common sense

The first principle is to break with what Bourdieu (1991) calls 'the illusion of immediate knowledge'. The diplomats and military officers I studied use all kinds of concepts and categories – that is, social representations – that I needed to understand and contextualize. For example, the phrase 'national interest' is ubiquitous in the diplomatic field. When I asked diplomats why their government decided to support such and such initiative relative to ESDP, they would often respond: 'Because that was in our national interest.' Not surprisingly, many political scientists also use the national interest as an explanatory variable. They say that France supports an independent Europe because it sees it as a way to multiply its declining power while Britain is Atlanticist because it wants to nurture a special relationship with the United States. This would explain why France is strongly in favour of ESDP while Britain is not. But then the same national interest made Britain oppose European defence 15 years ago, and France 40 years ago. Surely the national interest means something to diplomats, but what exactly? And since its content has a tendency to change, can it be an explanatory variable?

This is the sort of question for which qualitative analysis is useful. Sociologists have developed tools to interpret, classify, and link discourses to structural and historical factors. Max Weber, for example, proposed that we interpret (*verstehen*) such information by constructing typologies which help us make sense of ideas that are grounded in social structures. This is one of the ways in which we can try and go beyond common sense to uncover motives and logic of people's action. One thing that quickly became clear to me in my research was that different diplomats had different understandings of what the national interest is. It turned out that when they said the European security and defence policy was in their national interest, British diplomats really meant a better *security policy*, while the French emphasized the need for stronger *defence*, and the Germans underscored *European* unity. Going back to the foreign policy history of these countries, I found out that the British had always tried to shape the European security architecture from outside while the Germans were steeped in a federalist ideology that prizes everything European. As for the French, they adhere to a political theory that draws a close connection between the existence of a polity and the need to defend it. These understandings, I argued, had more to do with social representations of the role of the state and the future of European integration than with an objective definition of the national interest.

Constructing the research object

A sociologically sound research design begins with mapping out a research object, one that is clearly delineated and produces effects that are relevant for our research question. My own question was, why was ESDP created in the late 1990s? I called the object I ended up constructing the European security and defence *field*, or the arena in which statesmen, diplomats and military leaders interact and struggle over shaping European security policies. Studying the field over a long period, roughly from 1950 to 2000, I tried to identify the dominant players, their social representations, the rules of the game – what can be done and what cannot be done – and the evolution of practices. Social fields and social representations are social facts: they are *intersubjective*, that is, they exist only insofar as social actors agree on a given set of meanings. We must define fields and representations on the basis of the social relations that we observe empirically and the analytical framework that we use. In my research, I conducted around 100 interviews with policy makers, asking them about their social relations, worldviews and practices rather than about defence policy proper.

A research object is not an artefact: both are constructs, but the former is analytically constructed on the basis of empirical observation while the latter is reified (transformed into a 'real' object) on the basis of theoretical models that bear no relation to practices. The mapping out of a social field around a meaningful practice (shaping policy) led me to believe that 'the state' was in this way often an artefact that people talked about but in fact concealed more interesting social relations. Most of the research on ESDP treats the state as if it were the only kind of actor interacting with similar ones. Although this can be acceptable as shorthand for describing a situation (for example, 'Berlin asked for new procurement rules'), we should never lose sight of the fact that the state is a historical construct, which corresponds to what Bourdieu calls a field of power, in which power holders struggle to control the enormous advantages bestowed by what Weber calls the 'monopoly over legitimate coercion'.

This cautionary knowledge was useful to me because I was trying to understand how the actors most closely associated with the formation of nation-states

– diplomats, soldiers, statesmen – had come to support a project that seeks, ironically, to transcend the nation-state. By constructing my research object differently from the way most other scholars did – that is, by focusing on social fields rather than states – I was able to show that the state is made up of different government *actors*, with different social representations and levels of influence. I tried to trace who, inside the French, British and German governments, had supported ESDP and who had opposed it, and what sorts of compromise had emerged at the executive level. I came to the conclusion that diplomats have a *foreign policy*-based approach to ESDP while defence planners have a *capability*-based approach. While defence actors push for solutions to their problems of capabilities and military interoperability, diplomats see themselves as involved in a larger game, which is to make the EU, and their countries within it, more influential in world affairs. That is why diplomats tend to favour the EU while defence planners tend to prefer NATO solutions; each provides a better fit with their perceived needs. ESDP, which combines EU and NATO elements, is a *bricolage* of these two ways of seeing the world.

Now diplomats and soldiers possess different amounts of influence in France and the United Kingdom. The French foreign ministry exerts more influence on the definition of France's ESDP position because it enjoys greater symbolic and political leverage in the domestic arena than the defence ministry, which is often sidelined in the process. Conversely, the British Foreign Office is less able to impose its European concerns in the defence policy process because it is structurally more 'equal' to the Ministry of Defence. As a result, capabilities are given more importance in Whitehall than in Paris. Characterized by conflict-ridden social relations among government officials, the European security and defence field that I mapped out is much more complex than a bargaining process between unitary states.

Taking practices seriously

Taking practices seriously, rather than imposing theoretical models on actors, involves fieldwork. In my case, fieldwork involved three techniques. First, I conducted approximately 40 semi-structured interviews, usually lasting one to two hours, with diplomats, defence policy makers and politicians in France, the UK, Germany and in Brussels. To draw up the list of interviewees, I used the *decisional method*: I scanned the roster of every government department or interest group interested in defence policy with a view to identifying decision makers and observers in France, Germany, the UK, and in EU institutions. I also used snowballing, asking interviewees to provide other names, to get a few more interviews. I used interviews to get a better sense of what policy makers did and how they thought. Of course I could not just go out and ask them,

'What are your social representations?' This is a concept that the sociologist uses but the subject does not – unless he has a PhD in sociology. But I could ask a French official, for example, 'What do you think about the British? Why? Do you meet British officials often? What would be your typical day preparing for a Franco-British summit?' On that basis I tried to reconstruct the everyday life of a typical official, which was useful for me to understand his/her practices, social relations, and worldview.

Second, I distributed 70 questionnaires to a larger group of policy actors in the same country. The questionnaire contained questions on their position *vis-à-vis* certain issues, their social relations, and their involvement in specific ESDP-related decisions. The information I gathered was not as rich as with face-to-face interviews, but it was more systematic. By ESDP actors I meant officials, academics and lobbyists, working in an organizational unit or alone, but whose primary responsibility was to deal with ESDP. In addition to the decisional method, two methods were used to identify the sample: (1) I did an in-depth study of ESDP-related conferences, seminars, summits, etc. in order to extract actors who took a stand on ESDP issues (the *positional method*); (2) I submitted the resulting list containing several hundred names to a small group of ESDP experts, who added key individuals they thought were missing, but also subtracted those they thought were too marginal to ESDP debates (the *reputational method*).

Third, I did participant observation, for example by going to seminars organized by think tanks, or attending a military academy for a month. I would have liked to do more of it but defence policy is a secretive world: we do not have access to private meetings. For the same reason, I could not tape the interviews, so I always wrote down my notes. But getting interviews proved easier than I thought: actors usually like to talk about what they do, and I experienced only very few rejections. When ethnography is possible, you can supplement your research material with discursive analysis (speeches or official documents), archival data or opinion surveys, depending on what is available. To get a better sense of how military leaders saw European defence, for example, I analyzed surveys conducted among military officers and systematically analyzed publications written by military officers (Mérand 2003).

When it comes to ethnography, two pitfalls must be avoided. The first is to think that whatever we feel or our interviewees tell us is true; this is what we call the *subjectivist bias*. The second danger is to believe that the theoretical models we reconstruct are real; this is the *objectivist bias*. In the case of ESDP, it is interesting to note that, while many scholars believe that ESDP was created for what it *does*, others think that it was created for what it *could* do. Both are functionalist arguments of sorts. For example, many commentators say that ESDP was launched to facilitate civilian–military coordination in crisis management. That is what it does today but it was in no-one's mind back in 1998; neglecting the genesis of a social field can lead us to false conclusions. Conversely, so-called realist scholars argue that ESDP was created to balance the US; although this fits their theoretical model, in which international politics hinges on the balance of power, there is not a shred of evidence that this motive makes sense for the actors involved, who in interviews rejected it with amusement. In sum, extreme subjectivism and extreme objectivism are both flawed.

To chart a middle course, we again need to pay attention to practices. In particular, decision-making is a practice that takes place in time; in this temporal process, structural conditions and motives may change. As I said, we must patiently trace back this evolution and resist the temptation to reconstruct a series of decisions from the end result. The reality is that, back in 1998, no one knew what ESDP would look like ten years later. Interviewing some of the officials who participated in the negotiations that launched ESDP, at the Saint-Malo Summit of 1998, I came to the conclusion that, although French and British diplomats had different social representations about European defence, they had shared on this occasion an equal urge to conclude a successful summit – in diplomatic language, to find a 'deliverable'. Remember that France and the UK are the two most important countries when it comes to European defence because they are the biggest military powers, with seats on the UN Security Council, and conceptually, they have often been at odds with each other; consequently, any deal by Paris and London is usually welcomed by the other capitals.

The joint declaration signed in Saint-Malo states that: 'the Union must have the capacity for autonomous action, backed up by credible military forces, the means to decide to use them, and a readiness to do so, in order to respond to international crisis'. This language was discussed until late at night during the summit. The word 'autonomous' was the most controversial. Did it mean that Europe should develop an independent decision-making structure in the area of defence, as the French hoped for? Or did it simply mean that Europe should enhance its military capabilities, as the British insisted? Thus understood, the launching of ESDP had more to do with strategies to find mutually acceptable language on the basis of an ambiguous vocabulary, the implications of which were more or less understood, than with cold calculations of interest. French and British officials were simply experimenting with ways to find a common ground which would appear as a diplomatic success. So they *bricolaged* a policy that drew on dominant social representations, placated extant power structures, and offered a way out of the deadlock. In other words, they mobilized their practical knowledge of each other.

Keeping a critical perspective

A critical eye must be applied to our research object but also to ourselves. There is a strong tendency among policy analysts to take the answers of interviewees at face value. On the contrary, answers must be cross-referenced with the social context, to the actor's position within it, to his/her social trajectory, and to possible inconsistencies between their stated self-perceptions and the social reality as it is interpreted by the external observer. For example, many of the officials I met told me that the reason why ESDP was created was to solve the Balkan crisis, which dominated the 1990s. While we should not cynically assume that interviewees are concealing the truth, we must always check their assertions against the research object we have constructed. In this case, it struck me that, while the name ESDP was invented after the Balkan war and justified as a means of solving it, the social relations, social representations and practices that characterize the European security and defence field pre-existed this conflict. So clearly there was something going on that interviewees themselves did not see, could not acknowledge, or had simply forgotten.

Conversely, keeping a critical perspective implies that we should always question the research object we have constructed. The subjectivist bias of assuming that everything people say is true should not be replaced by the objectivist bias that assumes that our 'model' is necessarily true, that we know best. For example, I found that, while diplomats seemed quite fond of EU procedures, soldiers were more attached to NATO procedures. I concluded that social representations of diplomats were largely Europeanized while those of the military were 'NATOized'. But had I met other actors whose views contradicted this typology, I would have had to reconsider it. In the event I ended up adding nuances to my argument. After all, there is always interpretation involved on our part. As the anthropologist Marcel Mauss argued, the analyst is both native and alien to the practice s/he is trying to interpret. Although we construct a research object from the outside, we cannot interpret a social practice without in one way or another taking part in it, putting oneself in the position of an actor, rationalizing the logic of practice, and absorbing dominant social representations (Mauss 1979; Turner 1994). This empiricist strategy defies easy answers and requires some work, and it also means that we can often be wrong, but the payoff is well worth it.

Conclusion

In this chapter, we have seen what kind of sociological argument can be made about policy-making in the EU. Economics and political science in particular have developed sophisticated models of policy-making. To some extent, political scientists have also incorporated insights from the sociological tradition, such as the importance of framing and socialization. A sociological approach should be able to gather these insights in a coherent framework with a distinct methodology. The one I have outlined in this chapter borrows heavily from the sociology of Lévi-Strauss, Bourdieu, Mauss, and Goffman.

To sum up, I have argued that the world of EU policy-making is made up of social fields populated with a variety of actors. Each social field has its own structure, dominant social representations, and logic of practice. As a rule, we observe that policy-making looks more like *bricolage*, whereby policy actors experiment and strategize on the basis of their practical knowledge, than a series of rational decisions leading to a clearly defined outcome. And to get a grip on these practices, there is no better way than fieldwork. I identified four principles that fieldwork must try to uphold: going beyond common sense, constructing the research object, taking practices seriously, and keeping a critical perspective.

The sociology of EU policy-making faces two challenges. The first is access to the policy makers themselves. To go beyond formal institutions, we must be able to observe concrete social practices. Without ethnography, we may end up practising a sort of armchair sociology. But it is more difficult to get accepted in the world of policy makers. Internships in Brussels would be one way of doing it but one is often limited by strict rules of confidentiality and disclosure. Some great examples of this kind of work exist, though, such as Iver Neumann's (2004) participant observation in the Norwegian foreign ministry or George Ross's (1994) one-year ethnography of Jacques Delors' cabinet. The second challenge is to show that a sociological approach can explain or illuminate elements of the policy process that mainstream, institution-focused political science cannot account for. This involves developing clearly controlled research designs and finding ways to present a sociological argument that will bring real added value to policy sciences. The present chapter has developed a way towards this goal.

CHAPTER 9

Social Theory and European Integration

Hans-Jörg Trenz

> **Key concepts:** social theory, theory of society, integration, differentiation, modernization, rationality, social sense, meaning, moral integration, *Gemeinschaft*, *Gesellschaft*, mechanical and organic solidarity, methodological nationalism, structuration, securitization, capital, field, habitus, public sphere, network society, civil society, macro-micro-meso, globalization
>
> **Key references:** Weber, Durkheim, Münch, Delanty and Rumford, Haas, Parsons, Beck, Giddens, Eisenstadt, Rokkan, Bartolini, Foucault, Bigo, Bourdieu, Habermas, Castells

---

What would be a specific way of *theorizing* the European Union that might distinguish a sociological approach from other political, legal or normative accounts of European integration? This chapter addresses the role that contemporary social theory can play in helping us rethink EU studies, by building on the Durkheimian and Weberian traditions in sociological theory. In particular, it focuses on the sociological exploration of the concept of 'integration' in our discussion of the notion of 'European integration'. The very presence of the concept integration in discussions about the building of the EU signals the need for a deeper, sociological reflection on the kinds of theory of society that must lie behind other discussions about the EU, which typically are limited either to its institutional and policy dimensions, or which focus on the EU in normative terms. The chapter thus distinguishes between two dimensions by which a sociological understanding of integration might be brought to debates on European integration.

A first way, building on Max Weber's notion of *social sense* as the basic category of sociological thinking, would be to consider the process of European Union not simply as a *useful* arrangement of governance and problem solving, but also as a distinct structure of *meaning* that guides collective expectations and constitutes new social relations. A second, that will be developed more fully, would be to build on Durkheimian conceptions of *societal integration*, conceiving the object of sociological reflection (the European Union) at a new level of abstraction, and detailing how this process both integrates and differentiates European society in new ways, something which is accelerating social change in Europe and leading to new dimensions of diversity and unity. The chapter argues that a more specifically social theory based approach to rethinking European Union can go beyond the more classically empiricist approaches presented by other chapters in this volume, notably in moving the sociological study of the EU towards an understanding of European society, better able to work at macro-, micro- and meso-levels of reflection. The chapter thus represents a conclusion to our volume, as well as an invitation to further research.

Weberian approaches in the study of the European Union

The Weberian legacy laying the foundations of a sociological approach to European integration can be thought of in a number of ways. In contrast to his contemporary Emile Durkheim – who focused more on the role of values and cultural traditions in explaining action – Max Weber was more interested in the rational aspects of social action. He was sceptical with regard to the possibilities of moral integration of society – a constant theme in Durkheim's work – and the steering of social processes through political design and education. Nevertheless, his insights are highly relevant, for example, in understanding European integration as an expansion of the logic of free markets and capitalism. Weber (1978, ch. 8), for example, shows in an exemplary way how the ever-expanding capitalism in European history needed to be tamed by state intervention and the consolidation of a legal order. In a similar way, the European Union has repeated this experience of simultaneous de-regulation and re-regulation that characterized the expanding late nineteenth-century nation-state. At the same time it has established political authority and higher levels of secularized legitimacy that go beyond the nation-state.

Weber's diagnosis of modernity also classically draws attention to the loss of individual liberties and the restricted capacities for controlling global change as modernizing processes develop. European integration can thus be seen as an expression of scientific-technical civilization and bureaucratic domination (Bach 1999), devaluing, at the same time, existing resources of meaning and tradition. In contrast to Durkheim, Weber would be more pessimistic with regard to the possibilities of restoring the moral integration of the society emerging at a larger European level. European integration would rather unfold as a more or less civilized play of power and interests. The 'social' dimension of society would be restricted to instrumental action, and the chances for the building of community as a carrier of democracy and collective self-determination would be low.

Weber's sociology is nevertheless helpful to understand the dynamic aspects of European integration as a modern form of political order that expands around a bureaucratic apparatus in constant search of legitimacy. As a legislator and public authority the European Union produces and reproduces *social sense*, which according to Weber (1978) should be considered the basic category of sociological thinking. It is this machinery for the production of knowledge and social meaning that has turned the European Union from a common market project into a much broader political and social entity. The EU has thus become committed to a *normative* project of society building, in addition to its legal/political institutional construction. There is, however, a huge discrepancy between the concern with the normative deficits of European integration – which dominate the literature – and the lack of a genuine *theory* of this new society. This, I would argue, is where sociological reflection is most lacking.

Two theorists who have pursued this sociological reflection into a comprehensive social theory of the EU are Gerard Delanty and Chris Rumford (2005). In their joint work, the Weberian insights into how social reality is created by shared knowledge and meaning is taken as a starting point to formulate a constructivist theory of European integration. In contemporary Europe, such a constructivist perspective is useful to understand the restructuring of social relations by collective actors and institutions that are embedded in the particular context of the EU. European integration can in this sense be interpreted as a process of meaning production and justification that is organized around competing conceptions of political community (ibid.:12ff.). The European Union is, in this Weberian sense, institutionalized as a new type of polity, which needs to safeguard its basic legitimacy not only through the formal rationality of its procedures but also through the loyalty of its citizens.

Durkheimian approaches in the study of the European Union

Regarding the lack of an encompassing theory of European society, the alternative to a Weberian path is, of course, the legacy of Emile Durkheim. Indeed, Durkheim's legacy may prove even more enlightening, in that his work directly tackles the processes and dynamics of societal integration as its core theme. It was he who delivered the classical account of there being two forms of societal integration: that is, two different mechanisms of fabricating the 'unity' of society – either through cultural bonds of similarity (what Durkheim referred to as 'mechanical solidarity') or through a complex division of functional tasks in society ('organic solidarity'). He also emphasized that the stability of social order is based on an equilibrium between its collectivizing and differentiating forces. European integration is, in effect, experimenting with both modes of social integration, on a territorial and political scale vastly different to the classical unit of society: the nation-state.

The Durkheimian legacy is generally not familiar in EU studies despite the frequent invocation of processes and theories of European 'integration' which evoke this core Durkheimian concept. Yet a Durkheimian logic sits at the heart of classical contributions to this discussion. When Ernst Haas (1958) in the late 1950s theorized the dynamics of European integration, his expectation was that integration would unfold through functional spillover. 'Neo-functionalism', as this early theoretical strand was labelled, is sociological precisely in the sense that it assumes a link between political integration and social integration, describing the social forces that determine societal change. It thus postulates the existence of endogenous social laws that promote the unity of Europe. European integration is, in effect, not only political, it is also consequential. It is not simply a political construction, depending on the good will and intentions of particular actors, but rather objective destiny, dictated by the laws of the social.

If neo-functionalism was ideologically inspired by the federal thinking of Jean Monnet, one step back, it was intellectually inspired by the grand social theory of Talcott Parsons. In this sociological tradition, society is conceived holistically as an internally differentiated and externally delimited social system. It is stabilized through the interchange between different sub-systems, each part contributing to the maintenance of social order: the economic system through adaptation to the environment, the political system through goal attainment, the social community through membership, and the cultural system through value attachment (Parsons 1967:3ff.). The European Union could be conceived as a social system to the extent that it provides services with regard to each of these sub-systems. Neo-functionalism could therefore postulate the emergence of a European society as a structured entity in line with the national society. The European society would evolve as a new layer in a federal model of social and political order.

In the classical definition of Ernst Haas the concept of *integration* was thus indeed used in this wide sense comprising both political and social integration. Political integration is 'the process whereby political actors in several distinct national settings are persuaded to shift their loyalties, expectations and political activities toward a new centre, whose institutions possess or demand jurisdiction over the pre-existing national states' (Haas 1958: 16). The optimism of early integration theorists referred to a societal perspective of European integration: 'The end result of a process of political integration is a new political community, superimposing over the pre-existing ones' (ibid.: 16).

Durkheim was the missing reference underlying this theoretical logic. This was something that the connection of neo-functionalism to Parsonian thinking in functionalist political and social science should have made clear, since Parsons was a theorist who essentially naturalized Durkheimian modes of thought into an American empirical sociological context. To trace back this unspoken sociological heritage of European integration theory it is thus useful to recall the basic categories that were introduced by Emile Durkheim to explain the integration of a modern, differentiated society. In Durkheim's classical work on the 'division of social labour', he in fact already postulated a spontaneous movement towards a 'European society, which has, at present, some idea of itself and the beginning of organization' (Durkheim 1984: 405). How could Durkheim already, during the peak years of European nationalism, have arrived at such a prescient conclusion?

Translated into contemporary political vocabulary, Emile Durkheim was in fact a federal thinker. He stands at the beginning of a long line of tradition of conceiving the European society in terms of a federation: as a society held together by functional necessity and shared interests and embracing several national communities under a common economic and political umbrella. This federal vision of a European society operates through the distinction between *society* (*Gesellschaft*) represented by the heterogeneity of purposive and interest-based social relationships, and *community* (*Gemeinschaft*) represented by the homogeneity of primary and more intimate social relationships (Tönnies [1887] 1963). For Durkheim community and society are linked to two different mechanisms of social integration: one based on the primordial bonds of sameness between the members of the traditional (national) community (mechanical solidarity); the other based on the functional ties of difference between the members of a plural and multi-ethnic society (organic solidarity). This evolutionary process of modern society included further the transition from traditional collectivism to modern individualism. The segmental differentiation of societies as territorially confined units would slowly be replaced by the functional differentiation of society as a unity made up of the mutual dependencies of its plural elements. The socially and culturally homogeneous nation-state is therefore only transitory to a higher level of unity in diversity. It was because of this background assumption that Durkheimian sociology was so attractive for American sociology – in particular for Parsons – to explain the integration of the US in the twentieth century as a heterogeneous society based on plurality and difference. For the same reasons, Durkheimian sociology is highly relevant for explaining the integration of the European society as a 'unity in diversity' today.

Putting this core EU question in Durkheimian terms, then, sociology would need to test out to what extent the European society is *more* than an object of utopian (that is, normative) thinking and is rather becoming a *social fact* (Durkheim 1982). In a Durkheimian sense, the integrity of such a European society depends on the establishment of stable patterns of behaviour between EU actors and institutions and the people of Europe, that are bound together by a set of shared norms and expectations into a unifying whole. Sociology would focus on this evolving space of the 'social' as a *constraining factor* of European integration, that shapes the present choices and preferences of the actors involved. It could also analyze the conditions under which this society becomes an *enabling factor* of European integration, accounting for accelerated change in the behavioural patterns and expectations of the Europeans.

Despite its potential application to the emergence of European society, Durkheimian thinking, as with nearly all contemporary social theorizing, is limited by the fact that most of social science's analytical categories were developed within the nation-state framework. Several scholars have thus criticized the implicit 'methodological nationalism' that still dominates sociology: that nation-states and nationally bounded societies are still considered as the basic units of sociological analysis, something that limits the extension of classical terms of analysis to evolving contemporary forms, whether transnational or cosmopolitan (Wimmer and Glick Schiller 2002; Beck 2003). The nation-state model has also profoundly shaped our understanding of the stability of society and the possibility of social order. By relying on certain basic commonalities, such as language, culture and tradition, national society was able to accommodate internal diversity and to appease redistributive conflicts. Its historical achievement consists further in recognizing its members as equals and thus laying the foundations for trust and solidarity among the citizens.

The European Union is a double challenge with regard to this traditional thinking of society as a hierarchically organized and culturally homogeneous space. On a European scale, it is not necessarily the case that mechanisms which developed historically at the national level would work in the same way. We might be looking for a different kind of society.

First, the EU has consolidated as a non-state entity. Political authority is not centralized but dispersed over a variety of state and non-state actors, administrators and experts at the regional, national and supranational level of political aggregation (Marks *et al.* 1996; Kohler-Koch and Jachtenfuchs 2004). From this new form of political organization as a complex system of multilevel and multi-centred governance, it would be mistaken, though, to assume that the EU is also a non-society entity (Rumford 2002: 46ff). The overcoming of the traditional state focus rather becomes a dynamic element for societal forces to leave the national container behind, to engage in the 'social' in different ways.

Second, the EU has set out to accommodate enhanced social and cultural diversity within an open and still largely *undefined* societal (and territorial) space. On the one hand, it is committed to *positive integration*, with the aim of guaranteeing the social cohesion and stability of the continent. The EU has, for instance, been particularly successful in promoting economic development in structurally weak regions. Certain policies have also defended the rights of workers, of women and of minorities. Hence European integration has direct and indirect redistributive effects, which reconfigure the space of solidarity among the citizens. At the same time, the EU acts increasingly as a constraint on the integrity of the national society. These *disintegrating* effects are manifested in the opening of internal borders, the new mobility and competition in the labour market, the breaking of local traditions and solidarity, and a new heterogeneity of social milieus and practices – forms of *negative integration*, for the most part. These simultaneous processes of social opening and social closure are highly relevant in sociological terms, when thus rethought within a Durkheimian frame.

Rethinking in terms of the sociological tradition also helps extend our conception of *Europeanization*. Rather than limiting this to the study of institutional policy effects of European integration, Europeanization as a concept can refer to an encompassing process of social change; a transformation that can be also labelled the Europeanization of the nation-state and of national societies.

In sociological terms, then, Europeanization is not simply process of domestic change that is caused by European integration, as defined in the conventional EU literature (Börzel and Risse 2003). It proceeds rather through the very patterns of social integration and transformation identified by Durkheim around a century ago. Accordingly; Europeanization unfolds through internal differentiation and external adaptation. It makes national societies more dynamic and accounts for accelerated social change. As such, it is linked to harmonizing processes through which national societies become increasingly similar, but at the same time is also manifested in new heterogeneous practices, which increase internal diversity. The sociological challenge here is to conceive social integration at this new level of abstraction. The European society *integrates* by enhancing organic solidarity – i.e., the dependencies and functional links between and across national societies – while national societies within Europe *differentiate* by lowering the threshold of mechanic solidarity: the primordial bonds and commonalities within the nation-state.

The possible contributions of sociology to an understanding of European integration as a *social fact* can thus be fixed as follows. Sociological insights are needed to understand first, the 'meaning' of European integration beyond rational design and purposeful action, that is, the constraining and/or enabling factors of integration as a teleological project that stretches from market building to polity building and society building; and second, the dynamics and mechanisms of integration and disintegration, of binding and un-binding, of internal differentiation and external adaptation that demarcate the conflictive field of the emerging European society, as society is reconceived from a national to transnational European level.

In the remaining part of the chapter, I will focus mainly on the second, Durkheimian, question of reconceiving European society via a mapping of the evolving unity and diversity of the social space of Europe. Applying a variety of tools and concepts taken from contemporary social theory, the emergent European society can then be understood at a variety of levels: at macro-, micro- and meso-levels. We see how European Union can thus be conceived more deeply in Durkheimian terms, as a unitary social order built through particular integrating and differentiating efforts and mechanisms, which are linked to new social imaginaries of Europe as a meaningful whole.

Contemporary social theory and European integration

Much of the empirical sociology of EU – such as has been developed – delivers a comparative account of the *parallel* development of European nation-states. Applied to the European integration process, the idea is that European societies have developed structural similarities that group them together into one distinctive cluster of societies on a global scale. In order to prove this European distinctiveness, sociologists usually seek to describe the existence (or the emergence) of a European *social model* that separates European from non-European societies (Therborn 1995; Kaelble 1987 Crouch 1999; Lane and Ersson 1999; Bettin Lattes and Recchi 2005; Bach, Lahusen and Vobruba 2006).

Many of these works centre on the question of which elements of 'Europeanness' can be distinguished which impart a certain unity to all Western – and possibly also Eastern – European societies? Colin Crouch and Göran Therborn, who delivered the most comprehensive answers to this question, link the European social model to the major concern with social equality and welfare that distinguishes European societies from American society. The European social model would thus refer to a particular *European* way of relating to diversity: Europe as an 'ordered, limited and structured diversity', as compared to the American way of 'unstructured and pluralistic diversity' (Crouch 1999:

405). As such, the European social model has widespread implications for the system of values – for example for the design of the welfare state – as well as a broader emphasis on social policies and on the accommodation of internal diversity, such as dealing with minorities, mobility and immigration. One can argue that Europe is also more affected by internal cultural differentiation, as it is in fact characterized by exceptional cultural homogeneity as world region and hence displays a strong will to defend its cultural heritage. European integration can thus be understood as one way European societies have sought to defend social rights and welfare from the perceived threat of globalization.

Yet the European social model evoked by the EU is so far not substantiated in a European society as a socio-structural entity of its own. The European social model as such has only limited internal structuring effects on unifying the people of Europe or enhancing transnational solidarity and identity. The question of the possibilities of social integration *beyond* national society is not answered in conventional comparative empirical approaches; only whether societies in a similar socio-structural, political and historical position can be characterized along parallel and convergent (that is, *isomorphic*) processes of structural adaptation.

What such comparative empirical sociology does not provide is an adequate account of sociological Europeanization *over and above* the Europe of nation-states. Its description of the plurality of European societies tends to either look at measurements of difference or convergence between nation-states as the main indicator of Europeanization. Cross-country comparison by itself, however, allows only indirect conclusions about the possible demarcation of a European *society* in the singular. Particular findings, such as the specificity of a European family structure or of the European welfare state, rarely apply to the whole of Europe (Crouch 1999). In addition, one could criticize that these presumably 'European' features of society are not much more than variables in social research. They are only discovered *post hoc* from the analysis of statistical data and are rarely in the minds of the people who should constitute such a society. To get beyond this problem, which lies in comparative empirical sociology's inherently static view of social structures, we need to move towards an explanation of the more dynamic aspects of an evolving European society: what might be called, after Giddens, a *structuration* of European society.

The theory of structuration is useful here because it helps us avoid social determinism, which might result from either treating social structures as inviolable and permanent or agency as omnipotent. Giddens' concept of structuration aims to combine the dynamics of action with the 'stickiness' of structures, as well as transcending the micro- and macro-components of society. Social reality, then, is composed of the dynamic interrelation of different micro contexts of agencies with macro contexts of social structures. Sociology needs to understand how agents constantly reproduce social structures, which in turn enforce and maintain the dynamics of their action (Giddens 1984). Following this line of thinking, the structuration of contemporary European social space can be analyzed at the macro, the micro, and the meso level. We will consider each of these in turn.

A macro-sociology of European integration would analyze the consolidation of the European Union as a large-scale social system, as a polity and as a market. It would also reflect historical perspectives that might consider European society in terms of its distinctive civilizational features, as well as reconstructing the driving forces and dynamics of integration along new cleavages and constellations of interest. A micro-sociology would analyze to what extent Europeanization affects the everyday life of the individuals who inhabit the European space. It would investigate face-to face interactions at the basis of new forms of social organization that carry forward the European integration process. It would also consider the elementary relations among the citizens of Europe and their attitudes towards the EU. Meso-studies of European integration, meanwhile, would be necessary to understand how the macro- and the micro-configurations of Europe are inter-related. This includes, above all, an understanding of the mechanisms of intermediation through communication, the diffusion of knowledge and the building of trust and legitimacy.

Integration as macro-structural transformation

The question of macro-structural transformation immediately calls for an historical comparative perspective on the process of European integration. The dynamic notion of structuration works well in terms of historical analysis of the phenomenon. Historical approaches are particularly helpful in identifying longer-term developments that affect the constellation of European societies, and that constitute its internal value structure and belief system. A classical example of this approach is Max Weber's reconstruction of the link between the Protestant ethic and the development of modern capitalism in Western societies (Weber 2002[1905]). Against materialistic explanation of its social history, Weber emphasized the role of ideas and values as the driving forces in shaping the modern world. This refers to a general argument made in contemporary sociology that modernity takes multiple forms. It is thus possible to identify a specific path of modernization that European society has followed (see also Therborn 1999; Eisenstadt 2003).

Comparative historical sociology has thus aimed at an explanation of the distinctiveness of modern European society when compared to traditional societies, or when compared to processes of modernization in other parts of the world. Historical sociologists of Europe often operate with the concept of civilization, unifying a family of societies, which are shaped by the same basic cultural orientations and institutional settings. According to Shmuel Eisenstadt (1987), the particularity of European civilizational development lies in the parallel existence of multiple, competing centres. This has spurred competition across the European territorial and cultural space about who is the best within this civilizational constellation. European history reflects this continual experience of competition for hegemony in terms of ideology and power, although in practical terms the predominance of a single centre has never been achieved. The major effect of this competitive framework in the relationship between European societies was the consolidation of a European space of dense socioeconomic, cultural and political interchange. In the history of European state and nation building, the formation of political centres, collectivities and identities was closely related and developments within one sub-centre had immediate repercussions in others.

Stein Rokkan (1999) used these historical insights to formulate a configurational approach of the emergence of European societies. Rokkan traces back the macro-configuration of Europe as a political, territorial, social and cultural space that is marked by the parallel development of four fields (or 'systems' in the Parsonian sense): economy, political power/force, law and culture/religion. This allows him to account for the internal consolidation of centre–periphery links within established political systems as well as for the mapping of the variations in centre–periphery relations across the European space.

In the contemporary sociology of European integration, several authors have followed these lines of historical comparison identified with the work of Eisenstadt and Rokkan. Charles Tilly's work (1990) focused on modern state formation in the highly competitive framework of Europe, which co-occurred with the concentration of capital and military force. Bo Stråth (2000) pays attention to the question of European cultural commonality, which is found in a discourse on European civilization, in which issues of shared cultural heritage and values were constantly debated. Most recently in this vein, there has been the work of Stefano Bartolini (2005), who analyzes European integration in terms of new centre building. Considering the EU as an enlarged territorial and functional system, he elaborates some fundamental differences of EU centre formation from traditional state building. The novelty of the European experience lies in its attempt at centre formation *without* nation building. This alters fundamentally the nature of the European nation-states. Boundaries are removed at the national level, but do not necessarily reappear at the supranational level. In this sense, integration has introduced a new phase in the history of Europe, that dissolves the taken-for-grantedness of the national societies and rediscovers the diversity of the European space – both between and within nation-states.

The sociologically relevant question here is whether the un-bounding of the national configuration of societies can be also related to the *re*-bounding of a potentially 'post-national' configuration of a European society *sui generis*. To a certain extent European integration has already become a laboratory for testing out such new forms of social integration. The European laboratory has not only launched a large-scale experiment in political organization and governing. It has also experimented with new forms of democracy, with new forms of collective action and with the construction of new identities. But how can the political re-structuring and the social re-structuring of Europe be combined? To answer this, we must go beyond comparative historical sociology, delving more deeply into contemporary social theory. The retrospective view of the European configuration, presented by the historically-minded authors mentioned above, is useful for understanding path dependencies and for modelling ideal types of social order. It is less useful for understanding the forward-looking dynamics of European integration and the chances for or limits of European society building.

At this point, then, we need to supplement the perspective of the historical-retrospective structuration of Europe with a contemporary-prospective outlook of the structuring of an emerging European polity and a corresponding European society. Fossum (2006: 117), for example, stresses that an ecompassing strategy of comparison is needed to establish the uniqueness of the European experience. This would result not necessarily in the singling out of a distinct and clearly bounded entity but in the description of the complex inter-weaving of the EU with other entities, whether national, transnational or global. Europe is, in this view, no longer the fragmented space of national societies but both a unified space of new alliances and a polarized space of cross-cutting social cleavages and conflicts.

Macro-sociology should thus not only be concerned with the reconfiguration of the social and political order of society but also with general processes of societal development and change. A comprehensive answer to how European integration relates to modernization, for example, can be found in Ulrich Beck's theory of *reflexive modernization*. According to this author, Western societies have entered a new period, a 'second modernity', which is distinguished by the way in which a new logic of reflexivity is applied to all forms of social life. Reflexivity points to the constant questioning of the taken-for-grantedness of the social, the consideration of alternatives, and the need to constantly revise political choices. This is fundamentally different from the logics of necessity, stability and fixity of meaning that characterized 'first modernity' – as enshrined in the Parsonian social model, for example. The ongoing transformation of the basic institutions of modern society also affects the available forms of political organization. The national constellation of societies (in the plural) is replaced by a post-national constellation of society (in the singular).

What is the place of Europe in this emerging global order? First, European integration is seen as less specific, but rather as the systemic expression of a general symptom in the transformation of modern societies globally. The European Union is one model of regional integration, but it is also part of the (global) cosmopolitan society. Beck and Grande (2007) therefore propose to conceive the unity of Europe in terms of what they term a 'cosmopolitan empire', because it is only under cosmopolitan assumptions that Europe is able to uphold its internal diversity and stabilize its external relations. As an empire, the European Union cannot rely on any hegemony of power of fixed hierarchies, but unfolds through a new horizontal, network type of power. The European empire is further characterized by its open and variable territorial structure, its shifting borders with an inclusive tendency, and the loose organization of the territorial space. Last but not least, the multi-national societal structure of the EU is characterized by asymmetric memberships, with rights being granted and opportunities for participation being offered at the supranational, national and regional level (see also Eder and Giesen 2001).

Europeanization adds to these dynamics which represent a new drive towards the consolidation of social order. The German sociologist Richard Münch (2001: 180ff.) therefore builds on the Durkheimian legacy identified above to explain Europeanization in terms of *negative* and *positive integration*. Negative integration, for example, is achieved through the building of the single market, and the removal of obstacles to the free movement of capital, goods, services and people. As such, it enhances what Durkheim (1984: 111ff.) has called *negative solidarity*: the granting of individual rights of freedom and the accommodation of these rights in a way that creates distributive justice and avoids conflicts between individual profit maximizers. On the other hand, Europeanization has also increasingly turned into *positive integration* in the sense of developing new techniques of governance, and hence management of this economy. As such, it refers to what Durkheim (ibid.) has called *positive solidarity*: the commitment to collective goals which opens up possibilities for re-regulation and collective government at a European level.

A more gloomy answer to how European integration links with modernization is given by the defenders of the 'new security theory' of European integration. In the tradition of Michel Foucault, Barry (2001) sees the EU as a disciplinary institution that establishes 'technological zones' of control and regulation. As such, it demarcates a space within which differences of social practices have been reduced through the setting of common standards and control mechanisms, which in turn put increasing demands on the identities of the people living within that space. Bigo (1998), meanwhile, also a clearly Foucauldian-style thinker, explains European integration in the context of the ongoing securitization of modern society. While this securitization increasingly becomes global, the link to Europe can be established with reference to new techniques of 'security governance' developed by the EU. As such, the EU extends the regime of governmentality originally identified historically by Foucault, and associated with the control institutions of the modern nation-state. The regulatory regime established by the EU, rather, is based on the assumption that shared risks are in principal manageable at the European level and that corresponding techniques of control should thus be arranged for at this level. To uphold this regime of control, the EU needs to promote a discourse of insecurity and threat, thus leading to a kind of fortress mentality that affirms the role of European institutions and governments as the principal 'managers' in the 'governmentality of unease'. At the same time, this discourse of threat relates macro processes of power and control to the micro-spaces where these control techniques act upon individuals.

Integration as micro-structural transformation

A micro-sociology of European integration would turn towards the individuals who populate the European space. Eurobarometer provides an ample dataset about citizens' preferences and attitudes towards the EU and its policies. Only little is known, however, about how attitudinal change is linked to the behavioural change of European citizens. Theoretically, this raises the question of what kind of interpersonal ties and interactions develop between individuals and how they relate to political authority. Micro-sociological knowledge is important to assess how citizens can participate in European governance at different levels of political aggregation. It thus delivers information about how abstract citizenship rights are turned into what Wiener (1997) called 'citizenship practice'. Within the traditional structural-rationalistic paradigm of sociology, individual behaviour is situated within an established social order made up of power relations, rules and normative expectations. The activities of individuals or social groups are linked to the particular opportunities offered to them for accumulating resources and pursuing interests. In this sense, the European Union can also be analyzed as a new opportunity structure that is occupied by particular actors and groups who begin to organize their interests transnationally.

Bottom-up approaches to European integration frequently start with identifying those particular groups within society who are potentially affected by the EU and its policies. Drawing on classical sociological accounts of group formation and collective action, one could then expect that standardized life forms and expectations also lead to transnational alliances and solidarity among European citizens. A micro-sociology of European integration might also be useful to explain elite behaviour. This would include the analysis of the role perceptions of officials involved in bureaucratic decision-making (Egeberg 1999), the socialization of EU civil servants (Ross 1995; Hooghe 2002), competition and the struggle for recognition among the members of the European Parliament (Abélès 1996), associational behaviour in transnational advocacy coalitions including NGOs and social movement actors (Ruzza 2004), or the mindsets of journalists and EU correspondents (Meyer 1999; Baisnée 2002). In all these different accounts, the EU is portrayed as a 'playground' for new elites which, in Bourdieusian terms, accumulate new forms of capital (see below) to generate ideas, renew legitimatory beliefs or initiate advance policies in support of or in opposition to European integration (Ross 2008).

All this raises the question whether there is also a bottom-up process of 'ordinary Europeans' growing together and socializing across national borders. How does European integration affect the everyday life of the citizens? It is possible to observe the rapid Europeanization of individual behaviour through indicators such as cross-country marriages, changing identity patterns, social mobility and professional relationships across borders. In these terms, Steffen Mau and collaborators (Mau *et al.* 2008) have shown that cross-border transactions on the individual level have become a mass phenomenon in Germany. This perspective contrasts perhaps with the more sceptical findings presented in this volume by Díez Medrano. From traditional sociology of group behaviour we would expect that enhanced social mobility is also linked to attitudinal changes and opens up the possibility of creating new cosmopolitan lifestyles (Mau *et al.* 2008). From the perspective of political sociology, how this turned into support or opposition for the EU and its policies needs to be analyzed further. The growing awareness of citizens of the impact of the EU on their everyday life chances affects political preferences and is increasingly turned into political activism. A micro-sociology of European integration can thus contribute to our understanding of the conditions under which individuals learn to become a citizen of the EU – something which also implies learning to say 'no' to the EU and its policies.

As it appears relatively certain by now that the Europeanization of behavioural patterns is not restricted to a transnational elite, a micro-sociology of European integration from below will certainly grow in significance. More than partnerships with society, the EU has opened a new conflictual field, in which actors struggle for resources and legitimate positions in new configurations. This requires a sociological perspective which looks at the distinctive practices through which Europeanization proceeds as a struggle over changing social positions.

Structural-constructivist approaches in social theory, however, can take us beyond the behavioural-style explanations favoured by the more classical empirical sociologists mentioned above. Their focus is not simply on how individuals causally relate to pre-established social structures, but on how social practice unfolds over time and space constructing larger societal structures, as well as the subjectivity of persons.

This is a core theme of the sociology of Pierre Bourdieu, which explains how specific subjective positions defined through particular skills and capacities (*habitus*) are distributed unequally across what he calls the social field (*champ social*). The ensemble of distributive struggles over power and resources constitutes the particular field of social practice and the actors' roles and positions within it (Bourdieu 1977). In order to describe the European Union as a field of social practice, it is necessary to trace back the particular logics through which relevant actors position themselves within the field and relate to each other. In contrast to Marx, Bourdieu assumes that social positions are not simply determined by the distribution of economic capital, but by the complex entwinement of three additional forms of capital: *social capital*, which refers to the capacities of social actors to occupy social positions and to make use of power and resources in social networks – objectified, for instance, in prestige or recognition; *cultural capital*, which refers to actors' capacities to make use of more or less institutionalized forms of *distinction* – objectified, for instance, in university diplomas; and *symbolic capital*, which refers to their capacities to push through dominant interpretations of the particular historic situation and to set criteria for inclusion and exclusion – objectified, for instance, in historical narratives or in images of the collectivity (Bourdieu 1984, 1993).

European integration has a clear impact on the reconfiguration of the social field through the re-evaluation of these three forms of capital. It re-distributes power and resources, it re-organizes knowledge and information, and it re-shapes collective identities. The question, then, is how European integration stabilizes distinctively new norms, routines and practices. How will a new *eurohabitus* develop within the evolving social and political field of the new European elite? These new Europeans are distinguishing themselves through transnational power positions and privileged relational ties (social capital), go through a European educational career, acquiring specifically 'European' degrees and PhDs (cultural capital), and develop particular cosmopolitan attitudes, lifestyles and identities related to the transnational society they see themselves living in (symbolic capital). Empirical work is already being developed along these lines, as seen in the chapters in this volume by Favell and Recchi, and Kauppi.

Integration as meso-structural transformation

Perhaps the most interesting theoretical developments, however, can be viewed at the meso-level of study on Europe. Meso-structural approaches stand at the forefront of contemporary sociological theory with their intention to overcome the macro–micro split and a conviction that the two levels of analysis are complementary and synthetic, not opposed (Alexander *et al.* 1987). In highlighting the interwovenness of the social, sociology always moves between structure and agency to explain processes of intermediation, construction of meaning and signification. The practical turn in micro-sociology has thus been accompanied by a constructivist turn in macro-sociology, which focuses no longer on socio-structural determinants but locates society within an evolving discursive field. Applied to the EU, this implies the need to go beyond the presumed congruence between state, culture and people that makes up the idea of the classical nation-state society. From Bourdieu, the insight is taken that the emerging European society is not so much materialized in social structure but perpetuated in social practices, which again are activated by new social actors and forms of discourse. Two complementary concepts applied to the EU can help us grasp these intermediary, meso-level processes: Europe as a *public sphere* and Europe as *civil society*.

Public sphere approaches locate society in the processes of communication and discourse that bind Europeans together. It is communication that accounts for the interwovenness of the European social space. It was Jürgen Habermas (1989) who delivered the most influential historical account of the emergence of the national public sphere unfolding through critical discourse and the normative force of arguments. In modern anonymous societies, the public sphere relies on the mass media with its capacity to address a general audience and involve individual members of society in public opinion making and hence political will formation. As such, the public sphere has been analyzed, above all, as the communicative infrastructure of national democracy. Sociology has gone on from the work of Habermas to describe how the social unfolds through networks and how it is represented in shared discourse. The *network society* as described by Manuel Castells (2000), for example, is principally global. It is about spaces of information flows that operate through new types of electronic communication. Networks of information flows are the basic infrastructure of economic globalization. The *network state* is the political response to these new challenges: the European Union might be its clearest manifestation (ibid.: 364). Europe could thus be described as a particular nodal point in the global network of communication that is characterized by intensified communicative exchange. As such, it relates to other nodal points of the global network society for which it generates new information and becomes an addressable entity. Connecting back to mainstream EU studies, Castells' conceptualization of the European network state might be read as a variant of political science approaches, which have characterized the particular nature of the EU as a form of network governance (Eising and Kohler-Koch 1999).

The model of the network society is useful to locate Europe within the dynamic and accelerated processes of global change. It is less useful, however, to describe the normative and institutional underpinning of the emerging European communicative space. This latter aspect is at the heart of European *public sphere* theorizing, that has also developed in the wake of Habermas' work. The European public sphere refers to a space of mass communication that fulfils a particular function with regard to the cohesion of the EU polity: it intermediates between rule making at the supranational level and rule application at the national and sub-national level, and it articulates various degrees of societal adhesion to the European project. The European public sphere makes European politics transparent to the citizens – or, at least, is supposed to. Through its intermediary structures of communication, the performance of the political apparatus of the EU can be observed and evaluated (Trenz 2004). The European public sphere offers, at the same time, opportunities to become involved in common debates, to express shared concerns and to mobilize support or resistance. Ideally speaking, the public sphere is the space for collective public opinion and political will formation of European citizens. As such, it fulfils an important function for the normative integration of the emerging European society (Eriksen 2005) and, equally so, in the narrative construction of Europe's new boundaries (Eder 2006). Ultimately, public sphere research has contributed to the re-conceptualization of the role and functions of democracy in the EU. In the Durkheimian tradition, Trenz and Eder (2004) have formulated a theory of democratic functionalism, which understands democracy as an organizing principle and as a factor pushing European political integration. In a complex governmental arrangement like the EU, democratic procedures are required as the basic integrating mechanism facilitating interchange between political institutions and their environment. This functional necessity of democracy becomes a catalyst for institutional change and reform – in other words, for the further democratization of the EU. European integration in this sense is linked to collective learning processes among the different actors, institutions and publics involved. Such learning coincides with new forms of organized collective action and interest representation, the expansion of citizens' rights and practices and, finally, the introduction of processes of collective will formation.

The majority of authors in this line of work have discarded the possibility of an encompassing European public sphere built with the template of the national public sphere (Gerhards 2000; Fossum and Schlesinger 2007). Most importantly, the emergence of a pan-European media system is recognized as difficult, if not impossible. Due to the diversity of languages, media cultures and traditions, European audiences remain nationally segmented. Political communication in Europe is thus still mainly channelled through national organizations, parties or elected representatives. This results in a differentiated practice of news production with regard to the EU. The research agenda has shifted consequently to the *Europeanization* of public and media communication at the national level. This form of Europeanization – what might be referred to as a 'European public sphere lite' (as in Coke Lite!) – can be observed by measuring different degrees of Europeanization of existing national media spheres (Trenz 2004).

Similar to the concept of the public sphere, the idea of a European *civil society* refers to the intermediate sphere of public life found between official governmental or institutional actors of the EU and the private life of the citizens at the national or local level (Rumford 2003). When de Tocqueville delivered his classical account of democracy in America, he described how civil society comes into existence through activating a collective way of 'doing things together'. As such, civil society is constituted as the autonomous sphere of collective action and association among free and equal citizens. It requires a minimum degree of organization and it builds a particular kind of social capital which must be constantly renovated by holding the associational life and the communal practice alive, as for example explored in the widely known work of Robert Putnam (1993).

New concepts of civil society have surged to prominence in the social sciences in the wake of the democratic revolutions in post-communist Europe, and as a response to new global challenges. Jeffrey Alexander (2006), for example, discards both the traditional concept of civil society as *'bürgerliche Gesellschaft'* linked to the idea of free and equal citizens, and the critical concept of civil society as the realm of selfish economic interests denounced by Marx. Rather, in the contemporary world, civil society denotes the realm of civic justice and solidarity, and its sociological use lies precisely in pointing out the conditions for the maintenance and renewal of the social bond in globalizing societies. Alexander thus emphasizes the growing impact of legal and institutional guarantees, which make it crucial for civil society to build coalitions with states and governments. To maintain democracy in the post-national constellation, it becomes increasingly necessary for civil society to enter into the non-civil sphere and to become a partner in new governance arrangements (Caparoso and Tarrow 2008). The European Union might be the exemplary case where this new type of civil society emerges.

The debate on European civil society has therefore rightly focused on the notion of civil society as a partner in a new European system of governance. In the European Union, civil society building takes place in relationship to polity building: that is, the allocation of political authority and jurisdiction to the supranational level (Fossum and Trenz 2006). In this way, *governance* provides the key concept for describing the changing relationship between political power and civil society set in motion by European Union. Furthermore, in the tradition of the work of Charles Tilly (1978), who analyzed civic contention as a dynamic element of nation building, contentious politics are expected to become the motor for a process of Europeanization from below that is carried primarily by all those who feel in some way affected by European governance. These are themes explored in more depth in Chapter 6 by Guiraudon in this volume.

Conclusion

Social theory-based reflection provides an alternative way of rethinking European Union sociologically to the more empiricist sociological approaches that have been presented elsewhere in this volume. In these, the European 'society' being imagined is still often thought of as the mirror of the classical nation-state society and the sociological methodologies developed to understand it. The dominant view of comparative structural analysis in Europe has not really changed the national frame of reference, rather simply multiplied it for the purpose of empirical investigation. All macro-structural views of social system analysis put a strong consensual emphasis on social unity. Society is ultimately perceived as an internally differentiated and externally delimited entity, which is substantiated in an identitarian form (an ethnos) and in a political organization (a demos or a state).

However, sociology also has a long and outstanding tradition of breaking the 'iron cage' that is socio-structural analysis of national societies. More dynamic elements in the study of contemporary society are thus brought in by introducing social theory that has been developed in the wake of thinking about modernity and globalization. Within the European-global framework major shifts in modernity can now be seen to occur, with the EU emerging as a new post-national and/or cosmopolitan model for the legitimation of political order. Such generalized accounts of a Europe of 'reflexive modernisation' (Beck 2000) or the 'network society' (Castells 2000), and so on, of course, encounter the reverse problem that in their analysis the internal consolidation and external delimitation of the European societal space often remain empirically underspecified. At this point, micro- and meso-sociological approaches will offer a useful supplement that can sharpen our view of new actors' relations across borders and changing forms of social practice – a point which again underlines the centrality of Bourdieusian-style thinking to the study of European Union. The question of European integration processes is thus an ideal theoretical context for re-establishing the macro–micro link at the heart of all successful sociological analysis.

Moreover, this chapter underlines that to understand the encounter of competing logics of Europeanization we will need a theory of society. This chapter has mostly taken the position that a Durkheimian theory of society is likely to be the most effective; others such as Díez Medrano in this volume have taken a more Weberian line. A sociology of European Union building on these legacies will add to the understanding of the complex logics of Europeanization in several dimensions. Against political science's emphasis of Europeanization from above through the imposition of EU law and regulation, sociologists highlight the relevance of Europeanization from below, which takes place in the form of spontaneous associations of citizens, transnational and intercultural relations and new contentious politics. Further, against political scientists' trust in Europeanization as a process of integration through purposeful design, which unifies the European space, sociologists also focus on Europeanization as differentiation, which enhances diversity and contingency and which establishes new cleavages and exclusions. Finally, a sociological account goes beyond the traditional understanding of Europeanization as the interpenetration of national societies. As this chapter has repeatedly emphasized, Europeanization is more than simply interlinking existing structures and actors across borders. It is also, indeed mainly, about transforming these structures and actors; about, in short, the emergence of a *new* social entity. Sociology thus ultimately arrives at a new constructivist understanding of Europeanization as a form of 'reflexive creation', in the words of Delanty and Rumford (2005: 12). In this last sense, the notion of European society is not simply the other side of EU governance to be addressed and domesticated by EU institutions. It is, above all, an emergent reality, indicating a major reconfiguration of the European social, political, economic and cultural space. Addressing this question is where a sociology of the European Union finds its core vocation and purpose.

POSTSCRIPT

Arriving Late at the EU Studies Ball

Dilemmas, Prospects and Strategies for a Sociology of the European Union

George Ross

Imagine that you are a disorganized but ambitious outlier group attending a popular ball which has long been organized by others. This is a difficult situation, especially when your group is filled with people who dislike the ball's standards and norms, including those about how to dance. How should the group behave? Should it hide its differences and dance in the ways expected by those who run the ball? Should it announce its differences from the start and dance in its own ways, in the hope that the ball's organizers will accept in a spirit of choreographic pluralism? Or should it stay away altogether and organize its own ball? These are not easy choices. Each one bears different risks – of self-obliteration, slow co-optation, eventual expulsion, or marginalization. Something like these choices confronts many sociologists in the EU studies field today. Discussing this risk of exclusion is the goal of *Sociology of the European Union*.

Institutionalizing EU studies

It is in part an accident of intellectual history as well as disciplinary interests that 'EU studies' came to be dominated by political scientists and that those deploying various forms of institutionalism now organize the main EU studies balls. It has always made sense that the EU would fascinate political scientists. European integration was recognized as the vanguard of schemes for regional integration in the post-1945 world from the moment when Robert Schuman announced Jean Monnet's plan for a European Coal and Steel Community at the Quai d'Orsay in June 1950. The project was eminently appealing politically, promising the transcendence of what had been murderous national rivalries through unique supranational institutions. Even more intriguing for political scientists was that the emergent European Union challenged the holy grail of political analysis. Political scientists had always assumed the nation-state to be the final destination of political development. What if European integration meant that there was something beyond it? The answer might change the entire discipline.

In the beginning, even if sociologists were largely absent from the first frameworks for EU studies, sociological perspectives were not. Political scientists along with others at the time were drawing heavily on classic traditions of European social theory in which the building of modern states and societies were centre stage. Studying state and society-building had become central in the immediate post-1945 decades for other reasons as well. Ambitious American social scientists were attempting to apply their structural-functionalist theoretical project to project trajectories, often out of decolonization, toward the modern industrial societies which were for them the endpoint of political development. This, in retrospect, might be called the social scientific age of modernization

In this context, it was not surprising that some asked whether what was happening in post-war Europe was a novel form of nation building. Ernst Haas, mentioned many times in this volume, was perhaps the most influential figure who posed this question. His neo-functionalist theoretical framework led him to suggest that supranational but sectoral integration incentives would stimulate the emergence of supranational social forces and because of the sectoral interdependence of industrial societies this could promote spillover. These insights were eagerly taken up in the fields of international relations and comparative politics. Those who hoped that the Westphalian state system could be transcended were excited. Others, particularly realists in the IR field such as Stanley Hoffmann, disagreed. They produced their own sophisticated arguments, assisted enormously by General de Gaulle's hard-nosed efforts in the 1960s to bring EEC supranationality and spillover to an abrupt halt.

By the 1970s the EEC had settled into uneasy inter-governmental compromise and faced a deeply challenging international economic crisis. Euro-enthusiasm among political scientists, and most Europeans, shrivelled. Haas reconsidered his theoretical optimism and his students moved away from neo-functionalism towards liberal institutionalism. One of these, John Gerard Ruggie, describes his movement toward understanding that the international system was capable of organizing real cooperative action without any 'snowballing momentum ... leading to a 'higher' form of sociopolitical organization' (Ruggie 1998).

The renaissance of European integration, after years of deep Euro-pessimism, caught most analysts by surprise. Starting in 1985, a hyperactive Delors Commission, backed by a re-energized Franco-German couple, quickly produced the Single Market Programme and Economic and Monetary Union, setting off an explosion of new interest in European integration. Again EU studies would be dominated by a flock of young and largely Anglo-American political scientists. But these newcomers, who would cast the main intellectual debates about the EU, its dynamics and its directions, were different from the Haases and Hoffmanns – a point well made by Perry Anderson (2009), who foregrounds the problematic predominance of American and Anglophone theories and methods in the study of European integration. Social theory was out, often replaced by forms of economism as a result of the powerful institutionalist turn that American political science had undergone. Among other things, this turn also involved abandoning any vestige of sociological determinism and society-centric theorizing, whether neo-Marxian, Weberian or Parsonian.

The basic reasoning behind this was blindingly obvious. Reading politics off social structures was an error. Political events were best explained by what happened in political arenas. Given this, new institutionalist approaches fell easily to hand. To paraphrase the title of Peter Evans, Dietrich Rueschemeyer, and Theda Skocpol's important 1985 collection, the state should 'be brought back in'. It remained to define what this catchy turn of phrase meant, of course.

Two different and competing forms of institutionalist reasoning dominated political science, which, alas, pretty much overlooked the third sociological form discussed in Peter Hall and Rosemary Taylor's influential article (1996). The first, originating in the study of American politics, was a rational choice approach combining utilitarian methodological individualism and careful institutional modelling, both borrowed from economics. The second, coming more from comparative politics, was historical institutionalism. This approach also placed institutions at the centre of things, but less in the form of abstract models and more as ideal types drawn from comparative analysis of real-world practices, seen over time. Parallel to this, international relations specialists adopted many institutionalist approaches to explain the emergence of forms of interstate cooperation, often analyzed as institutionalized or informal 'regimes'. In the IR field states had never been displaced by societies, but scholars still needed to understand where cooperation came from in the supposedly anarchic world theorized by strict realists. Another reason that eager political scientists of all kinds were attracted to the EU at this point was because European events involved big new puzzles to the discipline. Interactions between supranational and national institutions begged for sophisticated analysis of 'Europeanization'. The EU's renaissance also brought back the troubling matter of the transcendence of the national state – was the Union essentially intergovernmental or a new form of polity?

The debates were very lively, and the number of participants grew greatly, for a number of reasons. Universities in Europe as well as North America had expanded since the EU's founding years in the 1950s and were absorbing a larger percentage of each age cohort. As the EU became a hot issue again, political science departments could make space for courses on it, something that helped focus research interests. For Europeans, moreover, careful observation of and teaching about the EU politics was not only a contribution to scientific knowledge but also a matter of civic education. Secondly, as the world globalized, so too did academic disciplines. National traditions of political analysis, drawn from constitutional law, political sociology or whatever, foundered as theoretical approaches traversed internal borders as well as the Atlantic. Finally the EU itself, and in particular the European Commission, played a key role. It eagerly subsidized debate about the EU and its institutions, through research programmes, EU Centres, Jean Monnet chairs, the European University Institute in Florence, numerous conferences, and a new openness to academic inquiry. The EU knew that knowledge of what it was up to was in short supply beyond the Rue de la Loi and that getting academics into the jobs of providing it was an important investment.

The years between Delors' 1985 announcement of the Single Market Programme and the sequels of the Maastricht Treaty in the 1990s brought the consolidation of today's 'EU studies'. As it did so, the different tribes of neo-institutionalist political scientists were well positioned to dominate as well as structure the terms of debate. What generated the most turbulent discussions in EU studies was the indeterminacy of the EU as an object. There were rational choice specialists, who were in fact less concerned with understanding the EU itself than with modelling some of its unique institutional structures and the strategies of actors within them. Principal–agent theory, drawing analytically on long-standing economic theorizations, became a preferred approach because it allowed analysts to sidestep the state transcendence issue with *a priori* assumptions that the EU's member states were the 'principals'of EU institutions. There were many historical institutionalists who were fascinated by the possibility of examining path dependency (or not), the role of ideas, multilevel governance and so on, in this complicated institutional setting. The possibility existed for them that the EU might be precipitating a huge 'critical juncture' itself, not only because of the development of its own institutions, but also because these institutions might be providing large 'exogenous shocks' producing serious change in national institutions. On the international relations side an elaborated liberal institutionalism emerged that was intent on explaining the new EU situation in ways that defended the analytical supremacy of the national state.

A place for sociology?

Serendipity and disciplinary good fortune allowed institutionalist political scientists to dominate the EU studies ball, with the help of a few lawyers and economists. Their theoretical traditions and interests structured the debate, identifying the puzzles, the unresolved questions and the matters in dispute. Fascinated by the institutional complexity of the European Union, they deployed their analytic tools to understand those institutions. As they did so, they closed down space for the sociologists' traditional questions about state–society relations, about power, and about social relations more generally. Sociology's questions about state–society relations and power – that is sociology writ large – were not altogether absent. They could be found, for example, in studies of elections to the European Parliament, Euro-level lobbying, gender and discrimination issues, immigration studies, social movements, and the analysis of EU-level social policies. Sociological theory often crept into ongoing debate about the EU's alleged democratic deficit as well, but this was largely because normative theory was exempted from the institutionalist turn. However, as Favell and Guiraudon point out in their earlier survey of the field (2009), sociologists were very much present, in examining the evolution of the different varieties of the European social model of welfare states and employment relations systems. Here important comparative work on national models thrived, testing and elaborating Esping-Andersen's famous taxonomy and/or filling in 'varieties of capitalism' analyses. There was not much reference to the EU in this, though, at least until the brief flurry of discussion about the Open Method of Coordination and the Lisbon Strategy in the new century. As this suggests, the evolution of the discipline of sociology is not without fault in this story. Indeed it contributed to its own marginalization. After its golden years as a potential master social science, it fragmented into smaller sub-disciplinary groups which studied a vast range of objects which were not always, or even often, connected – social problems, situations of social injustice, social policies, professional practices, theoretical rebellions against positivism and the Enlightenment, in addition to more traditional socio-demographic concerns. Persistent and large national differences in Europe contributed to this fragmentation, consecrating smaller national theoretical clans that often did not travel well. All of this made for disciplinary bad fortune: the discipline of sociology happened to be moving in seriously dispersed order at precisely the moment when European integration took off again in the 1980s. This left sociologists wondering about what place they might have at the dance.

Providing answers to this question has been the principal purpose of *Sociology of the European Union*. The core claim of the volume is that much more sociology is needed to understand today's EU. The book proceeds by identifying questions and sketching approaches that sociologists might undertake. These build on each author's own work, which itself is inspired by the standards of the sociological imagination. For example, Díez Medrano deploys class analytic categories to assess to what degree the EU fosters social classes, or fractions of them, whose identities are seriously European. Andreotti and Le Galès continue the class theme by examining how nationally-based elites with European perspectives combine feelings of European and national belonging. Sociologists could map and weigh the importance of the newly mobile populations of EU Europe sociodemographically and ethnographically to measure the effects of different dimensions of European integration – the free movement of people in particular (Favell and Recchi). EU Europe is the site of multiple social mobilizations – lobbies, protests, movements and cycles of discontent, but we need to know which of these have an EU focus, to what degree they play roles in EU governance, and what this might mean for the political sociology of the EU and/or its member states (Guiraudon). The EU is now a central actor in a broad range of public policies, but what actually happens in these different policy realms, how do which different actors attempt to construct their 'fields' of action, resource bases, and attribute meanings to what they do, and what differences do such things make for policy-making (Mérand)? How has the EU's restructuring of European markets affected the outlooks and strategies of firms and other market players (Fligstein)? And why not map in-depth the social profiles of different EU political and administrative elites and explore how such profiles influence policy-making (Kauppi)? No doubt, a much larger volume could have contained a great many more such suggestions.

From a methodological point of view, the essays propose a variety of approaches that goes well beyond the usual in the EU studies field. Ethnographic ingenuity often feeds into qualitative sampling and then toward even broader quantitative explorations, in ways that befit a social science that has not already decided what reality looks like. There are many proposals about new objects for research and how one might go about doing it. The essays are an eclectic but enticing collection of useful suggestions. Many refer to the theories and methods of Pierre Bourdieu, often by borrowing concepts such as 'fields' of action worth delineating and then examining, discerning the specific 'habitus' of those acting in these fields, pinpointing the plural sources of resources that these actors can deploy to attain their goals. An excellent concluding essay ties sociological EU studies in the vast literature of social theory (Trenz). What is most attractive in all this is the absence of dogma. We are invited seductively on an expedition into unexplored territory.

Confronting the hegemon

Does such a diverse and open-minded collection provide any definitive hints for latecomer sociologists who want to make a lasting impression at the EU studies ball? The volume does indicate the multiple ways in which sociology could help answer this question. But the EU studies ball is still highly structured, even if it is a congenial place. Newcomers could easily conclude that to be taken seriously they have to pay the large entry cost of subscribing to one of political science institutionalism's theoretical schools. It is clear from this volume, however, that paying such a cost would exclude most of what the authors really want to do. It is hard not to conclude, therefore, that the basic issue for a sociology of the European Union is to confront political science institutionalism head on, something which is much easier said than done.

In the most general of senses, there is nothing inherently wrong about institutionalism. Indeed, some kind of institutionalist theorizing is needed to guide our understanding of the thicket of very unusual institutions that make up the EU. But are those institutionalisms that presently dominate the field adequate to the task of explaining the kinds of things that this volume discusses? Scrutinizing the limits of these institutionalisms is therefore an important first step for EU sociologists. A first sociological criticism must be that the triumph of political science's institutionalisms has brought an eclipse of 'society' as a focus for analysis. Buying into approaches that *a priori* minimize these realities and linkages leaves very little space for sociology. Sociologists study society, and political sociologists, those most likely to want to dance at the EU studies ball, have to be concerned with the realities of state–institution–society linkages. Yet today's political scientists have ring-fenced their territory in such a way as to marginalize such issues. If one believes that there is a world of social process beyond political institutions, and that it matters, this is not simply a turf argument.

A second step would be to criticize these institutionalisms more thoroughly. Most have borrowed heavily from economics and imply clearly that economics should become the master theory of social science endeavours. The implications of this borrowing demand thorough scrutiny. Economics may gain parsimony by deploying a methodological individualism positing that actors are single-minded and rational utility maximizers. But such assumptions do violence to a much more complicated political reality where actors use multiple resources, including the symbolic resources of ideas, meanings and social capital, to maintain and advance their positions. However rationally they may behave, their rationalities are not focused in the same way as the hypothetical market actors of economists. They are not usually monotonically single-minded, they are not fully clear about what maximizing their own utility involves, and they do not possess sufficient information to anticipate accurately the consequences of their choices, nor can they, because they must place bets on a very uncertain future. Even in completely stable institutional situations, actors' preferences are far from given; EU institutions and their complex interactions are by no means that stable.

Historical institutionalism, in at least some of its declensions, is more open to sociological analysis, but still open to critique. To be sure, most institutions are indeed sticky and it usually takes major shocks to make them change direction in serious ways. Beyond such generalities, all institutions are not the same in the ways that they move in time. Weber was quite clear about this, positing that they will have particular ethics, deontologies and purposes which create great endogenous variability both in procedures and openness to change. Most important, while institutions are indeed relatively thick structures, they are far from impervious to inputs from their broader societies. Here sociology already has an accumulated stock of alternative, more complex ways of looking at institutions and organizations that should be invited to the debate. We could go deeper, but many other critics have done so already.

Such criticism is only a small beginning for sociologists of the EU. It is vastly more important to produce alternative analyses that explain things better. This is what *Sociology of the European Union* encourages so effectively. The fascinating complex of EU institutions is not the be all and end all of the EU saga. European integration is also a transnational state-building endeavour, even if we know that it is unlikely that the EU will become a transnational state. But denying that there is anything really state-like about the EU, as some strains of institutionalist political science do, is an essentially polemical exercise, however elegantly it may be undertaken. The EU should be viewed as an open-ended and uncertain thing – the famous 'unidentified political object' of which Jacques Delors and others have often spoken. Reducing it to something more familiar and more conventional ultimately does not really help understand it. One of sociology's great advantages at this point is that its intellectual universe is not afraid of open-ended and uncertain things, in part because it is not completely obsessed with the finality of the Westphalian state system.

Beyond this, it should not be news that state building goes with society building. If European integration is a peculiar kind of state building, it in all likelihood implies an equally peculiar kind of society building. Sociologists may be uniquely equipped to comprehend this, as several essays in this volume intimate. There is eminent sociological work on earlier state and society building by authorities such as Charles Tilly, Karl Deutsch, Stein Rokkan and others. But the EU is not well placed to engage in the open warfare to relocate boundaries and citizen identities that brought the nation-state into existence. It has very limited authority to constrain other jurisdictions to cooperate and it must explicitly recognize the desirability of cultural pluralism and a multiplicity of different identities. As Stefano Bartolini has helped us understand, this makes maps of past state and society building less reliable than many believe. The EU can survive and thrive if its member states need it to do things that they agree can only be achieved through international cooperation. But this can happen only if there is social support for such sovereignty pooling. Forward movement on both the Euro-political and social fronts is not inevitable. How much of either will happen remains very much an open question, as the essays in *Sociology of the European Union* almost all conclude. Both state and society building in the EU context need to be monitored and analyzed constantly, in particular because the processes are eminently capable of moving in two directions: more or less. EU studies presently do a reasonable job on institutional issues of cooperation and sovereignty pooling, even if a creative new political sociology could add a great deal. But it does not do much at all, beyond incessant deconstruction of unrevealing Eurobarometer polls for hidden meanings, to analyze society building. Sociology is really needed here, then.

Whether and how sociology ends up going to the EU studies ball is probably not the most important question. What matters more is that we need a flourishing sociology of the EU, no matter who goes to what ball. This volume is thus an invitation to build a *chantier*. There are real problems to be solved before such a *chantier* can be fully constructed, however. It may be a virtue that sociology looks much more intellectually pluralistic these days than political science. Lots of sociological flowers are blooming, and many of these are attractive. Such pluralism can be a problem, however, indicating intellectual dispersion, lack of broader focus and fragmentation, including fragmentation among relatively autonomous nationally-based sociologies. There is still a great deal of methodological nationalism out there in sociology, plus considerable national parochialism. How to bring things more together around the EU is the challenge, therefore. This volume often speaks of the promises of a sociology of a Bourdieusian approach. This is not at all misplaced because the promise is indeed there. Delicacy and care about strategies that prematurely create exclusivist paradigms is in order, however. There are many other ways of doing EU sociology that deserve to be heard. Revisiting the greats like Weber and Durkheim remains a useful thing to do, at least heuristically, as several authors suggest in this volume. The real issue is generating more EU sociology, whatever the approach and as long as it is plausible and serious. This means getting more sociologists to understand how important and interesting thinking sociologically about the EU really is. We learn from this volume that much has been done and many people out there are doing cutting-edge thinking and research, but there needs to be much more done by many more people. Truly understanding the EU is not only a worthy enterprise; it is also a fascinating one. So let us go forth and multiply, but as sociologists who have recognized the realities of the social world around us, let us do so intelligently!

Bibliography

Abbott, Andrew (1988) *The System of Professions. An Essay on the Division of Expert Labor*. Chicago, IL: University of Chicago Press.

Abbott, Andrew (2001) *Time Matters: On Theory and Method*. Chicago, IL: University of Chicago Press.

Abélès, Marc (1992) *La vie quotidienne au parlement européen*. Paris: Hachette.

Abélès, Marc (1996) 'La communauté européenne: une perspective anthropologique.' *Social Anthopology*, 4(1): 33–45.

Abélès, Marc, Irène Bellier and Maryon MacDonald (1993) *Approche anthropologique de la commission européenne*. Mimeo. Brussels: European Commission. URL: http://halshs.archives-ouvertes.fr/docs/00/37/43/46/PDF/ABELES_BELLIER_McDONALD_1993_CEfr.pdf

Adler-Nissen, Rebecca (2008) 'The diplomacy of opting out. A Bourdieusian approach to national integration strategies.' *Journal of Common Market Studies*, 46(3): 663–84.

Alba, Richard (1992) *Ethnic Identity: The Transformation of White America*. New Haven, CT: Yale University Press.

Alexander, Jeffrey C. (1998a) 'Civil society I, II, III: Constructing an empirical concept from normative controversies and historical transformations: Introduction', in Jeffrey C. Alexander (ed.), *Real Civil Societies: Dilemmas of Institutionalization*. London: Sage, 1–19.

Alexander, Jeffrey C. and Bernhard Giesen (1987) 'From reduction to linkage: the long view of the micro-macro debate', in Jeffrey C. Alexander, Bernhard Giesen, Richard Münch and Neil J. Smelser (eds) *The Micro-Macro Link*. Berkley, CA: University of California Press, 1–42.

Alter, Karen (2001) *Establishing the Supremacy of European Law*. Oxford: Oxford University Press.

Alter, Karen and Jeannette Vargas (2000) 'Explaining variation in the use of European litigation strategies: European Community law and British gender equality policy.' *Comparative Political Studies*, 33(4): 452–82.

Anderson, Chris (2008) *The Long Tail: Why the Future of Business is Selling Less of More*. New York: Hyperion.

Anderson, Perry (2009) *The New Old World*. London: Verso.

Andreotti, Alberta and Patrick Le Galès (2008) 'Middle class neighbourhood attachment in Paris and Milan: partial exit and profound rootedness', in T. Blockland and Mike Savage (eds) *Networked Urbanism. Social Capital in the City*. Aldershot: Ashgate, 127–44.

Appadura, Arjun (1996) *The Social Life of Things: Commodities in Cultural Perspective*. Cambridge: Cambridge University Press.

ARENA, University of Oslo. Working papers, http://www.arena.no
Atkinson, R. and G. Bridge (eds) (2005) *Gentrification in a Global Context: The New Urban Colonialism*. London: Routledge.
Bach, Maurizio (1999) *Die Bürokratisierung Europas. Verwaltungseliten, Experten und Politische Legitimation in der Europäischen Union*. Frankfurt a. M: Campus Verlag.
Bach, Maurizio, Christian Lahusen and Georg Vobruba (eds) (2006) *Europe in Motion: Social Dynamics and Political Institutions in an Enlarging Europe*. Sigma: Berlin.
Bagnasco, Arnaldo (ed.) (2008) *Ceto Medio: Perché e Come Occuparsene*. Bologna: Il Mulino.
Bagnasco, Arnaldo and Patrick Le Galès (2000) *Cities in Contemporary Europe*. Cambridge: Cambridge University Press.
Bagnasco, Arnaldo and N. Negri (1994) *Classi, Ceti, Persone*. Naples: Liguori.
Baisnée, Olivier (2002) 'Can political journalism exist at the EU level?' in Raymond Kuhn and Erik Neveu (eds) *Political Journalism*. London: Routledge, 108–28.
Baisnée, Olivier (2007a) 'En être ou pas. Les logiques de l'entre soi à Bruxelles.' *Actes de la recherche en sciences sociales* 166–7: 110–21.
Baisnée, Olivier (2007b) 'The European public sphere does not exist (at least it's worth wondering …).' *European Journal of Communication* 22(4): 493–503.
Baisnée, Olivier and Dominique Marchetti (2000) 'Euronews, un laboratoire de production de l'information "européenne".' *Cultures et Conflits*, 38–9: 121–55.
Baker, Wayne, Robert Faulkner and Gene Fisher (1998) 'Hazards of the market: the continuity and dissolution of interorganizational market relationships.' *American Sociological Review*, 63:147–77.
Balme, Richard and Didier Chabanet (2008) *European Governance and Democracy: Power and Protest in the EU*. Lanham, MD: Rowman & Littlefield.
Balme, Richard, Didier Chabanet and Vincent Wright (eds) (2002) *L' action collective en Europe*. Paris: Presses de Sciences Po.
Barry, Andrew (2001) *Political Machines: Regulating a Technological Society*. London: Athlone Press.
Barry, Andrew (2006) 'Technological zones.' *European Journal of Social Theory*, 9(2): 239–53.
Barry, Brian (1971) *Sociologists, Economists and Democracy*. Chicago, IL: Chicago University Press.
Bartolini, Stefano (1998) *Exit Options, Boundary Building, Political Structuring. Sketches of a Theory of Large-Scale Territorial and Membership 'Retrenchment/Differentiation' versus 'Expansion/Integration' (with Reference to the European Union)*, Firenze: EUI Working Papers, SPS No. 98/1.
Bartolini, Stefano (2005) *Restructuring Europe: Centre Formation, System Building and Political Structuring between the Nation State and the EU*. Oxford: Oxford University Press.

Bauman, Zygmunt (2000) *Liquid Modernity*. Oxford: Blackwell.
Baumgartner, Frank and Bryan Jones (1993) *Agenda and Instability in American Politics*. Chicago, IL: University of Chicago Press.
Beauvallet, Willy (2008) 'L'institutionnalisation d'une nouvelle figure politique: la professionnalisation des eurodéputés français (1979–2004). Unpublished PhD thesis, Institut d'études politiques, Strasbourg.
Beauvallet, Willy and Sébastien Michon (2008) 'Women in the European Parliament: effects of the voting system, strategies and political resources. The case of the French delegation.' GSPE Working Papers series. Strasbourg: GSPE-PRISME. URL: http://prisme.u-strasbg.fr/working papers/WPBeauvalletMichon.pdf
Beauvallet, Willy and Sébastien Michon (2009) 'General patterns of women's representation in the European Parliament: did something change after 2004?' Center for European Political Sociology Working Paper, available at http://gspe.eu.
Beauvallet, Willy and Sébastien Michon (2010) "Professionalization and socialization of the Members of the European Parliament." *French Politics*, 8 (2).
Beck, Ulrich (2000) *What is Globalisation?* Oxford: Blackwell.
Beck, Ulrich (2003) 'Toward a new critical theory with a cosmopolitan intent.' *Constellations*, 10(4): 453–68.
Beck, Ulrich (2006) *The Cosmopolitan Vision*. Cambridge: Polity.
Beck, Ulrich, Anthony Giddens and Scott Lash (1996) *Reflexive Modernization: Politics, Tradition and Aesthetics in the Modern Social Order*. Stanford, CA: Stanford University Press.
Beck, Ulrich and Edgar Grande (2007) *Cosmopolitan Europe*. Cambridge: Polity.
Beckfield, Jason (2006) 'European integration and income inequality.' *American Sociological Review*, 71 (December): 964–985.
Bellier, Irène (1994) 'La Commission Européenne: hauts fonctionnaires et culture du management.' *Revue Française d'Administration Publique* 70, (April–June issue): 253–62.
Bellier, Irène and Thomas Wilson (eds) (2000) *An Anthropology of the European Union: Building, Imagining, Experiencing Europe*. Oxford: Berg.
Benford, Robert and David Snow (2000) 'Framing processes and social movements.' *Annual Review of Sociology*, 26: 611–39.
Berezin, Mabel and Juan Díez Medrano (2008). 'Distance matters: place, political legitimacy and popular support for European integration.' *Comparative European Politics*, 6: 1–32.
Berger, Peter and Thomas Luckmann (1966) *The Social Construction of Reality*. London: Penguin.
Berger, Peter A. and Anja Weiß (eds) (2008) *Transnationalisierung sozialer Ungleichheit*. Wiesbaden: VS Verlag für Sozialwissenschaften.
Berger, Suzanne and Ronald Dore (1996) *National Diversity and Global Capitalism*. Ithaca, NY: Cornell University Press.
Bertaux, Daniel and Paul Richard Thompson (eds) (1997) *Pathways to Social Class*. Oxford: Clarendon.

Best, Joel (2002) 'Constructing the sociology of social problems: Spector and Kitsuse 25 years later.' *Sociological Forum*, 17(4): 699–706.

Bettin Lattes, Gianfranco and Ettore Recchi (eds) (2005) *Comparing European Societies: Towards a Sociology of the EU*. Bologna: Monduzzi.

Beyers, Jan and Jarle Trondal (2004) 'How nation states hit Europe: ambiguity and representation in the European Union.' *West European Politics*, 27(5): 919–42.

Bigo, Didier (1994) 'The European internal security field: stakes and rivalries in a newly developing area of police intervention,' in Malcolm Anderson and Monica Den Boer (eds) *Policing Across National Boundaries*. London: Pinter.

Bigo, Didier (1996) *Polices en Réseaux: L'Expérience Européenne*. Paris: Presses de Sciences Po.

Bigo, Didier (1998). 'Sécurité et immigration: vers une gouvernementalité par l'inquiétude?' *Cultures & Conflits*, 31–2, 13–38.

Billig, Michael (1995) *Banal Nationalism*. London: Sage.

Blakely, E. J. and M. G. Snyder (1997) *Fortress America: Gating Communities in the United States*. Washington, DC: Brookings Institute and Lincoln: Institute of Land Policy.

Boltanski, Luc (1982) *Les cadres*. Paris: Minuit.

Borjas, George (1989) 'Economic theory and international migration.' *International Migration Review* 23(3): 457–85.

Borjas, George (1999) *Economic Research on the Determinants of Immigration: Lessons for the European Union*. Washington, DC: World Bank Technical Paper 438.

Borneman, John and Nick Fowler (1997) 'Europeanization.' *Annual Review of Anthropology*, 26: 487–514.

Börzel, Tanja (ed.) (2006) *The Disparity of European Integration: Revisiting Neofunctionalism in Honour of Ernst B.Haas*. London: Routledge.

Börzel, Tanja and Thomas Risse (2003) 'Conceptualizing the domestic impact of Europe', in Kevin Featherstone and Claudio Radaelli (eds) *The Politics of Europeanization*. Oxford: Oxford University Press, 57–78.

Bouffartigues, Paul (2001) *Les cadres*. Paris: La Découverte.

Bourdieu, Pierre (1977). *Outline of a Theory of Practice*. Cambridge: Cambridge University Press

Bourdieu, Pierre (1981) *Questions de sociologie*. Paris: Minuit.

Bourdieu, Pierre (1984) *Distinction: A Social Critique of the Judgement of Taste*. Trans. Richard Nice. Cambridge, MA: Harvard University Press.

Bourdieu, Pierre (1989) 'Social space and symbolic power.' *Sociological Theory*, 4: 18–26.

Bourdieu, Pierre (1990) *The Logic of Practice*. Stanford, CA: Stanford University Press.

Bourdieu, Pierre (1991) *The Craft of Sociology: Epistemological Preliminaries*. New York: Walter de Gruyter.

Bourdieu, Pierre (1993) *Language and Symbolic Power*. Cambridge, MA: Polity Press.

Bourdieu, Pierre (1996) *The State Nobility: Elite Schools in the Field of Power*. Stanford, CA: Stanford University Press.
Bourdieu, Pierre, Jean-Claude Chamboredon and Jean-Claude Passeron (1968) *Le Métier de Sociologue*. Paris: Mouton
Bourdieu, Pierre and Loïc Wacquant (1992) *An Invitation to Reflexive Sociology*. Chicago, IL: University of Chicago Press.
Boyer, Robert and Daniel Drache (1996) *States Against Markets: The Limits of Globalization*. London: Routledge.
Brady, David, Jason Beckfield and Wei Zhao (2007) 'The consequences of economic globalization for affluent democracies.' *Annual Review of Sociology* 33: 313–34.
Braun, Michael and Ettore Recchi (2008) 'Interethnic partnerships of Western Europeans: between preferences and opportunities.' OBETS working paper 1: 73–89.
Breen, Richard (ed.) (2004) *Social Mobility in Europe*. Oxford: Oxford University Press.
Breen, Richard. and Ruud Luijkx (2004a) 'Social mobility in Europe between 1970 and 2000' in Richard Breen (ed.) *Social Mobility in Europe*. Oxford: Oxford University Press.
Breen, Richard and Ruud Luijkx (2004b) 'Conclusions', in Richard Breen (ed.) *Social Mobility in Europe*. Oxford: Oxford University Press.
Breen, Richard and David Rottman (1998) 'Is the national state the appropriate geographical unit for class analysis?' *Sociology*, 32 (1): 1–21.
Breuilly, John (1993) *Nationalism and the State*. Chicago, IL: University of Chicago Press.
Brinton, Mary and Victor Nee (1998) *The New Institutionalism in Sociology*. Palo Alto: Stanford University Press.
Brubaker, Rogers (1992) *Citizenship and Nationhood in France and Germany*. Cambridge, MA: Harvard University Press.
Brubaker, Rogers and Frederick Cooper (2000) 'Beyond identity', *Theory and Society*, 29(1): 1–47.
Bruter, Michael (2005) *Citizens of Europe? The Emergence of a Mass European Identity*. Basingstoke: Palgrave Macmillan.
Bruter, Michael and Yves Déloye (eds) (2007) *Encyclopaedia of European Elections*. Basingstoke: Palgrave Macmillan.
Bücker, Nicola (2008) 'Returning to Where? Images of 'Europe' and support for the process of European integration in Poland', in Ireneuscz Pawel Karolewski and Viktoria Kaina (eds) *European Identity: Theoretical Perspectives and Empirical Insights*. Berlin: LIT Verlag.
Burris, Val (2005) 'Interlocking directorates and political cohesion among corporate elites.' *American Journal of Sociology*, 111(1): 249–83.
Burtenshaw, David, Michael Batemen and Gregory. J. Ashworth. (1991) *The European City: A Western Perspective*. London: Fulton.
Butler, Tim (2005) 'Gentrification', in Nick Buck, Ian Gordon, Alan Harding and Ivan Turok (eds) *Changing Cities: Rethinking Urban Competitiveness, Cohesion and Governance*. Basingstoke: Palgrave Macmillan, 172–87.

Butler, Tim and Garry Robson (2003) *London Calling: The Middle Classes and the Remaking of Inner London.* Oxford: Berg.
Butler, Tim and Mike Savage (eds) (1995) *Social Change and the Middle Classes.* London: University College of London Press.
Cable, Vincent (1995) 'The diminished nation state: a study in the loss of economic power.' *Daedalus,* 124: 27–56.
Campana, Aurélie, Emmanuel Henry and Jay Rowell (eds) (2007) *La construction des problèmes publics en Europe: emergence, formulation et mise en instrument.* Strasbourg: Presses universitaires de Strasbourg.
Cárdenas, Julián (2008) 'The world corporate elite.' Unpublished PhD Dissertation: Universidad de Barcelona.
Castells, Manuel (1996) *The Rise of the Network Society.* Oxford: Blackwell.
Castells, Manuel (2000) *End of Millennium: The Information Age: Economy, Society and Culture.* Oxford: Blackwell.
Cavalli, Alessandro and Olivier Galland (1995) *Youth in Europe: Social Change in Western Europe.* Ann Arbor, MI: University of Michigan Press.
Cavallin, Jens (1998) 'European policies and regulation on media concentration.' *International Journal of Communication Law and Policy*: http://www.ijclp.net/ijclp_web-doc_3-1-1998.html.
Chabanet, Didier (2008) 'When the unemployed challenge the EU: the European marches as a mode of externalization of protest.' *Mobilization,* 13(3): 311–22.
Checkel, Jeffrey (1998a) 'The constructivist turn in international relations theory.' *World Politics,* 20: 324–48.
Checkel, Jeffrey (1998b) 'Social construction and integration.' *Journal of European Public Policy,* 6 (4): 545–60.
Checkel, Jeffrey (2005) 'International institutions and socialization in Europe: introduction and framework.' *International Organization,* 59(4): 801–26.
Checkel, Jeffrey (2006) 'Constructivism and EU politics', in Knud Erik Jørgensen, Mark Pollack and Ben Rosamond (eds) *Handbook of European Union Politics.* London: Sage Publications, 57–76.
Checkel, Jeffrey and Peter Katzenstein (eds) (2009) *European Identity.* Cambridge: Cambridge University Press.
Christiansen, Thomas and Emil Kirchner (2000) *Committee Governance in the European Union.* Manchester: Manchester University Press.
Christiansen, Thomas, Knud Erik Jørgensen and Antje Wiener (2001) *The Social Construction of Europe.* London: Sage.
Cini, Michelle (2007) *European Politics.* Oxford: Oxford University Press.
Claeys, Paul-Henri, Corinne Gobin, Isabelle Smets and Pascaline Winand (eds) (1998), *Lobbying, Pluralism and European Integration.* Brussels: European Interuniversity Press.
Coen, David and Jeremy Richardson (eds) (2009) *Lobbying the European Union. Institutions, Actors and Issues.* Oxford: Oxford University Press.

Cohen, Antonin and Antoine Vauchez (2007a) 'Introduction: law, lawyers, and transnational politics in the production of Europe.' *Law & Social Inquiry*, 32: 75–82.
Cohen, Antonin and Antoine Vauchez (2007b) *The European Constitution and its Discontents: Social Processes and Political Mobilization in the Making of a New Europe*. Brussels: Presses de l'Université libre de Bruxelles.
Cohen, Michael, James March and Johan Olsen (1972) 'A garbage can model of organizational decision-making.' *Administrative Science Quarterly*, 17(1): 1–25.
Cohen, Robin and Paul Kennedy (2007) *Global Sociology*. New York: New York University Press.
Coleman, James S. (1990) *Foundations of Social Theory*. Cambridge, MA: Harvard University Press.
Commission of the European Communities (2001) *European Governance. A White Paper*. COM(2001) 428 final. Brussels: CEC.
Commission of the European Communities (2006) *White Paper on a European Communication Policy*. COM (2006) 35 final. Brussels: CEC.
Constantelos, John (2004) 'The Europeanization of interest group politics in Italy: business associations in Rome and the regions.' *Journal of European Public Policy*, 11 (6): 1020–40.
Cowhey, Peter F. (1990) 'The international telecommunications regime: the political roots of regimes for high technology.' *International Organization*, 44: 169–99.
Cowles, Maria, Thomas Risse and James Caporaso (eds) (2001) *Europeanization and Domestic Change*. Ithaca, NY: Cornell University Press.
Crouch, Colin (1999) *Social Change in Western Europe*. Oxford: Oxford University Press.
Crouch, Colin and Alessandro Pizzorno (1978) *The Resurgence of Class Conflict in Western Europe since 1968*. New York: Holmes & Meier.
Crouch, Colin and Wolfgang Streeck (eds) (1997) *Political Economy of Modern Capitalism: Mapping Convergence and Diversity*. London: Sage.
Dahl, Robert (1961) *Who Governs? Democracy and Power in the American City*. New Haven, CT: Yale University Press.
Dakowska, Dorota (2009) 'The emergence of European political foundations: political entrepreneurs and transnational transfers.' Center for European Political Sociology Working Paper. URL: http://gspe.eu.
Daviter, Falk (2007) 'Policy framing in the European Union.' *Journal of European Public Policy*, 14(4): 654–66.
de Lassalle, Marine and Didier Georgakakis (2007) 'Who are the DG? Trajectories and careers of the directors-general of the Commission'. EU consent on line working papers. URL: http://www.eu-consent.net/library/deliverables/D17_Team7_georgakakis-delassalle.pdf.
de Vreese, Claes H. (2001) 'Europe in the news: a cross-national comparative study of the news coverage of key EU events.' *European Union Politics*, 2: 283–307.

Delanty, Gerard and Chris Rumford (2005) *Rethinking Europe: Social Theory and the Implications of Europeanization*. London: Routledge.
della Porta, Donatella and Manuela Caiani (2007) 'Europeanization from below? Social movements and Europe.' *Mobilisation*, 12 (1): 1–20.
della Porta, Donatella, Hans-Peter Kriesi and Dieter Rucht (eds) (1999) *Social Movements in a Globalizing World*. London: Macmillan.
della Porta, Donatella and Yves Mény (eds) (1997) *Democracy and Corruption in Europe*. London: Pinter.
della Porta, Donatella and Sidney Tarrow (eds) (2004) *Transnational Protest and Global Activism*. Lanham, MD: Rowman & Littlefield.
Denier, Nicole (2010) 'An interview with Neil Fligstein.' *McGill Sociological Review*, 1 (January): 59–65.
Deutsch, Karl W. ([1957] 1969) *Nationalism and Social Communication*. Cambridge, MA: MIT Press.
Deutsch, Karl, Sidney A. Burrell, Robert A. Kann, Jaurice Lee, Jr., Martin Lichterman, Raymond E. Lindgren, Francis L. Loewenheim and Richard W. Van Wagenen (1957) *Political Community in the North-Atlantic Area: International Organization in the Light of Historical Experience*. Princeton, NJ: Princeton University Press.
Deutsch, Karl W., Lewis. J. Edinger, Roy. C. Macridis, and Richard. L. Merritt (1967) *France, Germany, and the Western Alliance: A Study of Elite Attitudes on European Integration and World Politics*. New York: Charles Scribner's Sons.
Dezalay, Yves and Bryan G. Garth (1998) *Dealing in Virtue: International Commercial Arbitration and the Construction of a Transnational Legal Order*. Chicago, IL: University of Chicago Press.
Dezalay, Yves, Antonin Cohen and Dominique Marchetti (eds) (2007) *Constructions européennes*, special issue of *Actes de la recherche en sciences sociales*, 166–7: 4–13.
Diez, Thomas (1999) 'Speaking "Europe": the politics of integration discourse.' *Journal of European Public Policy*, 6(4): 598–613.
Díez Medrano, Juan (2003) *Framing Europe: Attitudes to European Integration in Germany, Spain and the United Kingdom*. Princeton, NJ: Princeton University Press.
Díez Medrano, Juan (2009) 'The public sphere and the European Union's political identity', in Jeffrey T. Checkel and Peter J. Katzenstein (eds) *European Identity*. Cambridge: Cambridge University Press, 81–109.
Díez Medrano, Juan (2010) 'Unpacking European identity', in Sophie Duchesne (ed.) *L'identité européenne entre science politique et science fiction*, *Politique européenne*, no.30: 45–66.
Díez Medrano, Juan and Paula Gutiérrez (2001) Nested identities: national and European identity in Spain. *Ethnic and Racial Studies*, 24(5): 753–78.
DiMaggio, Paul J. (1988) 'Interest and agency in institutional theory', in Lynne G. Zucker (ed.) *Institutional Patterns and Organizations*. Cambridge, MA: Ballinger, 3–22.

DiMaggio, Paul and Walter Powell (eds) (1991) *The New Institutionalism in Organizational Analysis*. Chicago, IL: Chicago University Press

Dinan, Desmond (2005) *Ever Closer Union: An Introduction to European Integration*. Basingstoke: Palgrave Macmillan.

Dobbin, Frank and T. Dowd (2000) 'The market that antitrust built: public policy, private coercion and railroad acquisitions, 1825 to 1922.' *American Sociological Review*, 65:631–57.

Dománski, Henryk (2000) *On the Verge of Convergence: Social Stratification in Eastern Europe*. Budapest: Central European University.

Dorandeu, Renaud and Didier Georgakakis (eds) (2002) *Les métiers de l'Europe politique: acteurs et professionnalisations de la construction européenne*. Strasbourg: Presses Universitaires de Strasbourg.

Dörr, Nicole (2007) 'Is "another" public space actually possible? Deliberative democracy and the case of "women without" in the European Social Forum process.' *Journal of International Women's Studies*, 8 (3): 71–87.

Duchesne, Sophie (2010) 'Introduction', in Sophie Duchesne (ed.) 'L'identité européenne entre science politique et science fiction', *Politique Européenne*, 30: 7–16.

Duchesne, Sophie (ed.) (2010) 'L'identité européenne entre science politique et science fiction', Politique Européenne 30.

Duchesne, Sophie, Florence Haegel, Elizabeth Frazer, Virginie van Ingelgom, Guillaume Garcia, André-Paul Frognier (2010) 'Europe between integration and globalisation: social differences and national frames in the analysis of focus groups conducted in France, Francophone Belgium and the United Kingdom, in 'L'identité européenne entre science politique et science fiction' no. 30, *Politique Européenne*, no. 30: 67–106.

Duchesne, Sophie and André-Paul Frognier (1995) 'Is there a European Identity?', in Oskar Niedermayer and Richard Sinnott (eds) *Public Opinion and Internationalized Governance*. Oxford: Oxford University Press, 193–226.

Duchesne, Sophie and André-Paul Frognier (1998) 'National and European identifications: a dual relationship.' *Comparative European Politics*, 6: 143–68.

Duchesne, Sophie and André-Paul Frognier (2002) 'Sur les dynamiques sociologiques et politiques de l'identification à l'Europe.' *Revue française de science politique*, 52(4): 355–73.

Dunford, Mick, Adrian Smith, Al Rainnie, Jane Hardy, Ray Hudson and David Sadler(2002) 'Networks of value, commodities and regions: reworking divisions of labour in macro-regional economies.' *Progress in Human Geography*, 26: 41–63.

Durkheim, Émile (1982) *The Rules of Sociological Method*. New York: Free Press.

Durkheim, Émile (1984) *The Division of Labor in Society*. New York: Free Press.

Eder, Klaus (2006) 'Europe's borders: the narrative construction of the boundaries of Europe.' *European Journal of Social Theory*, 9: 255–71.

Eder, Klaus. and Bernhard Giesen (eds) (2001) *European Citizenship: National Legacies and Transnational Projects*. Oxford: Oxford University Press.

Egeberg, Morton (1999) 'Transcending intergovernmentalism? Identity and role perceptions of national officials in EU decision-making.' *Journal of European Public Policy*, 6(3): 456–74.

Egeberg, Morten (2006) 'Executive politics as usual: role behaviour and conflict dimensions in the college of European commissioners.' *Journal of European Public Policy*, 13(1): 1–15.

Eisenstadt, Shmuel (1987) *The European Civilisations in Comparative Perspective*. Oslo: Norwegian University Press.

Eisenstadt, Shmuel (2003) *Comparative Civilisations and Multiple Modernities: A Collection of Essays*. Leiden and Boston: Brill.

Eising, Rainer and Beate Kohler-Koch (1999) 'Network governance in the European Union', in Beate Kohler-Koch and Rainer Eising (eds) *The Transformation of Governance in the European Union*. London: Routledge, 3–13.

Ekengren, Magnus (2002) *The Time of European Governance*. Manchester: Manchester University Press.

Elias, Norbert (1978) *The Civilizing Process*. London: Blackwell.

Eriksen, Erik O. (2005a) 'An emerging European public sphere,' *European Journal of Social Theory* 8(3): 341–63.

Eriksen, Erik O. (ed.) (2005b) *Making the European Polity: Reflexive Integration in the EU*. London: Routledge.

Erikson, Robert and John Goldthorpe (1992) *The Constant Flux*. Oxford: Oxford University Press.

Esping-Andersen, Gøsta (1990) *The Three Worlds of Welfare Capitalism*. Cambridge: Polity.

Esping-Andersen, Gøsta (ed.) (1993) *Changing Classes: Stratification and Mobilities in Post-Industrial Societies*. London: Sage.

Esping-Andersen, Gøsta (1999) *The Social Foundations of Post Industrial Economies*. Oxford: Oxford University Press.

Ester, Peter and Hubert Krieger (2008) *Labour Mobility in a Transatlantic Perspective. Conference Report*. Dublin: European Foundation for the Improvement of Living and Working Conditions.

Eurobarometer, European Commission, Brussels. URL: http://ec.europa.eu/public_opinion/index_en.htm.

European Commission (1983) Communication from the Commission to the Council on Telecommunications: *Lines of Action*. COM (1983) 573.

European Commission (1987) *Green Paper on the Development of the Common Market for Telecommunications Services and Equipment*. COM (1987) 290.

European Commission (2004a) *Report on Regulatory Framework for Electronic Communication in the EU*.

European Commission (2004b) *Report on the First Ten Years of the Single Market*.

European Social Survey (2004) *ESS Round 2: European Social Survey Round 2 Data*.

Eyal, Gil, Iván Szelényi and Eleanor Townsley (1998) *Making Capitalism without Capitalists: Class Formation and Elite Struggle in Post-communist Central Europe.* London: Verso.

Evans, Peter B., Dietrich Rueschemeyer and Theda Skocpol (1985) *Bringing the State Back In.* Cambridge: Cambridge University Press.

Falkner, Gerda (2000) 'Policy networks in a multi-level system: convergence towards moderate diversity?' *West European Politics,* 23(4): 94–120.

Favell, Adrian (1998) 'The Europeanisation of immigration politics.' *European Integration online Papers* 2(10): 1–24. URL: http://eiop.or.at/eiop/pdf/1998-010.pdf.

Favell, Adrian (2001) 'Integration policy and integration research in Europe: a review and critique', in Alexander Aleinikoff and Doug Klusmeyer (eds) *Citizenship Today: Global Perspectives and Practices.* Washington, DC: Brookings Institute/Carnegie Endowment for International Peace, 249–99.

Favell, Adrian (2004) 'London as Eurocity: French free movers in the economic capital of London.' *Global and World Cities Research Bulletin,* 150 (Sept): 1–16. URL: http://www.lboro.ac.uk/gawc/rb/rb150.html

Favell, Adrian (2005) 'Europe's identity problem.' *West European Politics,* 28 (5): 1109–16.

Favell, Adrian (2006) 'The sociology of EU politics', in Knud Erik Jørgensen, Mark A. Pollack and Ben Rosamond (eds) *Sage Handbook of European Union Politics Politics.* New York: Sage, 122–8.

Favell, Adrian (2008) *Eurostars and Eurocities: Free Movement and Mobility in an Integrating Europe.* Oxford: Blackwell.

Favell, Adrian and Andrew Geddes (2000) 'Immigration and European integration: new opportunities for transnational political mobilisation?' in Ruud Koopmans and Paul Statham (eds), *Challenging Ethnic Relations Politics in Europe: Comparative and Transnational Perspectives.* Oxford: Oxford University Press, 407–28.

Favell, Adrian and Virginie Guiraudon (2009) 'The sociology of the European Union: an agenda.' *European Union Politics,* 10 (4): 550–76.

Favell, Adrian and Ann Zimmermann (2009) 'Public sphere, political field or governmentality? Mapping the new political sociology of European Union'. Paper presented at the European Sociological Association conference, Lisbon, September 2009.

Featherstone, Kevin and Claudio M. Radaelli (eds) (2003) *The Politics of Europeanization.* Oxford: Oxford University Press.

Fielding, A. J. (1995) 'Migration and middle-class formation in England and Wales 1981–91', in Tim Butler and Mike Savage (eds) *Social Change and the Middle Classes.* London: UCL Press, 169–87.

Finnemore, Martha (1996) *National Interests in International Society.* Ithaca, NY: Cornell University Press.

Fligstein, Neil (2001a) *The Architecture of Markets.* Princeton, NJ: Princeton University Press.

Fligstein, Neil (2001b) 'Social skill and the theory of fields.' URL: http://www.irle.berkeley.edu/culture/papers/Fligstein01_01.pd.

Fligstein, Neil (2008) *Euroclash, the EU, European Identity, and the Future of Europe*. Oxford: Oxford University Press.

Fligstein, Neil and Jim Choo (2005) 'Corporate Governance and Economic Performance.' *Annual Review of Law and Social Science*. Palo Alto, CA: Annual Reviews.

Fligstein, Neil and Iona Mara-Drita (1996) 'How to make a market: reflections on the attempt to create a single market in the European Union.' *American Journal of Sociology*, 102: 1–33.

Fligstein, Neil and Frédéric Mérand (2002) 'Globalization or Europeanization? Evidence on the European economy since 1980.' *Acta Sociologica* 45:7–22.

Fligstein, Neil and Alec Stone Sweet (2002) 'Constructing polities and markets: an institutionalist account of European integration.' *American Journal of Sociology*, 107 (5): 1206–43.

Flora, Peter (ed.) (1986) *Growth to Limits: The Western European Welfare State since World War II*. Berlin: De Gruyter.

Fossum, John Erik (2006) 'Conceptualizing the European Union through four strategies of comparison.' *Comparative European Politics*, 4.

Fossum, John Erik and Philip Schlesinger (eds) (2007) *The European Union and the Public Sphere: A Communicative Space in the Making?* London: Routledge.

Fossum, John Erik and Hans-Jörg Trenz (2006) 'The EU's fledgling society: from deafening silence to critical voice in European constitution making.' *Journal of Civil Society*, 2(1): 57–77.

Foucault, Michel (2004) *Sécurité, territoire, population*. Paris: Gallimard/Seuil.

Gabel, Matt (1998) *Interests and Integration: Market Liberalization, Public Opinion, and European Union*. Ann Arbor, MI: University of Michigan Press.

Ganzeboom, Harry B.G, Ruud Luijkx and Donald J. Treiman (1989) 'Intergenerational class mobility in comparative perspective,' *Research in Social Stratification and Mobility*, 8: 3–84.

Garrett, Geoffrey (1998) *Partisan Politics in the Global Economy*. New York: Cambridge University Press.

Gaspar, Sofia (2009) 'Mixed marriages between Europeans: a sociological analysis on their evolution in Portugal.' Paper presented at the II International Conference on Intercultural Studies. ISCAP: April, 2009.

Gaxie, Daniel and Nicolas Hubé (2007) 'Projet CONCORDE: les conceptions ordinaires de l'Europe. Une approche de sociologie compréhensive.' *Politique européenne*, 23(3): 179–82.

Geddes, Andrew (2000) 'Lobbying for migrant inclusion in the European Union: new opportunities for transnational advocacy?' *Journal of European Public Policy*, 7(4): 632–49.

Geddes, Andrew and Virginie Guiraudon (2003) 'The emergence of a European Union policy paradigm amidst contrasting national models: Britain, France and EU anti-discrimination policy.' *West European Politics*, 27(2): 334–53.

Gellner, Ernest (1983) *Nations and Nationalism*. Ithaca, NY: Cornell University Press.
Georgakakis, Didier (2008a) 'European civil service as a group: sociological notes about the Eurocrats' common culture', in Joachim Beck and Franz Thedieck, *The European Dimension of Administrative Culture*. Baden Baden: Nomos
Georgakakis, Didier (2008b) 'La sociologie historique et politique de l'Union européenne: un point de vue d'ensemble et quelques contre points.' *Politique européenne*, 25(2): 53–85.
Georgakakis, Didier and Marine de Lassalle (eds) (2008a) *La 'nouvelle gouvernance' européenne: genèses et usages politiques d'un livre blanc*. Strasbourg: Presses Universitaires de Strasbourg.
Georgakakis, Didier and Marine de Lassalle (2008b) 'Where have all the lawyers gone? Structure and transformations of the top European Commission officials' legal training.' EUI Working Papers RSCAS 2008/ 38. URL: http://cadmus.eui.eu/dspace/handle/1814/10032.
Gerhards, Jürgen (2000) 'Europäisierung von Ökonomie und Politik und die Trägheit der Entstehung einer europäischen Öffentlichkeit', in M. Bach (ed.), *Die Europäisierung nationaler Gesellschaften: Sonderheft der Kölner Zeitschrift für Soziologie und Sozialpsychologie*. Opladen: Westdeutscher Verlag, 277–305.
Gerhards, Jürgen (2007) *Cultural Overstretch? Differences Between Old and New Member States of the EU and Turkey*. London: Routledge.
Gerhards, Jürgen (2010) *Mehrsprachigkeit in vereinten Europa: Transnationales sprachlichen Kapital als Ressource in einer globalisieren Welt*. Wiesbaden: VS-Verlag.
Gerth, Hans. H. and C. Wright Mills (eds) (1954) *Character and Social Structure: The Psychology of Social Institutions*. London: Routledge.
Giddens, Anthony (1971) *Capitalism and Modern Social Theory: An Analysis of the Writings of Marx, Durkheim and Weber*. Cambridge: Cambridge University Press.
Giddens, Anthony (1984) *The Constitution of Society: Outline of the Theory of Structuration*. Cambridge: Polity.
Giddens, Anthony (1990) *The Consequences of Modernity*. Palo Alto, CA: Stanford University Press.
Giddens, Anthony (1994) 'Living in a post-traditional society', in Ulrich Beck, Anthony Giddens and Scott Lash, *Reflexive Modernization: Politics, Tradition and Aesthetics in the Modern Social Order*. Cambridge: Polity Press, 56–109.
Glaser, Barney G. and Anselm L. Strauss (1967) *The Discovery of Grounded Theory*. New York: Aldine de Gruyter.
Glick-Schiller, Nina and Andreas Wimmer (2002) 'Methodological nationalism and beyond: nation-state building, migration and the social sciences.' *Global Networks*, 2 (4): 301–34.
Goffman, Erving (1974) *Frame Analysis: An Essay on the Organization of Experience*. Cambridge, MA: Harvard University Press.

Golthorpe, John (1982) 'On the service class, its formation and future', in Anthony Giddens and Gavin MacKenzie (eds) *Social Class and the Division of Labour.* Cambridge: Cambridge University Press, 47–64.

Goldthorpe, John, David Lockwood, Frank Bechhofer and Jennifer Platt (1969) *The Affluent Worker in the Class Structure.* Cambridge: Cambridge University Press.

Goodin, Robert and Hans-Dieter Klingemann (eds) (1996) *A New Handbook of Political Science.* Oxford: Oxford University Press.

Gouldner, Alvin W. (1957) 'Cosmopolitans and locals: towards an analysis of latent social roles – I.' *Administrative Science Quarterly,* 2: 281–306.

Granovetter, Mark (1985) 'Economic action and social structure: the problem of embeddedness.' *American Journal of Sociology,* 91: 481–510.

Graziano, Paolo and Maarten Vink (eds) (2006) *Europeanization: New Research Agendas.* Basingstoke: Palgrave Macmillan.

Green, David Michael (2007) *The Europeans: Political Identity in an Emerging Polity.* Boulder, CO: Lynne Rienner.

Greenwood, Justin (2007) *Interest Representation in the European Union.* 2nd edn. Basingstoke: Palgrave Macmillan.

Grossman, Emiliano (2004) 'Bringing politics back in: rethinking the role of economic interest groups in European integration', *Journal of European Public Policy* 11(4): 637–54.

Groux, Guy (1982) *Les cadres.* Paris: La Découverte.

Guiraudon, Virginie (2000) 'L'espace sociopolitique européen: un champ encore en friche?', *Sociologie de l'Europe: élites, mobilisations et configurations institutionnelles,* double issue of *Cultures et conflits,* 38–9: 7–37.

Guiraudon, Virginie (2001) 'Weak weapons of the weak? Mobilizing around migration at the EU-level', in Doug Imig and Sidney Tarrow (eds) *Contentious Europeans: Protest and Politics in an Emerging Polity.* Lanham, MD: Rowman & Littlefield, 163–83.

Guiraudon, Virginie (2003) 'The constitution of a European immigration policy domain: a political sociology approach.' *Journal of European Public Policy,* 10(2): 263–82.

Guiraudon, Virginie (2004) 'Construire une politique européenne de lutte contre les discriminations: l'histoire de la directive "race".' *Sociétés contemporaines,* 53: 11–32.

Guiraudon, Virginie (2006) 'Europe through Europeans' eyes: political sociology and EU studies.' *EUSA Newsletter,* 19(1): 1–7.

Guiraudon, Virginie (with Olivier Baisnée and Olivier Grojean) (2002) 'Mesurer la place de l'Europe dans les débats de politique publique nationaux: enjeux théoriques, protocole méthodologique et premiers résultats empiriques à partir du cas français.' Paper presented at the French Association of Political Science meeting, Lille, September 2002.

Guiraudon, Virginie and Paul Statham (2003) 'Europeanization, public debates and contentious politics in Britain and France. Two different paths?' Paper presented at the international conference 'Europeanisation of

public spheres? Political mobilisation, public communication, and the European Union' at the Wissenschaftszentrum Berlin für Sozialforschung', June 2003.
Haas, Ernst B. (1958) *The Uniting of Europe. Political, Social, and Economic Forces, 1950–1957*. Stanford, CA: Stanford California Press.
Haas, Ernst B. (1961) 'International integration: the European and the universal process.' *International Organization*, 15(3): 366–92.
Habermas, Jürgen (1969) *Strukturwandel der Öffenlichkeit: Untersuchungen zu einer Kategorie der bürgerlichen Gesellschaft*. Frankfurt-am-Main: Suhrkamp.
Habermas, Jürgen (1989) *The Structural Transformation of the Public Sphere*. Cambridge: Polity.
Habermas, Jürgen (2001) *The Postnational Constellation*. Oxford: Polity Press.
Hall, Peter and David Soskice (2001) *Varieties of Capitalism: The Institutional Foundations of Comparative Advantage*. Oxford: Oxford University Press.
Hall, Peter and Rosemary Taylor (1996) 'Political science and the three institutionalisms.' *Political Studies*, 44(5): 936–57.
Haller, Max (1993) *Class Structure in Europe: New Findings from East-West Comparisons of Social Structure and Mobility*. Oxford: Blackwell.
Haller, Max. (2008) *European Integration as an Elite Process: The Failure of a Dream?* New York: Routledge.
Hart, Jeffrey A. (1988) 'The politics of global competition in the telecommunications industry.' *The Information Society*, 5(3): 169–201.
Hawthorn, G. (1991) *Plausible Worlds: Possibility and Understanding in History and the Social Sciences*. Cambridge: Cambridge University Press.
Helfferich, Barbara and Felix Kolb (2001) 'Multilevel action coordination in European contentious politics: the case of the European Women's Lobby', in Doug Imig and Sidney Tarrow (eds), *Contentious Europeans: Protest and Politics in an Emerging Polity*. Lanham, MD: Rowman & Littlefield, 143–61.
Héritier, Adrienne, Dieter Kerwer, Christoph Knill, Dirk Lehmkuhl, Michael Teutsch and Anne-Cecile Douillet (2001) *Differential Europe. The European Union Impact on National Policymaking*. Lanham, MD: Rowman & Littlefield.
Herm, A. (2008) 'Recent migration trends: citizens of EU-27 member states become ever mobile while EU remains attractive to non-EU citizens.' *Statistics in Focus*. 98, Eurostat. URL: http://epp.eurostat.ec.europa.eu/cache/ITY_OFFPUB/KS-SF-08-098/EN/KS-SF-08-098-EN.PDF.
Hermann, Richard K., Thomas Risse, Marilynn B. Brewer (eds) (2004) *Transnational Identities: Becoming European in the EU*. Lanham, MD: Rowman & Littlefield.
Hewstone, Miles (1986) *Understanding Attitudes to European Integration*. Cambridge: Cambridge University Press.
Hills, J. (1986) *Deregulating Telecoms*. London: Frances Pinter.
Hirschman, Albert O. (1970) *Exit, Voice, and Loyalty: Responses to Decline in Firms, Organizations, and States*. Cambridge, MA: Harvard University Press.

Hix, Simon (1994) 'The study of the European community: the challenge to comparative politics.' *West European Politics*, 17(1): 1–30.
Hix, Simon (1998) 'The study of the European Union II: the "new governance" agenda and its rival.' *Journal of European Public Policy*, 5(1): 38 –65.
Hix, Simon (2005) *The Political System of the European Union*. Basingstoke: Palgrave Macmillan.
Holmes, Douglas (2000) *Integral Europe: Fast-Capitalism, Multiculturalism, Neofascism*. Princeton, NJ: Princeton University Press.
Hooghe, Liesbet (2001) *The European Commission and the Integration of Europe: Images of Governance*. Cambridge: Cambridge University Press.
Hooghe, Liesbet (2002) *The European Commission and the Integration of Europe*. Cambridge: Cambridge University Press.
Hooghe, Liesbet (2003) 'Europe divided? Elites vs. public opinion on European integration.' *European Union Politics*, 4 (3): 281–305.
Hooghe, Liesbet (2005) 'Several roads lead to international norms, but few via international socialization: a case study of the European Commission.' *International Organization*, 59(4): 861–98.
Hooghe, Liesbet and Gary Marks (2004) 'Does identity or economic rationality drive public opinion on European integration?' *Political Science and Politics*, 37 (3): 415–20.
Hooghe, Liesbet and Gary Marks (2005) 'Calculation, community, and cues: public opinion on European integration.' *European Union Politics*, 6(4): 419–43.
Hooghe, Liesbet and Gary Marks (2008) 'A post-functionalist theory of European integration: from permissive consensus to constraining dissensus.' *British Journal of Political Science*, 39: 1–23.
Hoskins, Catherine (ed.) (1996) *Integrating Gender. Women, Law and Politics in the European Union*. New York: Verso.
Howorth, Jolyon (2007) *Security and Defence in the European Union*. Basingstoke: Palgrave Macmillan.
Imig, Doug (2004) 'Contestation on the streets: European protest and the emerging Euro-polity.' *Comparative Political Studies*, 35(8): 914–33.
Imig, Doug and Sidney Tarrow (eds) (2001) *Contentious Europeans: Protest Politics in an Emerging Polity*. New York: Rowman & Littlefield.
Immerfall, Stefan and Göran Therborn (2010) *Handbook of European Societies: Social Transformations in the 21st Century*. Frankfurt: Springer.
Irondelle, Bastien (2003) 'Europeanization without the European Union? French military reforms, 1991–1996.' *Journal of European Public Policy*, 10(2): 208–26.
Irondelle, Bastien (2006) 'French political science and European integration: the state of the art.' *French Politics*, 4(3): 188–208.
Jachtenfuchs, Markus (2002) *Die Konstruction Europas: Verfassungsideen und Institutionelle Entwicklung* Baden-Baden: Nomos.
Jacquot, Sophie (2010) 'The paradox of gender mainstreaming: the unanticipated effects of new modes of governance in the gender equality domain.' *West European Politics*, 33(1): 118–35.

Jacquot, Sophie and Cornelia Woll (2003) 'Usage of European integration: Europeanization from a sociological perspective.' *European Integration Online Papers*, URL: http://eiop.or.at/eiop/texte/2003-012a.htm.

Jettinghoff, Alex and Harm Schepel (eds) (2005) *Lawyers' Circles: Lawyers and European Legal Integration*. The Hague: Elzevir Reed.

Joppke, Christian (1998) 'Immigration challenges the nation state', in Christian Joppke (ed.) *Challenge to the Nation State: Immigration in Western Europe and the United States*. Oxford: Oxford University Press.

Judt, Tony (2005) *Postwar: A History of Europe Since 1945*. London: Penguin.

Kaelble, Hartmut (1987) *Auf dem Weg zu einer Europäischen Gesellschaft*. Münich: Beck.

Kaelble, Hartmut (2007) *Sozialgeschichte Europas: 1945 bis zur Gegenwart*. Frankfurt-am-Main: C.H. Beck.

Kaiser, Wolfram (2008) 'History meets politics: overcoming the interdisciplinary *Volapük* in research on the EU,' *Journal of European Public Policy*, 15(2): 300–13.

Kaiser, Wolfram, Brigitte Leucht and Morten Rasmussen (eds) (2008) *The History of the European Union: Origins of a Trans- and Supranational Polity 1950–72*. London: Routledge.

Katz, Richard and Bernd Wessels (eds) (1999) *The European Parliament, National Parliaments, and European Integration*. Oxford: Oxford University Press.

Katzenstein, Peter (2005) *A World of Regions: Asia and Europe in the American Imperium*. Princeton, NJ, Cornell University Press.

Katzenstein, Peter (ed.) (1996a) *The Culture of National Security. Identity and Norms in World Politics*. New York: Colombia University Press.

Katzenstein, Peter (ed.) (1996b) *Cultural Norms and National Security: Police and Military in Postwar Japan*. Ithica, NY: Cornell University Press.

Kauppi, Niilo (1994) *The Making of an Avant-Garde, Tel Quel*. Berlin and NewYork: Mouton de Gruyter.

Kauppi, Niilo (1996a) *French Intellectual Nobility: Institutional and Symbolic Transformations in the Post-Sartrian Era*. Albany, NY: SUNY-Press.

Kauppi, Niilo (1996b) 'European Union institutions and French political careers.' *Scandinavian Political Studies*, 19(1): 1–24.

Kauppi, Niilo (2000a) *The Politics of Embodiment: Habits, Power, and Pierre Bourdieu's Theory*. Frankfurt: Peter Lang.

Kauppi, Niilo (2000b) 'La construction de l'Europe: le cas des élections européennes en Finlande 1999.' *Cultures et Conflits*, 38–39: 101–18.

Kauppi, Niilo (2003) 'Bourdieu's political sociology and the politics of European integration.' *Theory and Society*, 32 (5–6): 775–89.

Kauppi, Niilo (2005) *Democracy, Social Resources and Political Power in the European Union*. Manchester: Manchester University Press.

Kauppi, Niilo (2007) 'Légitimation politique et espaces publics européens: la communication comme ressource et pratique', in Aurélie Campana, Emmanuel Henry and Jay Rowell (eds) *La construction des problèmes publics en Europe*, Strasbourg: Presses universitaires de Strasbourg, 137–54.

Kauppi, Niilo (2009) 'Rationality, institutions and reflexivity in the EU: some ontological and epistemological considerations.' Center for European Political Sociology Working Paper. URL: http://gspe.eu.

Kauppi, Niilo and Mikael Rask Madsen (2007) 'European integration: scientific object or political agenda?' *Praktiske Grunde*, 1: 28–31. URL: http://www.hexis.dk/praktiskegrunde-01-2007.pdf.

Kazepov, Yuri (ed.) (2005) *Cities of Europe: Changing Contexts, Local Arrangements, and the Challenge to Urban Cohesion*. Oxford: Blackwell.

Keck, Margaret and Katheryn Sikkink (1998) *Activists Beyond Borders: Advocacy Networks in International Politics*. Ithaca, NY: Cornell University Press.

Kentor, Jeffery and Jank, Young Suk (2004) 'Yes there is a (growing) transnational business community: a study in interlocking directorates 1983–98.' *International Sociology*, 19(3), September: 355–68.

Kingdon, John (1984) *Agendas, Alternatives, and Public Policies*. New York: Longman.

Knill, Christopher (2001) *The Europeanization of National Administrations. Patterns of Institutional Change and Persistence*. Cambridge: Cambridge University Press.

Knudsen, Ann-Christina L. (2009) *Farmers on Welfare: The Making of the Common Agricultural Policy*. Ithaca, NY: Cornell University Press.

Kocka, Jürgen and Allan Mitchell (1993) *Bourgeois Society in 19th Century Europe*. Oxford: Berg.

Kohler-Koch, Beate, and Markus Jachtenfuchs (2004) 'Multi-level governance', in Antje Wiener and Thomas Diez (eds), *European Integration Theory*. Oxford: Oxford University Press, 97–115.

Kolher-Koch, Beate and Berthold Rittberger (eds) (2007) *Debating the Democratic Legitimacy of the European Union*. Lanham, MD: Rowman & Littlefield

Koopmans, Ruud (2007) 'Who inhabits the European public sphere? Winners and losers, supporters and opponents in Europeanised political debates.' *European Journal of Political Research*, 46(2): 183–210.

Koopmans, Ruud and Paul Statham (1999) 'Political claims analysis: integrating protest event and political discourse approaches.' *Mobilization*, 4(2): 203–22.

Koopmans, Ruud, and Paul Statham (2002) *The Transformation of Political Mobilisation and Communication in European Public Spheres: A Research Outline*. URL: http://europub.wz-berlin.de.

Koopmans, Ruud and Paul Statham (2003) 'How national citizenship shapes transnationalism: a comparative analysis of migrant and minority claims-making in Germany, Great Britain and the Netherlands', in Christian Joppke and Ewa Morawska (eds) *Toward Assimilation and Citizenship: Immigrants in Liberal Nation-States*. Basingstoke: Palgrave Macmillan, 195–238.

Koopmans, Ruud and Paul Statham (eds) (2010) *The Making of a European Public Sphere: Media Discourse and Political Contention*. Cambridge: Cambridge University Press.

Korpi, Walter (1987) *Class, Power and State Autonomy in Welfare State Development*. Stockholm: Swedish Institute for Social Research.
Kull, Michael (2008) *EU Multilevel Governance in the Making: The Community Initiative Leader + in Finland and Germany*. Helsinki: Acta Politica.
Lagneau, Eric and Pierre Lefébure (2000) 'The spiral of Vilvoorde: mediatization and politicization of protest.' *La Lettre de la Maison française d'Oxford*, 12, Trinity Term (June): 91–117.
Lagroye, Jacques (1997) *Sociologie Politique*. Paris: Dalloz-Presses de la Fondation nationale des sciences politiques.
Lamont, Michèle (1992) *Money, Morals and Manners: The Culture of the French and American Upper Middle Class*. Chicago, IL: Chicago University Press.
Lamont, Michèle (2000) *The Dignity of Working Men: Morality and Boundaries of Race, Class and Immigration*. Cambridge, MA: Cambridge University Press.
Lane, Jan-Erik and Ersson, Svante (1999) *Politics and Society in Western Europe*. London: Sage.
Lawler, Edward (1992) 'Affective attachments to nested groups: a choice-process theory.' *American Sociological Review*, 57(3): 327–40.
Le Galès, Patrick (2002) *European Cities: Social Conflicts and Governance*. Oxford: Oxford University Press.
Lenoir, Rémi, Dominique Merllié, Patrick Champagne and Louis Pinto (1996). *Initiation à la pratique sociologique*. Paris: Dunod.
Le Roux, Brigitte and Henry Rouanet (2004) *Geometric Data Analysis. From Correspondence Analysis to Structured Data Analysis*. Dordrecht: Kluwer Academic Publishers.
Lévi-Strauss, Claude (1963) *Structural Anthropology*. New York: Basic Books.
Lévi-Strauss, Claude (1968) *The Savage Mind*. Chicago, IL: University of Chicago Press.
Lindberg, Leon (1963) *Political Dynamics of European Economic Integration*. Oxford: Oxford University Press.
Lindblom, Charles (1959) 'The science of muddling through.' *Public Administration Review*, 19(2):79–88.
Lipsky, Michael (1980) *Street-level Bureaucracy: Dilemmas of the Individual in Public Services*. New York: Russell Sage.
Lockwood, David (1995) 'Introduction: making out the middle class(es)', in Tim Butler and Mike Savage (eds), *Social Change and the Middle Classes*. London: University College of London Press, 1–14.
Lombardo, Elisabeta, Petra Meier and Mieke Verloo (eds) (2009) *The Discursive Politics of Gender Equality. Stretching, Bending and Policymaking*. London: Routledge.
Lukes, Steven (2005) *Power: A Radical View*. London: Palgrave Macmillan.
Madsen, Mikael Rask (2005) 'L' émergence d'un champ des droits de l'homme dans les pays européens: enjeux professionnels et stratégies d'État au carrefour du droit et de la politique (France, Grande-Bretagne et Pays Scandinaves, 1945–2000).' PhD dissertation. Paris: École des hautes études en sciences sociales.

Madsen, Mikael Rask (2006) 'Transnational fields: elements of a reflexive sociology of the internationalisation of law.' *Retfærd*, 3(114): 23–41.
Majone, Giandomenico (1996) *Regulating Europe*. London: Routledge.
Mangenot, Michel (2003) 'Une chancellerie du Prince: le secrétariat général du Conseil dans le processus de décision bruxellois.' *Politique européenne*, 11.
Mangenot, Michel (2009) 'European games and institutional innovation: the making of Eurojust.' Center for European Political Sociology Working Paper URL: http://gspe.eu.
Mann, Michael (1993a) 'Nation-states in Europe and other continents: diversifying, developing, not dying.' *Daedalus*, 122 (3): 115–40.
Mann, Michael (1993b) *Sources of Social Power: The Rise of Classes and Nation-States*. Cambridge: Cambridge University Press.
Mann, Michael (1998) 'Is there a society called Euro?', in Roland Axtmann (ed.), *Globalization and Europe: Theoretical and Empirical Investigations*. London: Pinker, 184–207.
Mann, Michael (1999) 'Has globalization ended the rise of the nation-state?', in T.V. Paul and J.A. Hall, *International Order and the Future of World Politics*. Cambridge, Cambridge University Press: 237–61.
Manners, Ian (2007) 'Another Europe is possible: critical perspectives on European Union politics', in Knud Erik Jorgensen, Mark A. Pollack and Ben Rosamond (eds), *Handbook of EU Politics*. London: Sage, 77–96.
March, James and Johan Olsen (1984) 'The new institutionalism: organizational factors in political life.' *American Political Science Review*, 78(3): 734–49.
Marks, Gary and Doug McAdam (1996) 'Social movements and the changing structure of political opportunity in the European Community.' *West European Politics*, 19(2): 249–78.
Marks, Gary, Fritz W. Scharpf, Philippe C. Schmitter and Wolfgang Streeck (1996) *Governance in the European Union*. London: Sage.
Martin, Andrew and George Ross (1999) *The Brave New World of European Labor*. New York: Berghahn.
Martin, Bill (1998) 'Knowledge, identity and the middle class: from collective to invididualised classe formation?' *The Sociological Review*, 4: 653–86.
Martin, John Levi (2003) 'What is field theory?' *American Journal of Sociology*, 109(1):1–49.
Marx, Karl (1844[1977]) *Contribution to the Critique of Hegel's Philosophy of Right*. Cambridge: Cambridge University Press.
Marx, Karl (2000) *Economic and Philosophical Manuscript of 1844*. URL: http://www.marxists.org/archive/marx/works/1844/manuscripts/preface.htm.
Mattli, Walter (1999) *The Logic of Regional Integration: Europe and Beyond*. Cambridge, MA: Cambridge University Press.
Mau, Steffen (2010) *Social Transnationalism: Lifeworlds beyond the Nation State*. London: Routledge.
Mau, Steffen and Roland Verwiebe (2009) *Die Sozialstruktur Europas*. Konstanz: UTB/UVK Verlagsanstalt.

Mau, Steffen, Ann Zimmermann and Jan Mewes (2008) 'Cosmopolitan attitudes through transnational social practices?' *Global Networks*, 8(1): 1–24.
Mauss, Marcel ([1934]1979) 'The notion of body techniques', in *Marcel Mauss Sociology and Psychology: Essays*. London: Routledge & Kegan Paul, 95–123.
Mayntz, Renate and Fritz Scharpf (2001) 'L'institutionnalisme centré sur les acteurs.' *Politix*, 14(55): 95–123. (German original 1995.)
Mazey, Sonia and Jeremy Richardson (1993) *Lobbying in the European Community*. Oxford: Oxford University Press.
Mazower, Mark (2000) *Dark Continent: Europe's Twentieth Century*. London: Vintage.
McLaren, Lauren (2006) *Identity, Interests and Attitudes to European Integration*. Basingstoke: Palgrave Macmillan.
Meehan, Elizabeth (2000) 'Citizenship and the European Union.' Discussion Paper presented at the Zentrum für Europäische Integrationsforschung, Rheinische Friedrich Wilhelms-Universität Bonn.
Mendras, H. (1997) *L'Europe des européens: Sociologie de l'Europe occidentale*. Paris: Gallimard.
Menéndez-Alarcón, Antonio V. (2005) *The Cultural Realm of European Integration*. London: Praeger.
Menon, Anand (2008) 'French follies?' *Politique européenne*, 25(2): 217–230.
Mény, Yves (1999) *Le système politique français*. Paris: Montchrestien.
Mérand, Frédéric (2006) 'Social representations in the European security and defense policy.' *Cooperation and Conflict* 41(2): 131–52.
Mérand, Frédéric (2008) *European Defence Policy: Beyond the Nation State*. Oxford: Oxford University Press.
Mérand, Frédéric (2010) 'Pierre Bourdieu and the birth of European defense.' *Security Studies*, 19(2): 342–74.
Mérand, Frédéric and Sabine Saurugger (2010) 'Does European integration theory need sociology?' *Comparative European Politics*, 8: 1–18.
Merton, Robert K. (1957) 'Patterns of influence: locals and cosmopolitans', in *Social theory and social structure*. Glencoe: The Free Press.
Meyer, John and W.R. Scott (1983) *Organizational Environments: Ritual and Rationality*. Beverly Hills, CA: Sage.
Michel, Hélène (ed.) (2006) *Lobbyistes et lobbying de l'Union européenne*. Strasbourg: Presses universitaires de Strasbourg.
Michel, Hélène (2007) 'La "société civile" dans la "gouvernance européenne". Éléments pour une sociologie d'une catégorie politique.' *Actes de la recherche en sciences sociales* 166–7: 30–7.
Michel, Hélène (2009), 'The construction of a European interest through legal expertise: property owners' associations and the Charter of Fundamental Rights', in Michel Mangenot and Jay Rowell Jay (eds) *What Europe constructs*. Manchester: Manchester University Press.
Milward, Alan S. (1997) 'The social bases of monetary union', in Peter Gowan and Perry Anderson (eds) *The Question of Europe*. London: Verso, 149–61.

Milward, Alan S., George Brennan and Federico Romero (1992) *The European Rescue of the Nation-State* (revised edition 2000) London: Routledge.
Milward, Alan S., Ruggero Ranieri, Frances M.B. Lynch, Federico Romero and Vibeke Dorensen (1993) *The Frontier of National Sovereignty: History and Theory 1945-1992*. London: Routledge.
Mizruchi, Mark (1982) *The American Corporate Network, 1904-1974*. Beverly Hills, CA: Sage Publications.
Mizruchi, Mark (1992) *The Structure of Corporate Political Action: Interfirm Relations and their Consequences*. Cambridge, MA: Harvard University Press.
Moch, Leslie Page (2003) *Moving Europeans: Migration in Western Europe Since 1650*. Bloomington, IN: Indiana University Press.
Modood, Tariq, Richard Berthoud, Jane Lakey, James Nazroo, Patten Smith, Satnam Virdee and Sharon Beishon (1997) *Ethnic Minorities in Britain: Diversity and Disadvantage*. London: Policy Studies Institute.
Monforte, Pierre (2008) 'Europeanization from below? Protest against 'Fortress Europe'.' Florence, European University Institute PhD Thesis.
Moravcsik, Andrew (1998) *The Choice for Europe: Social Purpose and State Power from Messina to Maastricht*. Ithaca, NY: Cornell University Press.
Moravcsik, Andrew (1999) '"Is something rotten in the state of Denmark?" Constructivism and European integration.' *Journal of European Public Policy*, 6(4): 669-81.
Moravcsik, Andrew (2005) 'The European constitutional compromise', *EUSA Review*, 18(2): 1-7.
Mueller, Walter and Markus Gangl (eds) (2004) *Transitions from Education to Work in Europe: The Integration of Youth into Labour Markets*. Oxford: Oxford University Press.
Münch, Richard (2001) *Offene Räume. Soziale Integration diesseits und jenseits des Nationalstaats*. Frankfurt-am-Main: Suhrkamp.
Münch, Richard (2008) *Die Konstruktion der europäisches Gesellschaft: zur Dialektik von transnationaler Integration und nationaler Disintegration*. Frankfürt: Campus.
Myles, John and Adnan Turegun (1994) 'Comparative studies in class structure.' *Annual Review of Sociology*, 20: 103-24.
Nash, Kate and Alan Scott (2001) *The Blackwell Companion to Political Sociology*. Oxford: Blackwell.
Neumann, Iver (2005) 'To be a diplomat.' *International Studies Perspectives*, 6(1): 72-93.
Neveu, Erik (2004) 'L'Europe comme "communauté inimaginable"? L'échec du magazine français l'Européen (mars-juillet 1998)', in Dominique Marchetti (ed.) *En quête d'Europe: médias européens et médiatisation de l'Europe*. Rennes: Presses universitaires de Rennes.
Nikolaïdis, Kalypso (2007) 'Trusting the Poles? Constructing Europe through mutual recognition.' *Journal of European Public Policy*, 14(5): 682-98.
North, Douglas (1990) *Institutions, Institutional Change and Economic Performance*. Cambridge: Cambridge University Press.

OCS (Observation du changement social) (1987) *L'esprit des lieux*. Paris: CNRS éditions.
OECD (1998) *OECD Economic Outlook 1998* (2): 154.
Office for National Statistics (2006) *Labour Force Survey: Employment Status by Occupation and Sex, April–June 2006*.
Ohmae, Kenichi (1985) *Triad Power*. St. Petersberg, FL: Seashellbooks.
Olsen, Johan P. (2002) 'The many faces of Europeanization.' *Journal of Common Market Studies*, 40(5): 921–52.
Olson, Mancur (1971) *The Logic of Collective Action: Public Goods and the Theory of Groups*. Cambridge, MA: Harvard University Press.
Ostner, Ilona and Jane Lewis (1995) 'Gender and the evolution of European social policies', in Stephan Leibfried and Paul Pierson (eds) *European Social Policy: Between Fragmentation and Integration*. Washington, DC: The Brookings Institution, 159–93.
Outhwaite, William (2008) *European Society*. Cambridge: Polity.
Parsons, Craig (2003) *A Certain Idea of Europe*. Ithaca, NY: Cornell University Press.
Parsons, Craig (2010) 'How – and how much – are sociological approaches to the EU distinctive?' *Comparative European Politics*, 8: 143–59.
Parsons, Talcott (1951) *The Social System*. London: Routledge
Parsons, Talcott (1967) *Sociological Theory and Modern Society*. New York: Free Press.
Pauly, Louis and Simon Reich (1997) 'National structures and multinational corporation behavior.' *International Organization*, 51: 1–31.
Peixoto, J. (2001) 'Migration and Policies in the European Union: high-skilled mobility, free movement of labor and the recognition of diplomas.' *International Migration*, 39 (1): 33–61.
Peter, B. Guy (1994) 'Agenda setting in the European community.' *Journal of European Public Policy*, 1(1): 9–26.
Pierson, Paul (1996) 'The path to European integration: a historical institutionalist perspective.' *Comparative Political Studies*, 29:2 (123–63).
Pierson, Paul (2004) *Politics in Time: History, Institutions and Social Analysis*. Princeton, NJ: Princeton University Press.
Pinçon, Michel and Pinçon-Charlot Monique (1989) *Dans les beaux quartiers*. Paris: Seuil.
Pinçon, Michel and Pinçon-Charlot Monique. (2000) *Sociologie de la bourgeoisie*. Paris: La Découverte, 'Repères'.
Pinol, Jean-Luc (2002) *Histoire d'Europe urbaine*. Paris: Presses universitaires de France.
Podolny, Joel (2005) *Status Signals: A Sociological Theory of Market Competition*. Princeton, NJ: Princeton University Press.
Polanyi, Karl (1957) *The Great Transformation*. Boston: Beacon Press.
Pollack, Mark (1997) *The Engines of European Integration*. Oxford: Oxford University Press.

Pollack, Mark (1998) 'Constructivism, social psychology and elite attitide change: lessons from an exhausted research paradigm'. Paper presented at the 11th International Conference of Europeanists.

Poulantzas, Nicos (1968) *Pouvoir politique et classes sociales*. Paris: Maspéro.

Pouliot, Vincent (2008) 'The logic of practicality: a theory of practice of security communities.' *International Organization*, 62(2): 257–88.

Powell, Walter and Paul DiMaggio (eds) (1991) *The New Institutionalism in Organizational Analysis*. Chicago, IL: University of Chicago Press.

Pratschke, Jonathan (2007) 'L'articolazione territoriale dello svantaggio sociale in Italia: una nuova misura multidimensionale per piccole aree geografiche', in Andrea Brandolini and Chiara Saraceno, *Povertà e Benessere: Una geografia delle disuguaglianze in Italia*. Bologna: Il Mulino, 123–46.

Préteceille, Edmond (2006) 'La ségrégation contre la cohésion sociale, le cas de la métropole parisienne', in H.Lagrange (ed.), *L'épreuve des inégalités*. Paris: PUF.

Princen, Sebastian and Mark Rhinard (2006) 'Crashing and creeping: agenda-setting dynamics in the European Union.' *Journal of European Public Policy*, 13(7): 1119–32.

Putnam, Robert (1993). *Making Democracy Work*. Princeton, NJ: Princeton University Press.

Putnam, Robert (2000) *Bowling Alone: The Collapse and Revival of American Community*. New York: Simon & Schuster.

Radaelli, Claudio (1999) 'The public policy of the European Union: whither the politics of expertise?' *Journal of European Public Policy*, 6(5): 757–74.

Radaelli, Claudio (2000) 'Whither Europeanization? Concept stretching and substantive change.' *European Integration online Papers* (EIoP) 4 (8). URL: http://eiop.or.at/eiop/texte/2000-008a.htm (consulted 24 April 2009).

Recchi, Ettore (2006) 'The social mobility of mobile Europeans.' Paper presented at the RC28 (ECPR) Committee Meeting in Nijmegen.

Recchi, Ettore (2008) 'Cross-state mobility in the EU: trends, puzzles and consequences.' *European Societies*, 10: 197–224.

Recchi, Ettore and Adrian Favell (eds) (2009) *Pioneers of European Integration: Citizenship and Mobility in the EU*. Cheltenham: Edward Elgar.

Reif, Karlheinz, and Herman Schmitt (1980) 'Nine second-order national elections: a conceptual framework for the analysis of European election results.' *European Journal of Political Research*, 8(1): 3–44.

Ricciardi, F. (2004) 'Entre quadri et dirigenti: les cadres en Italie', in P. Bouffartigue and A. Grelon, *Les cadres d'Europe du sud et du monde méditerranéen*. Cahier du GDR Cadres, no. 8, 123–37.

Risse, Thomas (2001) 'A European identity? Europeanization and the evolution of nation-state identities', in Maria Cowles, Thomas Risse and James Caporaso (eds) *Transforming Europe: Europeanization and Domestic Change*. Ithaca, NY: Cornell University Press.

Risse, Thomas (2010) *A Community of Europeans? Transnational Identities and Public Spheres*. Ithaca, NY: Cornell University Press.

Risse, Thomas, Daniela Engelmann-Martin, Hans-Joachim Knope and Klaus Roscher (1999) 'To Euro or not to Euro? The EMU and identity politics in the European Union.' *European Journal of International Relations*, 5 (2): 147–87.

Risse, Thomas, Stephen Ropp and Kathryn Sikkink (1999) *The Power of Human Rights: International Norms and Domestic Change*. Cambridge: Cambridge University Press.

Roche, Maurice (2010) *Exploring the Sociology of Europe*. London: Sage.

Rodríguez, Josep, Julián Cárdenas and Christian Oltra (2006) 'Redes de poder económico en Europa.' *Sistema*, 194: 3–44.

Rodríguez-Pose, Andrès (2002) *The European Union: Economy, Society, and Polity*. Oxford: Oxford University Press.

Rodrik, Dani (1997) *Has Globalization Gone Too Far?* Washington, DC: Institute for International Economics.

Rodrik, Dani (2001) 'Why do more open economies have bigger governments?' NBER Working Paper 5537. Cambridge, MA: NBER.

Rokkan, Stein (1999) 'State formation, nation-building, and mass politics', in Peter Flora, Stein Kuhnle and Derek Urwin (eds) *State Formation, Nation-Building and Mass Politics in Europe. The Theory of Stein Rokkan*. Oxford: Oxford University Press.

Róna-Tas, Ákos (1994) 'The first shall be last? Entrepreneurship and communist cadres in the transition from socialism.' *American Journal of Sociology*, 100 (1): 40–69.

Rootes, Christopher (ed.) (2003) *Environmental Protest in Western Europe*. Oxford: Oxford University Press.

Rosamond, Ben (2000) *Theories of European Integration*. Basingstoke: Palgrave Macmillan.

Rosamond, Ben (2001) 'Discourses of globalization and European identities', in Thomas Christiansen, Knud Erik Jørgensen and Antje Wiener, *The Social Construction of Europe*. London: Sage, 158–75.

Rosamond, Ben (2003) '(European) integration theory, EU studies and the sociology of knowledge.' Paper presented to the 8th biennial conference of the European Union Studies Association, Nashville. URL: http://aei.pitt.edu/2915/01/152.pdf

Ross, George (1994) *Jacques Delors and European Integration*. Oxford and New York: Polity Press and Oxford University Press.

Ross, George (2008) 'What do 'Europeans' think? Analyses of the European Union's current crisis by European elites.' *Journal of Common Market Studies*, 46(2): 389–412.

Rucht, Dieter (2002) 'The EU as a target of political mobilisation. Is there a Europeanization of conflict?', in Richard Balme, Didier Chabanet and Vincent Wright (eds) *L'action collective en Europe*. Paris: Presses de Sciences Po, 163–94.

Ruggie, John Gerard (1998) *Constructing the World Polity: Essays on International Institutionalization*. London and New York: Routledge.

Rumford, Chris (2002) *The European Union: A Political Sociology*. Oxford: Blackwell.
Rumford, Chris (2003) 'European civil society or transnational social space? Conceptions of society in discourses of EU citizenship, governance and the democratic deficit: an emerging agenda.' *European Journal of Social Theory*, 6(1): 25–43.
Rumford, Chris (2008) *Cosmopolitan Spaces: Europe, Globalization, Theory*. London: Routledge.
Rumford, Chris (ed.) (2009) *The Sage Handbook of European Studies*. London: Sage.
Ruzza, Carlo (2004) *Europe and Civil Society: Movement Coalitions and European Institutions*. Manchester: Manchester University Press.
Ruzza, Carlo and Emanuela Bozzini (2008) 'Organised civil society and European governance: routes of contestation.' *European Political Science*, 7: 296–303.
Sabatier, Paul (1998) 'The advocacy coalition framework: revisions and relevance for Europe.' *Journal of European Public Policy*, 5(1): 98–130.
Sallaz, Jeffrey (2006) 'The making of the global gambling industry: an application and extension of field theory.' *Theory and Society*, 35(3): 265–97.
Salt, John (1992) 'Migration processes among the highly skilled in Europe.' *International Migration Review*, 26 (2): 484–505.
Sandholtz, Wayne (1993) 'Institutions and collective action: the new telecommunications in Western Europe.' *World Politics*, 45: 242–70.
Sandholtz, Wayne (1998) 'The emergence of a supranational telecommunications regime', in Wayne Sandholtz and Alec Stone Sweet (eds) *European Integration and Supranational Governance*. Oxford: Oxford University Press, 134–63.
Sandholtz, Wayne and Alec Stone Sweet (1998) *European Integration and Supranational Governance*, Oxford: Oxford University Press.
Sandholtz, Wayne and James Zysman (1989) '1992: recasting the European bargain.' *World Politics*, 42: 95–128.
Sapir, André, Philippe Aghion, Giuseppe Bertola, Martin Hellwig, Jean Pisani-Ferry, Dariusz K. Rosati, José Viñalsand Helen Wallace (2004) *An Agenda for a Growing Europe*. Oxford: Oxford University Press.
Saurugger, Sabine (ed.) (2008) Les approches sociologiques de l'intégration européennes: perspectives critiques. *Politique européenne*, 25 (2).).
Saurugger, Sabine (2009) 'Sociology and European studies.' *Journal of European Public Policy*,16(6): 937–50.
Savage, Mike, Gaynor Bagnall and Brian Longhurst (2005) *Globalisation and Belonging*. London: Sage.
Scharpf, Fritz (1999) *Governing Europe*. Oxford: Oxford University Press.
Schimmelfennig, Frank (2002) 'Goffman meets IR: dramaturgical action in international community.' *International Review of Sociology*, 12(3): 417–37.
Schimmelfennig, Frank, Stefan Engert and Heiko Knobel (2006) *International Socialization in Europe: European Organizations, Political Conditionality and Democratic Change*. Basingstoke: Palgrave Macmillan.

Schissler, Hanna and Yasemin Soysal (eds) (2004) *The Nation, Europe and the World: Textbooks and Curricula in Transition.* New York: Berghahn.

Schlesinger, Philip (1999) 'Changing spaces of political communication: the case of the European Union'. *Political Communication,* 16(3): 263–79.

Schmidt, Vivien (2006) *Democracy in Europe: The EU and National Polities.* Oxford: Oxford University Press.

Schmitter, Philippe (2000) *How to Democratize the EU ... and Why Bother?* Lanham, MD: Rowman & Littlefield.

Schmitter, Philippe C. (2003) 'Democracy in Europe and Europe's democratization.' *Journal of Democracy,* 14(4): 71–85.

Schnabel, Virginie (1998) 'Elites européennes en formation: les étudiants du collège de Bruges et leurs études.' *Politix,* 43: 33–52.

Schnapper, Dominique (1994) *La communauté des citoyens: sur l'idée moderne de la nation.* Paris: Seuil.

Schroedter, Julia H. (2004) 'Binationale Ehen in Deutschland.' Master's thesis, Mannheim: Universität Mannheim.

Semetko, Holli, Claes de Vreese and Jochen Peter (2000) 'Europeanised politics – Europeanised media? European integration and political communication.' *West European Politics,* 23(4): 121–41.

Shore, Cris (2000) *Building Europe: The Cultural Politics of European Integration.* London: Routledge.

Sinnott, Richard (1995) 'Bringing public opinion back in', in Oscar Niedermayer and Richard Sinnott (eds), *Public Opinion and Internationalized Governance.* Oxford: Oxford University Press, 11–33.

Sklair, Leslie (1995) *Sociology of the Global System.* New York: Harvester Wheatsheaf.

Sklair, Leslie (2001) *The Transnational Capitalist Class.* Oxford: Blackwell.

Smith, Andy (1999) 'L'espace public européen: une vie (trop) aérienne.' *Critique international,* 2 (hiver): 169–80.

Smith, Andy (2004a) *Le Gouvernement de l'Union européenne: une sociologie politique.* Paris: LGDJ.

Smith, Andy (ed.) (2004b) *Politics and the European Commission: Actors, Interdependence, Legitimacy.* London: Routledge.

Snow, David and Robert Benford (1988) 'Ideology, frame resonance and participant mobilization.' *International Social Movement Research,* 1: 197–217.

Soysal, Yasemin (1994) *Limits of Citizenship.* Chicago, IL: Chicago University Press.

Stafford, David and Richard Purkis (1989) *Directory of Multinationals.* London: Macmillan Press.

Stafford, David and Richard Purkis (1997) *Directory of Multinationals,* London, Macmillan Press.

Standard & Poor's (1999) *Standard Corporation Descriptions.* New York: Standard & Poor's.

Stone Sweet, Alec, Wayne Sandholz and Neil Fligstein (2001) *The Institutionalization of Europe.* Oxford: Oxford University Press.

Stråth, Bo (2000) 'Multiple Europes: integration, identity and demarcation to the other', in Bo Stråth (ed.), *Europe and the Other and Europe as the Other*. Brussels: PIE, 385–420.

Streeck, Wolfgang and Philippe Schmitter (eds) (1986) *Private Interest Government: Beyond Market and State*. London: Sage.

Suleiman, Ezra and Henri Mendras (1995) *Le recrutement des élites en Europe*. Paris: La Découverte.

Taleb, Nassim Nicholas (2008) *The Black Swan: The Impact of the Highly Improbable*. New York: Random House.

Tarrow, Sidney (1998) *Power in Movement: Social Movements and Contentious Politics*. Cambridge: Cambridge University Press.

Tarrow, Sidney (2001) 'Contentious politics in a composite polity', in Doug Imig and Sidney Tarrow (eds) *Contentious Europeans: Protest and Politics in an Emerging Polity*. Lanham, MD: Rowman & Littlefield, 233–51.

Tarrow, Sidney (2005) *The New Transnational Activism*. Cambridge: Cambridge University Press.

Taylor, Graham and Andrew Mathers (2004) 'The European Trade Union Confederation at the crossroads of change? Traversing the variable geometry of European trade unionism.' *European Journal of Industrial Relations*, 10(3): 267–85.

Taylor, Peter J. and Michael Hoyler (2000) 'The spatial order of European cities under conditions of contemporary globalisation.' *Tijdschrift voor Economische en Sociale Geografie*, 91: 176–89.

te Brake, Wayne (1998) *Shaping History: Ordinary People in European Politics, 1500–1700*. New York and Cambridge: Cambridge University Press.

Theodos, B.A. (2006) *Geographic Mobility and Geographic Labor Mobility in the United States*. Washington, DC: The Urban Institute.

Therborn, Göran (1995) *European Modernity and Beyond: The Trajectory of European Societies, 1945–2000*. Thousand Oaks, CA: Sage.

Therborn, Göran (1999) '"Europe" as issues of sociology', in Th.P. Boje, B. van Steenbergen and S. Walby (eds) *European Societies: Fusion or Fission?* London: Routledge, 19–29.

Tilly, Charles (1978) *From Mobilization to Revolution*. Reading, MA: Addison-Wesley.

Tilly, Charles (1990) *Coercion, Capital and European States AD 990–1992*. Oxford: Blackwell.

Tönnies, Ferdinand ([1887] 1963) *Community and Society (Gemeinschaft und Gesellschaft)*. New York: Harper & Row.

Treiman, Donald and Harry Ganzeboom (2000) 'The fourth generation of comparative stratification research', in Stella Quah and Arnaud Sales (eds) *The International Handbook of Sociology*. Newbury Park, CA: Sage.

Trenz, Hans-Jörg (2004) 'Media coverage on European governance: testing the performance of national newspapers.' *European Journal of Communication*, 19(3): 291–319.

Trenz, Hans-Jörg (2007) 'Reconciling diversity and unity: language minorities and European integration.' *Ethnicities* 7(2): 157–85.
Trenz, Hans-Jörg and Klaus Eder (2004) 'The democratising dynamics of a European public sphere: towards a theory of democratic functionalism.' *European Journal of Social Theory*, 7(1): 5–25.
Tribalat, Michèle, Patrick Simon and Benoît Riandey (1996) *De l'Immigration à l'assimilation: Une enquête sur la population étrangère en France*. Paris: INED.
Tsebelis, George (1994) 'The power of the European Parliament as a conditional agenda-setter.' *American Political Science Review*, 88(1): 128–42.
Tsebelis, George and Xenophon Yataganas (2002) 'Veto players and decision-making in the EU after Nice.' *Journal of Common Market Studies*, 40(2): 283–307.
Turner, Stephen (1994) *The Social Theory of Practices*. Chicago, IL: University of Chicago Press.
Urry, John (1997) *Mobilities*. Cambridge: Polity.
Urry, John (2000) *Sociology Beyond Societies*. London: Routledge.
Uzzi, Brian and Ryon Lancaster (2004) 'Embeddedness and price formation in the corporate law market.' *American Sociological Review*, 69: 319–44.
Vandenbrande, Tom, Laura Coppin and Peter van der Hallen (2006) *Mobility in Europe: Analysis of the 2005 Eurobarometer Survey on Geographical and Labour Market Mobility*. Dublin: European Foundation for the Improvement of Living and Working Conditions.
Vauchez, Antoine (2008) 'The force of a weak field: law and lawyers in the government of the European Union.' *International Political Sociology*, 2 (2): 128–44.
Veblen, Thorsten ([1899] 1994) *The Theory of the Leisure Class*. London: Penguin.
Vetters, Regina, Erik Jentges and Hans-Jörg Trenz (2009) 'Whose project is it? Media debates on the ratification of the EU Constitutional Treaty.' *Journal of European Public Policy*, 16 (3): 412–30.
Wade, Robert (1996) 'Globalization and its limits: reports of the death of the national economy are greatly exaggerated', in Suzanne Berger and Ronald Dore (eds) *National Diversity and Global Capitalism*. Ithaca, NY: Cornell University Press.
Wæver, Ole (2004) 'Discursive approaches', in Antje Wiener and Thomas Diez (eds), *European Integration Theory*. Oxford: Oxford University Press, 197–215.
Wagner, Anne-Catherine (2007) *Les classes sociales dans la mondialisation*. Paris: La Découverte, "Repères".
Walters, William and Jens Henrik Haahr (2005) *Governing Europe: Discourse, Governmentality and European Integration*. London: Routledge.
Warleigh, Alex (2004) 'In defence of intra-disciplinarity: "European Studies", the "New Regionalism" and the issue of democratisation.' *Cambridge Review of International Affairs*, 17(2): 301–18.
Waters, Mary (1990) *Ethnic Options: Choosing Identities in America*. Berkeley, CA: University of California Press.
Watson, William (1964) 'Social mobility and social class in industrial communities', in Max Gluckman (ed.) *Closed Systems and Open Minds: The*

Limits of Naivety in Social Anthropology. Edinburgh: Oliver and Boyd, 129–57.

Weber, Eugen (1976) *Peasants into Frenchmen: The Modernization of Rural France 1870–1914.* Palo Alto, CA: Stanford University Press.

Weber, Max (1922) *Gesammelte Aufsätze zur Religionssoziologie.* Tübingen: (Mohr) Siebeck.

Weber, Max, Guenther Roth and Claus Wittich (eds) (1978) *Economy and Society.* Berkeley, CA: University of California Press.

Weber, Max (2002[1905]) *The Protestant Ethic and the Spirit of Capitalism.* London: Penguin Classics.

Weisbein, Julien (2008) 'L'Europe à contrepoint. Objets nouveaux et classicisme théorique pour les études européennes.' *Politique européenne*, 25(2): 115–35.

Wendon, Bryan (1998) 'The Commission as image-venue entrepreneur in EU social policy.' *Journal of European Public Policy*, 5(2): 339–53.

Wendt, Alexander (1999) *Social Theory of International Politics.* Cambridge: Cambridge University Press.

Wessler, Hartmut, Bernhard Peters, Michael Bruggemann, Katharina Kleinen-V. Konigslow and Stéfanie Sifft (2008) *Transnationalization of Public Spheres.* Basingstoke: Palgrave Macmillan.

White, Harrison (1981) 'Where do markets come from?' *American Journal of Sociology*, 87: 517–47.

White, Jonathan (2010) 'Europe and the common'. *Political Studies* 58(1):104–122.

Wiener, Antje (1997) 'Making sense of the new geography of citizenship: fragmented citizenship in the European Union.' *Theory and Society*, 26 (4).

Wiener, Antje (2008) *The Invisible Constitution of Politics: Contested Norms and International Encounters.* Cambridge: Cambridge University Press.

Wiener, Antje and Thomas Diez (eds) (2003) *European Integration Theory.* Oxford: Oxford University Press.

Willis, Paul (1981) *Learning to Labor: How Working Class Kids Get Working Class Jobs.* New York: Columbia University Press.

Wimmer, Andreas and Nina Glick Schiller (2002) 'Methodological nationalism and beyond: nation-state building, migration and the social sciences.' *Global Networks*, 2(4): 301–34.

Woll, Cornelia (2007) 'Leading the dance? Power and political resources of business lobbyists.' *Journal of Public Policy*, 27(1): 57–78.

World Trade Organization Annual Report 1996.

World Trade Organization Annual Report 2004.

World Trade Organization Annual Report 2006.

Woodward, Alison (2004) 'Building velvet triangles: gender and informal governance', in Simona Piattoni and Thomas Christiansen (eds), *Informal Governance and the European Union.* London: Edward Elgar, 76–93.

Woodward, Alison (2007) 'Challenges of intersectionality in the transnational organization of European women's movements: forming platforms and maintaining turf in today's EU', in Ilse Lenz and Charlotte Ullrich (eds)

Gender Orders Unbound: Towards New Reciprocity and Solidarity? Opladen and Berlin: VS Verlag für Sozialwissenchaften/Leske & Budrich, 9–27.

Wright, Erik O. (1996) *Class Counts: Comparative Studies in Class Analysis*. Cambridge: Cambridge University Press.

Zaiceva, Anzelika and Klaus Zimmermann (2008) *Scale, Diversity, and Determinants of Labour Migration in Europe*. IZA DP No. 3595. Bonn: Forschungsinstitut zur Zukunft der Arbeit.

Zeitlin, Maurice and Richard Earl Radcliff (1988) *Landlords and Capitalists*. Princeton, NJ: Princeton University Press.

Zunz, Olivier, Leonard Schoppa and Nobuhiro Hiwatari (eds) (2002) *Social Contracts under Stress: The Middle Classes of America, Europe, and Japan at the Turn of the Century*. New York: The Russell Sage Foundation.

Zürn, Michael (2004) 'Global governance and legitimacy problems.' *Government and Opposition* 39(2): 260–87.

Index

Abbott, A. 58, 154
agency, embedded 156, 170
agenda-setting 175–6
Alexander, J. 209, 211
alliances 117, 119
Amsterdam 68–72
Anderson, B. 42, 43
Anderson, P. 217
anthropology 11–12, 20
anti-discrimination legislation 144
Appaduraï, A. 79
artefacts 187
Article 13 144
Article 119 (now Article 141) 145
Asia 107, 122
autonomization 161–2

Bagnasco, A. 16
Baisnée, O. 141
Balkan crisis 191
Balme, R. 131
Barry, A. 205
Barry, B. 6
Bartolini, S. 19–20, 79, 203, 223
Bauman, Z. 13, 65, 72
Baumgartner, F. 175
Beauvallet, W. 22, 161
Beck, U. 3, 13, 14, 57, 72, 204–5, 212
Beckfield, J. 17, 30
Belgium 40, 137
bell curve 66, 67
Berezin, M. 45
Berger, P. 8, 154
Bertaux, D. 69
Bigo, D. 205–6
Billig, M. 47
Blair, T. 185
Bolkestein directive 41, 178
boomerang effect 129
Borjas, G. 60
bottom-up approaches 130, 206–8

bounded nation-state-society *see*
  methodological nationalism
Bourdieu, P. 3, 21, 32, 35, 73, 125, 126,
  142, 151, 158, 176, 177, 179, 180,
  181, 183, 186, 187, 192, 208, 209,
  220, 223
bourgeoisie see middle classes
Breen, R. 56–7
bricolage 126, 182–5, 190, 192
British Telecom 115, 117, 119, 120, 123
Brubaker, R. 13
Brussels 68–72
Business Europe 182
Butler, T. 82, 83, 86, 90

cadres supérieurs 87
capability-based approach to ESDP 188
capital 3
  forms of 21, 156, 208
  social capital *see* social capital
capitalism 78–9, 194
  mercantile 81
  varieties of 14, 17, 29–30, 78, 122,
    219
career trajectories 165–6
cartels 103
Castells, M. 13, 209, 212
Catalonia 47
centralization 47
Chirac, J. 185
Christiansen, T. 8
cities
  elites, middle classes and 26–7, 76–99
  selection and local contexts 88–9
  social and spatial mobility of Eurostars
    68–72, 74
citizenship, European 33, 58, 71
civil society 134, 211–12
  organized 129, 136
civilization 202–3
claims-making 129, 137
  quantitative analysis 139–42

257

class   25–6, 28–49, 220
    Europeanization vs European social
        classes   32–42
    middle classes   *see* middle classes
    position   32; and spatial mobility   60,
        62–4
    prospect for European classes   48–9
    reproduction of class cultures   52
    social groups and classes   29–30
    social mobility   *see* social mobility
    social structure, Europeanization and
        30–2
'class for itself'   31–2
'class in itself'   31–2
Cohen, M.   176
cohesion funds   45
collective resources   157
Common Agricultural Policy (CAP)
    184–5
common sense, going beyond   186–7
Communist Party of France (PCF)   168
community   *see Gemeinschaft*
comparative sociology   3, 11–18
    gender equality and mobilizations
        145–7
    historical   202–4
    upper-middle classes in European cities
        86–92
competition policy   103, 105, 184
composite polity   19–20
conflict dimension, Europe as   139–40
constructivism   8–11, 176, 180–1
    structural   152
    theory of European integration   195,
        213
consumption   34–5
    elites, cities and   91–2, 93, 96–7
cooperation, interstate   217
cosmopolitan empire   205
cosmopolitans and locals   53
costs and benefits   124
    of Europeanization   120–3
Council of Ministers   19, 46
counterfactual analysis   68
critical perspective   191
Crouch, C.   3, 15, 30, 34, 78, 200, 201
cultural capital   21, 208
cultural resources   155, 178
culture   7–8

Dahl, R.   131
De Gaulle, C.   216

decentralization   47
defence planners   188, 191
Delanty, G.   195, 213
delegitimation   158
democratic deficit   168–9
democratic functionalism   210
de-nationalization   71–2
Deutsch, K.   4–5, 5–6, 42–3, 132, 223
Deutsche Telecom   115, 117, 119, 120,
    123
Díez Medrano, J.   26, 44, 45, 127
differentiation   81–2, 85, 197–8, 199
DiMaggio, P.J.   152
diplomats   188, 191
distinction   30, 32, 208
domination   154
Durkheim, E.   2, 9, 66, 78, 127, 176, 180,
    194, 195–200, 205, 223

EADS   113
Eastern Europe
    migration from   74–5
    trade   109–10
Economic and Monetary Union   217
economic sociology
    and EU studies   123–4
    and the study of integrated market
        economies   102–7
economics   6–7, 221–2
    neo-classical   102
Eder, K.   210
education   43–4, 161, 178
efficiency   103
Eisenstadt, S.   203
elective belonging   85–6
Elias, N.   47, 152
elites   26–7, 76–99, 220
    comparison of elites in European cities
        86–92
    elite consensus   158
    European integration   206–7
    part of a virtual global society   92–8
embedded agency   156, 170
embodied institutions   157, 170
embourgeoisement   83–4
employment relations   219
Engels, F.   40, 48–9
engineers   88–99
epistemology   6
Erasmus programme   33
escalator effect   53, 65
Esping-Andersen, G.   3, 17, 29–30, 219

ethnography 68, 182, 189–90
EU Migrants Forum 144, 146
EU policies 126–7, 163, 172–92
  bricolage 126, 182–5, 190, 192
  defence policy 185–91
  political science approaches 173–6
  social fields 177–9
  social representations 179–81, 186–7
  sociological approach to EU policy-making 177–85
  typology of 174
EU politics 126, 150–71
  advantages of the sociological approach 157–60
  fields and power 151–4
  immigration and race 142–5
  political sociology of 3, 18–23
  roles and resources 154–7
  social practices in the European Parliament 163–9
  Strasbourg school 160–3
Eurobarometer 206
European citizenship 33, 58, 71
European classes
  Europeanization vs 32–42
  prospect for 48–9
European Coal and Steel Community 216
European Commission 19, 22, 123, 128–9, 161, 174, 218
  budget 173
  civil society and 134–5
  telecommunications industry 116
European Commissioners 162, 165–6
European Court of Justice (ECJ) 19, 21, 123, 174, 177
European Defence Community (EDC) 185
European Defence Initiative 185
European identity 10, 35–7, 47–8, 97–8
European integration 4–6, 12, 17, 127, 170, 179
  economic theories 58–60
  European mobilizations and 130–1;
    symptom or cause 132–5
  macro-structural transformation 202–6, 212
  meso-structural transformation 202, 208–12
  micro-structural transformation 202, 206–8, 212
  social theory and 127, 193–213

European Internal Migrants Social Survey (EIMSS) 61, 62
European Network against Racism 146
European Ombudsman 157
European Parliament 19, 22, 46, 138, 151, 158, 174
  elections 159–60, 164, 167–8
  social practices in 163–9
European public sphere 23, 125, 129, 139–42, 209–11
European Security and Defence Policy (ESDP) 185–91
European Social Forum 129–30, 137–8
European social model 200–1
European Social Survey 54, 55–6
European Women's Lobby 146, 147
Europeanization 2, 3, 11–12, 148, 199, 211
  class, social structure and 30–2
  costs and benefits of 120–3
  vs European social classes 32–42
  globalization vs 107–13
  mixed method approach to studying mobilization 139–47
EUROPUB project 40–1, 44, 125, 139–41
Eurostars 68–72, 74
Eurovision Song Contest 47
Evans, P. 217
executive power 152–4
exit strategies 26–7, 77, 84, 85–6, 92–8

family 71–2, 92–3
Favell, A. 41, 68–72, 85, 144
federalism 197
fields 3, 21, 125, 126, 142, 208
  EU policy-making 177–9
  European field of mobility 73–5
  European security and defence 187–8
  immigration 142–5
  and power 151–4
Finland 108, 109
  and EU politics 159, 163, 166, 168
firms 27, 100–24
  costs and benefits of Europeanization 120–3
  co-ownership and social ties 39–40
  globalization vs Europeanization 107–13
  investment 106, 111–13
  telecommunications industry 106–7, 113–20, 122–3
Fligstein, N. 11, 37, 42, 43, 142
foreign-born residents 58, 59

foreign languages 96
foreign policy-based approach to ESDP 188
Foucault, M. 14, 152, 205–6
fragmentation of sociology 219
frames/framing 144, 147, 164, 176, 180
France 47, 84, 88, 122–3
    ESDP 186–7, 188, 190
    and EU politics 159, 160, 163, 165–7; European Parliament elections 1999 167–8
    immigrants, surveys 61–2
    MEPs 161
    social mobility 55, 56, 63, 70
    telecommunications industry 115, 116, 123
    trade 109
France Telecom 115, 117, 119, 120, 123
freedom of mobility 73–5
friends 92–3
functionalism 4–5, 6, 189
    democratic 210
    neo-functionalism 5, 131, 196–7, 216
    structural 53, 66–7

Gans, H. 84
garbage-can model 176
Gellner, E. 2, 43, 45
Gemeinschaft (community) 197–8
gender equality 145–7
gentrification 83–4
Georgakakis, D. 162, 163
Germany 40, 122–3
    ESDP 187
    and EU politics 161
    social mobility 55, 63, 64
    telecommunications industry 115, 116, 123
    trade 109
Gesellschaft (society) 197
Giddens, A. 8, 72, 79, 201–2
Guiraudon, V. 4, 14, 19, 22, 23, 33, 41, 45, 125, 126, 140, 142, 144, 145, 160, 172, 175, 190, 212, 219, 220
Glick-Schiller, N. 57
global justice movement 129
globalization 13–14, 17, 65, 77, 101, 120–2
    vs Europeanization 107–13
    social theory, nation building and 78–82

Globalization and World Cities project 89, 109
Goffman, E. 2, 8, 126, 164, 180, 192
Goldthorpe, J. 2, 86
Gouldner, A. 53
governance 163, 211–12
governments 103
    ownership in telecommunications firms 114, 117
Granovetter, M. 38, 102
Green Paper of 1987 116

Haas, E. 4, 5, 131, 132, 196–7, 216
Habermas, J. 3, 14, 129, 134, 209, 210
habitus 3, 21, 69, 144, 180, 208
Hall, P. 8–9, 14, 122, 217
hidden population problem 67
Hirschman, A.O. 85
historical institutionalism 8–9, 217, 218–19, 222
history/historians 15–17
Hix, S. 8, 128
Hoffmann, S. 216
homology 158
horizontal Europeanization 139–40
Hungary 56

ideal types 68–72
idealism 8
ideas 179
identification 10–11, 35–7, 97–8
identity 7
    European 10, 35–7, 47–8, 97–8
    and European social class 34, 35–7
    national 36–7, 46–8, 97–8
    sub-national 47–8
imagined communities 42, 43
Imig, D. 40–1, 128, 130
immigration
    claims-making 140–1
    politics of 142–5
    see also spatial mobility
increased national focusing on Europe 139–40
individual resources 157
institutionalism 8–9, 66–7, 217–19
    European integration 132
    historical 8–9, 217, 218–19, 222
    liberal 216–17, 219
    limitations of 221–2
    rational choice 8–9, 131, 217, 218
    sociological 9

institutionalization 154–5
  EU studies 215–19
  European Parliament 167
institutions 22–3
  embodied 157, 170
  market 103, 104
  political 151–2
integrated market economies 102–7
integration 193
  European *see* European integration
  moral 194–5
  political 132, 196–7
  positive and negative 199, 205
  societal 194, 195–200
interest groups 130–1, 135–6, 175, 182
interests, and ideas 179
intergovernmental policies 174, 184, 185
intermarriage 38–9
international non-governmental organizations (INGOs) 148
interpretation 186–7, 191
intersectionality 147
interstate cooperation 217
interviews 188–9
intra-EU trade 108–9, 110
investment 106, 111–13
Ireland 45, 56, 108, 109
isomorphism 184
Italy 84, 88
  social mobility 56, 63, 64
  telecommunications industry 116, 117

joint-decision trap 175
joint ventures 117–20
Jørgensen, K.E. 8
Judicial Cooperation Unit (Eurojust) 161

Kaelble, H. 3, 15–16
Kalanke v. Freie Hansestadt Bremen 145–6
Katzenstein, P. 7, 9, 122
Keck, M. 129
Kingdon, J. 176
KPN 119
Krivine, A. 168

Laffan, B. 17
Lagroye, J. 81

Laguiller, A. 168
Lamont, M. 52
languages, foreign 96
law 21–2
  legal integration 161
  legal mobilization 137
Lawler, E. 45, 47
Le Galès, P. 16
legislative elite 167
legislative power 152–4
Lévi-Strauss, C. 126, 152, 176, 183, 192
Lewis, J. 146
liberal institutionalism 216–17, 219
liberal intergovernmentalism 133
Lindberg, L. 131
Lisbon, Treaty of 46
Lisbon Agenda 17, 58
lobbying 130, 144, 146, 162–3, 182
locals and cosmopolitans 53, 86
Lockwood, D. 83
logic of practice 179
London
  Eurostars and social mobility 68–72
  urban elites 88–99
Luckmann, T. 8, 154
Lyon 88–99

macro-structural transformation 202–6, 212
Madrid 88–99
mainstreaming 145
Majone, G. 173
managers 88–99
Mangenot, M. 161, 178
Mann, M. 48, 78
manufacturing trade 108–9
March, J. 152, 176
markets 27, 100–24
  costs and benefits of Europeanization 120–3
  economic sociology and integrated market economies 102–7
  globalization vs Europeanization 107–13
  telecommunications industry 106–7, 113–20, 122–3
Marks, G. 133
Marx, K. 2, 31–2, 40, 48–9, 78, 91, 131, 211
material resources 155–6
Mattli, W. 122

Mau, S. 207
Mauss, M. 176, 191, 192
McAdam, D. 133
meaning 194–5
mechanical solidarity 196, 197–8, 199
media 96–7, 140–1, 210–11
　socialization 43–4, 44–5
Members of the European Parliament (MEPs) 161, 165–6
　national and international political experience 167
　professionalization and specialization 166–7
Mendras, H. 3, 16
Merton, R.K. 53
meso-structural transformation 202, 208–12
meta-theory 6
methodological nationalism 13, 51, 57–60, 158, 198
micro-structural transformation 202, 206–8, 212
middle classes 26–7, 37, 41–2, 48, 76–99
　comparison of upper-middle classes in European cities 86–92
　dynamics of formation 82–6
　upper-middle classes as part of a virtual global society 92–8
migration *see* spatial mobility
Migration Policy Group 144
Milan 88–99
military, as agent of socialization 43–4
Milward, A. 15, 16, 28, 46
mixed methods research 139–47
mobilities 220
　elites and cities 26–7, 76–99
　European field of mobility 73–5
　Social *see* social mobility
　spatial *see* spatial mobility
mobilizations 20, 125–6, 128–49, 178–9, 220
　and European integration 130–1; symptom or cause 132–5
　European social class 34, 35, 40–2
　gender equality 145–7
　qualitative study of immigration and race politics 142–5
　quantitative analysis of claims-making 139–42
　studying EU-related contention 135–8

modernization 194–5, 202
　reflexive 204–5, 212
Monnet, J. 196, 216
moral integration 194–5
Moravcsik, A. 9–10, 133
multilevel policies 174, 184
multinational corporations (MNCs) 136
　investment 111–13
　see also firms
Münch, R. 205

nation building 12–13, 130, 203, 222–3
　European society and 42–5, 46, 47
　social theory and globalization 78–82
nation-state 46–8, 77, 187, 198–9
national identification 36–7
national identity 36–7, 97–8
　enduring salience 46–8
national interest 186–7
national phone companies 115
national policy preferences 133
national social representations 181
national structures 74
national/supranational dimension 152–4
NATO 188, 191
negative integration 199, 205
negative solidarity 205
neo-classical economics 102
neo-functionalism 5, 131, 196–7, 216
neo-liberalism 120–2
network society 209–10, 212
network state 209
networks 91, 92, 138, 166
　transnational 91, 93–4, 146
Neumann, I. 192
new security theory 205–6
newspapers 140–1
non-governmental organizations (NGOs) 129, 143, 148, 162
　and EU organizational structures 134–5
norms 7, 66, 67–8, 71–2, 145–6
　postnational 143
North America 107, 122
　see also United States (US)
North American Free Trade Area (NAFTA) 107

objectivist bias 189–90, 191
occupational structure 54–6
Olivetti 117

Index

Olsen, J. 152, 176
Olson, M. 131
ontology 6
open-endedness 222
operationalization 4, 29, 51, 131–2
   comparison of upper-middle classes in European cities 86–92
   European social classes 34–42
   mobilizations 135–47
   social mobility and spatial mobility 61–72
organic solidarity 196, 197–8, 199
organizational sociology 9
organizational structures 134–5
organized civil society 129, 136
Ostner, I. 146

Paris 88–99
Parsons, T. 4, 6, 66, 196, 197
partial exit 85–6, 92–8
participant observation 189
path dependency 67
patterns of social mobility 60, 64–5
phenomenological approach 69–70
physical resources 155
Pinçon, M. 82
Pinçon-Charlot, M. 82
PIONEUR project 62, 73
place 89–90
pluralism
   political 130–1
   in sociology 223
Poland 56
Polanyi, K. 102
policy, EU *see* EU policies
policy convergence 184
policy entrepreneurs 175
policy sectors 154
policy stream 176
political experience 161
political integration 132, 196–7
political mobilization *see* mobilizations
political resources 152–3, 156, 165–6, 178
political science 6–7
   approaches to EU policies 173–6
political sociology 3, 18–23
political stream 176
politics, EU *see* EU politics
Portugal 109
positive integration 199, 205

positive selection 59–60
positive solidarity 205
'postnational norms' 143
post-war Europe 104
power 178–9
   fields and 151–4
practice, logic of 179
practices 208
   bricolage as practice 182–5
   ESDP and taking practices seriously 188–90
   social practices in the European Parliament 163–9
   urban elites 91–2, 96–7
preliminary rulings 177
Préteceille, E. 89
principal–agent theory 218
privatization 114, 117, 118
problem stream 176
process, EU as 51
professionalization 162
   MEPs 166–7
professionals 20, 21, 22
property rights 103, 105
prosopographic studies 161
protest 133, 137–8
protest event analysis 137
public sector 93
public sphere 77
   European 23, 125, 129, 139–42, 209–11
public sphere school 134
Putnam, R. 38, 156, 211

qualitative research 2, 51
   EU politics 161
   immigration and race politics 142–5
   social mobility and spatial mobility 65–72
quantitative research 2, 51
   claims-making 139–42
   social mobility and spatial mobility 61–6
   statistical analysis of groups involved in EU politics 160–1
questionnaires 189
   constructing 89–92

race to the bottom 121, 122
race politics 142–5
rational actors 59, 73, 221–2

rational choice institutionalism 8–9, 131, 217, 218
rationality 194
RECON project 141
reflexive modernization 204–5, 212
regional aid 105
regulatory state 173
relational sociology 177
Renault 137
rent-seeking 103
reproduction of class cultures 52
research object 187–8
researchers 46
residential career 91
resources 178
  EU politics 152–3, 154–7
  social practices in the European Parliament 165–6
Risse, T. 7, 10
Rodríguez, J. 40
Rokkan, S. 79, 203, 223
roles 154–7
Ross, G. 20, 192
routines 183
Rueschemeyer, D. 217
Ruggie, J.G. 216–17
Rumford, C. 195, 213
Ruzza, C. 133
Ryder Cup 47

Sandholtz, W. 132
Sapir report 17
Savage, M. 82, 83–4, 85–6, 90–1, 93
Sbragia, A. 17
scale 73, 79, 82
  exit strategies 84, 85
Scharpf, F. 175
Schengen Treaty 33
Schmitter, P. 131
Schuman, R. 216
Scotland 47
securitization 205–6
security 45
selection bias 138
Senior Officials Group for Telecommunications (SOGT) 115–16
service class 87–99
Sikkink, K. 129
single market 100, 104
  and anti-discrimination provisions 144

Single Market Programme (SMP) 104–6, 111, 113, 116, 122, 217
  positive results 121
  trade 107, 108, 110
Sklair, L. 79–80
Skocpol, T. 217
Smith, A. 162
social capital 21, 156, 208, 211
social class *see* class
social constructivism 8–11, 176, 180–1, 195
social differentiation 81–2, 85, 197–8, 199
social exclusion 144
social fluidity 56–7
social integration 196–7
social mobility 26, 29, 50–75, 77, 207
  data analysis 54–7
  European field of mobility 73–5
  hypotheses 60–1
  and immobility in Western societies 52–4
  patterns of 60, 64–5
  qualitative approach 65–72
  quantitative approach 61–5
social movements 128–30
  see also mobilizations
social practices *see* practices
social protection for workers 121, 122
social representations
  EU policy-making 179–81, 191
  EU politics 165–9
  national interest 186–7
social resources 154–7, 166, 178
social sense 194, 195
social spiralism 53, 60, 70–1
social structure *see* structure
social systems 196
social theory 13–14, 127, 193–213
  contemporary and European integration 200–12
  Durkheimian approaches 195–200
  nation building and globalization 78–82
  Weberian approaches 194–5
social ties 34, 35, 37–40
social transactions 42–3
socialization 5, 43–5, 176, 180–1
societal integration 194, 195–200
socio-history 21–2
sociological approaches in EU studies 3, 4–11

sociological institutionalism 9
SOS Racisme 145
Soysal, Y. 143
Spain 36, 38–9, 109, 116
  social mobility 56, 63
  upper-middle class 88
spatial mobility 26, 39, 50–75, 77
  European field of mobility 73–5
  hypotheses 60–1
  and immobility in Western societies 52–4
  qualitative approach 65–72
  quantitative approach 61–5
  urban elites 94–6
specialization 154–5
  MEPs 166–7, 170
spillovers 5, 158, 196
sports 47
Starting Line Group 144, 145
state aid 105
state building 222–3
Stone Sweet, A. 132
Strasbourg school 21–2, 126, 160–3
Stråth, B. 203
stratification 29–30, 50
strong ties 34, 35, 37–40
structural constructivism 152, 207–8
structural funds 45
structuration 201–12
structure 15, 51
  class, Europeanization and 30–2
  transformation of occupational structure 54
subjectivist bias 189–90, 191
sub-national identities 47–8
subsidiaries 117, 119
suburbanization 83–4
supranational/national dimension 152–4
supranational policies 174, 184
supranationalization 139–40
Switzerland 36
symbolic capital 208
symbolic resources 156
symbolism 51

Tarrow, S. 19–20, 40–1, 128, 130
Taylor, R. 8–9, 217
te Brake, W. 19–20

technological change 115
technological zones 205
Telecom Italia 117, 119
telecommunications industry 106–7, 113–20, 122–3
Telia 117, 119
territory 80–1
theory of society 195, 213
Therborn, G. 3, 16, 28, 80, 200
Tilly, C. 81, 130, 203, 212, 223
Tocqueville, A. de 78, 211
Tönnies, F. 197
top-down activism 130
trade 100, 105, 106, 107–10, 122
trade unions 179
transactionalism 5, 42–3
'Transformation of Political Mobilisation and Communication in European Public Spheres' (EUROPUB) project 44, 139–41
translation 183–4
transnational capitalist class 39–40, 77, 79–80
transnational collective action 129
  see also mobilizations
transnational networks 91, 93–4, 146
transnational social groups 31
travel practices 94–6
Trenz, H.-J. 210
turf wars 161–2

United Kingdom (UK) 122–3
  class analysis 84
  ESDP 186–7, 188, 190
  immigrants, surveys 61–2
  social mobility 55, 63, 65
  telecommunications industry 115, 116, 123
  trade 108–9
United States (US) 52, 57, 104
'unity in diversity' 198
Urry, J. 13, 72, 77

variation 66
varieties of capitalism 14, 17, 29–30, 78, 122, 219
venue shopping 175
vertical Europeanization 139–40
Viag 117
Vilvoorde Renault car factory 137

virtual global society 92–8
Vodaphone 115, 117, 119
voice 85

Wagner, A.-C. 86
Weber, E. 43, 45, 47
Weber, M. 2, 32, 35, 68, 78, 80, 81, 127, 151, 152, 176, 186, 187, 194–5, 202, 222, 223
welfare regimes 29–30, 219
Wendt, A. 8

White, H. 103
White Paper on European Governance 163
Wiener, A. 8
Wimmer, A. 57
women MEPs 22
working career 90–1
World Social Forum 130
World Trade Organization Seattle protest 138
Wright, V. 16